Insider lending

Banks in early nineteenth-century New England functioned very differently from their modern counterparts. Most significantly, they lent a large proportion of their funds to members of their own boards of directors or to others with close personal connections to the boards. In *Insider Lending*, Naomi R. Lamoreaux explores the workings of this early nineteenth-century banking system – how and how well it functioned and the way it was regarded by contemporaries. She also traces the processes that transformed this banking system based on insider lending into a more impersonal and professional system by the end of the century. In the particular social, economic, and political context of early nineteenth-century New England, Lamoreaux argues, the benefits of insider lending outweighed its costs, and banks were instrumental in financing economic development. As the banking system grew more impersonal, however, banks came to play a more restricted role in economic life. At the root of this change were the new information problems banks faced when they conducted more and more of their business at arm's length. Difficulties in obtaining information about the creditworthiness of borrowers and in conveying information to the public about their own soundness led them to concentrate on providing short-term loans to commercial borrowers and to forsake the important role they had played early on in financing economic development.

NBER *Series on Long-term Factors in Economic Development*

Editor

CLAUDIA GOLDIN

Also in the series

Claudia Goldin
Understanding the Gender Gap: An Economic History of American Women
(Oxford University Press, 1990)

Roderick Floud, Kenneth Wachter, and Annabel Gregory
Height, Health and History: Nutritional Status in the United Kingdom, 1750–
1980 (Cambridge University Press, 1990)

Robert A. Margo
Race and Schooling in the South, 1880–1950: An Economic History (University of Chicago Press, 1990)

Samuel H. Preston and Michael R. Haines
Fatal Years: Child Mortality in Late Nineteenth-Century America (Princeton University Press, 1991)

Barry Eichengreen
Golden Fetters: The Gold Standard and the Great Depression, 1919–1939
(Oxford University Press, 1992)

In preparation (tentative titles)

Lance E. Davis, Robert E. Gallman, Karin J. Gleiter, and Teresa D. Hutchins
In Pursuit of Leviathan: Technology, Institutions, Productivity, and Profits in American Whaling, 1816–1906

Ronald N. Johnson and Gary Libecap
The Federal Civil Service System and the Problem of Bureaucracy: The Economics and Politics of Institutional Change

Robert W. Fogel
The Escape from Hunger and Early Death: Europe and America, 1750–2050

Richard H. Steckel
Families on the Move: A History of Migration within the United States, 1700–
1990

Kenneth L. Sokoloff
The Means to Private Comfort: Early Industrialization in the American Northeast

Relation of the Directors to the Work and Publications
of the National Bureau of Economic Research

1. The object of the National Bureau of Economic Research is to ascertain and to present to the public important economic facts and their interpretation in a scientific and impartial manner. The Board of Directors is charged with the responsibility of ensuring that the work of the National Bureau is carried on in strict conformity with this object.

2. The President of the National Bureau shall submit to the Board of Directors, or to its Executive Committee, for their formal adoption all specific proposals for research to be instituted.

3. No research report shall be published by the National Bureau until the President has sent each member of the Board a notice that a manuscript is recommended for publication and that in the President's opinion it is suitable for publication in accordance with the principles of the National Bureau. Such notification will include an abstract or summary of the manuscript's content and a response form for use by those Directors who desire a copy of the manuscript for review. Each manuscript shall contain a summary drawing attention to the nature and treatment of the problem studied, the character of the data and their utilization in the report, and the main conclusions reached.

4. For each manuscript so submitted, a special committee of the Directors (including Directors Emeriti) shall be appointed by majority agreement of the President and Vice Presidents (or by the Executive Committee in case of inability to decide on the part of the President and Vice Presidents), consisting of three Directors selected as nearly as may be one from each general division of the Board. The names of the special manuscript committee shall be stated to each Director when notice of the proposed publication is submitted to him. It shall be the duty of each member of the special manuscript committee to read the manuscript. If each member of the manuscript committee signifies his approval within thirty days of the transmittal of the manuscript, the report may be published. If at the end of that period any member of the manuscript committee withholds his approval, the President shall then notify each member of the Board, requesting approval or disapproval of publication, and thirty days additional shall be granted for this purpose. The manuscript shall then not be published unless at least a majority of the entire Board who shall have voted on the proposal within the time fixed for the receipt of votes shall have approved.

5. No manuscript may be published, though approved by each member of the special manuscript committee, until forty-five days have elapsed from the transmittal of the report in manuscript form. The interval is allowed for the receipt of any memorandum of dissent or reservation, together with a brief statement of his reasons, that any member may wish to express; and such memorandum of dissent or reservation shall be published with the manuscript if he so desires. Publication does not, however, imply that each member of the Board has read the manuscript, or that either members of the Board in general or the special committee have passed on its validity in every detail.

6. Publications of the National Bureau issued for informational purposes concerning the work of the Bureau and its staff, or issued to inform the public of activities of Bureau staff, and volumes issued as a result of various conferences involving the National Bureau shall contain a specific disclaimer noting that such publication has not passed through the normal review procedures required in this resolution. The Executive Committee of the Board is charged with review of all such publications from time to time to ensure that they do not take on the character of formal research reports of the National Bureau, requiring formal Board approval.

7. Unless otherwise determined by the Board or exempted by the terms of paragraph 6, a copy of this resolution shall be printed in each National Bureau publication.

(Resolution adopted October 25, 1926, as revised through September 30, 1974)

Insider lending

Banks, personal connections,
and economic development
in industrial New England

NAOMI R. LAMOREAUX
BROWN UNIVERSITY

NBER

CAMBRIDGE
UNIVERSITY PRESS

Published by the Press Syndicate of the University of Cambridge
The Pitt Building, Trumpington Street, Cambridge CB2 1RP
40 West 20th Street, New York, NY 10011-4211, USA
10 Stamford Road, Oakleigh, Melbourne 3166, Australia

First published 1994

Printed in the United States of America

Library of Congress Cataloging-in-Publication Data
Lamoreaux, Naomi R.
Insider lending : banks, personal connections, and economic
development in industrial New England / Naomi R. Lamoreaux.
p.   cm.
Includes bibliographical references and index.
ISBN 0-521-46096-4
1. Banks and banking – New England – History – 19th century.
2. Commercial loans – New England – History – 19th century.
3. Economic development projects – New England – Finance –
History – 19th century. 4. Asset-backed financing – New England –
History – 19th century. I. Title.
HG2601.L36   1994
332.1'753 – dc20   93-32161

A catalog record for this book is available from the British Library.

ISBN 0-521-46096-4 hardback

FOR
DAVID AND STEPHEN

Contents

Acknowledgments

Scholarship is a collective endeavor, and this particular study is no exception. I owe a tremendous debt to the many people who have helped me research and write this book. Charles P. Calomiris, David Lamoreaux, James T. Patterson, Edwin J. Perkins, and Richard Sylla deserve special thanks for reading and commenting on the entire manuscript, some of them more than once. The work is much the better for their suggestions. I am also greatly indebted to Daniel M. G. Raff and Peter Temin, who encouraged me to think about the subject in the context of imperfect information, and to Louis Galambos for his support and helpful comments. At the risk of omitting the names of some of the many other people who have given me the benefit of their knowledge, I would like to thank Etsuo Abe, John Brooke, Howard Chudacoff, Sally Clarke, Lance Davis, Konstantin Dierks, John S. Gilkeson, George D. Green, Timothy Guinnane, Michael J. Haupert, Carol Heim, Richard John, Geoffrey Jones, Yoichi Kawanami, Jane Knodell, Mark Kornbluh, John Landry, Thomas K. McCraw, David Meyer, Kerry Odell, Martha Olney, William N. Parker, Glenn Porter, Duncan M. Ross, Larry Schweikart, Frank Smith, Kenneth L. Sokoloff, Myron Stachiw, Jean Strouse, Steven Tolliday, Thomas Weiss, and Gordon Wood, as well as participants in seminars and lectures at American University, Columbia University, Dartmouth College, Harvard University, Indiana University, the Johns Hopkins Univeristy, Northwestern University, Meiji University, Rice University, the University of Arizona, the University of California – Los Angeles, the University of Illinois, the University of Kansas, the University of Massachusetts, the University of Michigan, Yale University, the American Antiquarian Society, Old Sturbridge Village, and the National Bureau of Economic Research. I would especially like to thank the faculty members and graduate students who attended the several Brown University History Department Workshops at which I presented preliminary drafts of chapters. They provided me with some of the most rigorous and thought-provoking criticism I received. Earlier versions of some of this material appeared in the *Journal of Economic History*, the *Business History Re-*

view, Business History, and *Inside the Business Enterprise: Historical Perspectives on the Use of Information,* edited by Peter Temin and published by the University of Chicago Press for the National Bureau of Economic Research. I am grateful for the suggestions of the anonymous referees solicited by each of these publications.

I would also like to express my appreciation to the managers and staffs of the Bank of Boston, the Bank of New Hampshire, Fleet National Bank, and the Shawmut Bank, who graciously granted me access to their historical records and provided me with a great deal of hospitality during the months I spent poring over old minute books and ledgers. My research was also made easier by the invaluable assistance of librarians, curators, and other officials at the Boston Athenaeum, the Boston Public Library, Brown University Libraries, Harvard University's Baker Library (as well as other libraries at Harvard), the Massachusetts Historical Society, the Massachusetts State Library, the Maine Historical Society, the Mendon Historical Society, the New Hampshire Historical Society, Old Sturbridge Village's Research Library, the Rhode Island Historical Society, the Rhode Island State Library and Archives, the Society for the Preservation of New England Antiquities, and the University of Rhode Island Library's Special Collections Department.

Fellowships from the American Council of Learned Societies, the John Simon Guggenheim Memorial Foundation, and the National Endowment for the Humanities enabled me to take time from teaching to pursue my research, and a fellowship at the Charles Warren Center gave me access to Harvard University's rich library resources. Thanks to grants from Brown University's Undergraduate Teaching and Research Assistantship Program, I benefited from the assistance of an able group of students. Christopher Glaisek, Andrew Morris, Ellie Stoddard, and Melissa Zimkin were all energetic and resourceful researchers who were a pleasure to work with as well. I want especially to give them my thanks.

Introduction

Banks in early-nineteenth-century New England were very different from the banks we know today, and perhaps the best way to begin this study is to explain how. Currently the region's financial sector is dominated by a handful of very large institutions, headquartered in major cities, whose influence extends throughout the area as a result of branch offices and mergers. The largest early-nineteenth-century banks were also located in cities, but because branch banking was not allowed, their operations were confined mainly to their local communities. Each bank was an independent, separately incorporated entity that raised its own funds and retained full control over its own lending decisions. There were a great many of them, too – more than three hundred by the mid 1830s and more than five hundred on the eve of the Civil War. By that time most small towns in the region had several banks each, and cities like Boston and Providence had as many as forty apiece.[1]

Despite their large numbers, early banks – unlike modern institutions – rarely provided financial services to ordinary households. Their customers consisted almost entirely of local businessmen whose borrowings took a very different form from what is common today. Typically, early-nineteenth-century businessmen brought notes (IOUs) to their banks to have them "discounted." Banks would advance borrowers an amount equal to the face value of their notes less an interest charge, and borrowers were then liable for the full value of the notes at maturity. Discounts were usually granted for only short periods of time (often for as

1. J. Van Fenstermaker, *The Development of American Commercial Banking, 1782–1837* (Kent, Ohio: Bureau of Economic and Business Research, Kent State University, 1965), 186–247; Richard Eugene Sylla, *The American Capital Market, 1846–1914: A Study of the Effects of Public Policy on Economic Development* (New York: Arno, 1975), 249–52; Massachusetts, Secretary of the Commonwealth, *Abstracts of the Returns from the Banks* (1860), 78–9; Rhode Island, State Auditor, *Annual Statement Exhibiting the Condition of the Banks* (1860), 35.

I

little as sixty days), after which the notes might be renewed upon payment of an additional interest charge. Banks typically required all notes to be endorsed (that is, signed by one or more parties who would guarantee payment in the event of default). Sometimes borrowers were permitted to offer collateral security for their notes instead, but this practice was not very common. Personal security was considered safer than collateral security, because the notes were backed by all the resources of the endorser(s) as well as those of the borrower.

Early-nineteenth-century banks discounted two basic kinds of notes: commercial paper and what was known at the time as accommodation paper.[2] Commercial paper consisted of notes generated in the course of actual business transactions. When a manufacturer sold his wares to a merchant, for example, the merchant would often pay for them by giving the manufacturer an IOU, which he pledged to redeem in cash by a certain date (presumably selling the goods in the interim). If the manufacturer needed his money sooner, he could take the note to a bank and have it discounted, adding his endorsement to the merchant's name as security for the loan. Because of the self-liquidating nature of the debt, this type of note was rarely renewed. Typically the bank would collect payment from the merchant when the note matured, and the transaction was thus completed.

Accommodation loans, on the other hand, were entirely unrelated to any specific commercial transaction. They were a means for borrowers to obtain credit for a variety of purposes, including investments in manufacturing plant and equipment. The borrower drew up a note listing himself as payer, obtained one or more endorsers who were willing to guarantee the debt, and brought it to a bank to be discounted. Although the bank would discount the note only for a short period of time, it was often understood that the note would be renewed at maturity – sometimes repeatedly. In this way early banks transformed what was technically a short-term obligation into a long-term debt. The ratio of accommodation to commercial paper varied from one bank to the next, but it was common for the ratio greatly to exceed one.[3]

2. For further discussion of the nature of early banks' loans, see Fritz Redlich, *The Molding of American Banking: Men and Ideas* (New York: Hafner, 1947), pt. i, 10–12. In the discussion that follows, and throughout the rest of the book, I use male pronouns to refer to merchants, manufacturers, bank officers, and bank directors. Although women frequently owned stock in banks and occasionally borrowed from them, the kinds of transactions I am describing involved men almost exclusively. Men also monopolized bank directorships and staff positions throughout the nineteenth century.

3. There are two ways to measure the amount of accommodation paper in a bank's portfolio. The best way, but unfortunately one that is possible in only

Early banks obtained the funds they lent to borrowers from very different sources than modern banks. Today, for example, the most important component of a bank's liabilities is deposits, but these were relatively insignificant during the early nineteenth century, making up only about 10 to 20 percent of the total, depending on locality (see Table 3.7). Unlike modern institutions, early banks were allowed to issue currency in the form of banknotes, that is to say, non-interest-bearing IOUs, and these notes constituted the bulk of the circulating media of the period. Notwithstanding their importance for the operation of the economy, however, banknotes also occupied a relatively insignificant position on early banks' balance sheets. Instead, as Table 3.7 indicates, the preponderance of the banks' liabilities consisted of shares of their own capital stock. This pattern contrasts sharply with that of modern banks. Today such securities account typically for only a minuscule part of total liabilities – a few percentage points at most.[4]

Finally, early-nineteenth-century banks had very different management structures from modern ones. Large banks today have extensive managerial hierarchies consisting of professionals who are responsible for their day-to-day operations. Early banks, by contrast, had only a few salaried workers. The largest might employ a cashier (the effective head of operations), several tellers and clerks, and perhaps a bookkeeper. The smallest might employ only a cashier. Regardless of size, the real managers of an

a few cases, is to look at who actually benefited from the discount. If the proceeds went to the note's endorser, the note was most likely commercial paper. On the other hand, if the proceeds went to the principal, the note was most likely accommodation paper. By this measure, 84% of the notes outstanding at the Eagle Bank of Bristol, R.I., in October 1818 were accommodation paper. Discount Book, 1818–24, Eagle Bank, Fleet National Bank Archives.

The other way to estimate the proportion of accommodation paper is to look for loans denominated in round numbers, on the presumption that commercial paper represented actual transactions and therefore was likely to be in odd amounts. The overwhelming majority of notes in the portfolios of banks from this period were denominated in round numbers. For examples, see Discount Book, 1820–34, New England Commercial Bank, Newport, R.I., Mss. 781, Baker Library, Harvard Graduate School of Business Administration; list of Notes, Jan. 1, 1824, Concord (N.H.) Bank, Mss. 1989–011, Box 5, Folder 7, New Hampshire Historical Society; and list of Notes, Dec. 20, 1842, in Directors' and Stockholders' Minute Book, 1815–85, Pawtuxet Bank, Warwick, R.I., Rhode Island Historical Society Manuscript Collections.

4. Some scholars have suggested that early banks' capital stock was largely fictitious, but, as I will argue in Chapter 1, this was true only during the initial years of a bank's existence.

early-nineteenth-century bank were its directors, one of whom was chosen by the others to act as president. Although the president was sometimes paid a small salary, the directors typically received no remuneration
at all for their services. Nevertheless, they were responsible for such important managerial functions as verifying the cashier's accounts, deciding
how much money the bank could afford to lend, and, most significantly,
deciding who should receive the loans.

As Chapter 1 will demonstrate, an examination of bank records, government investigations, and other sources from the early nineteenth century reveals that directors often funneled the bulk of the funds under their
control to themselves, their relatives, or others with personal ties to the
board. Though not all directors indulged in this behavior, insider lending
was widespread during the early nineteenth century and most conspicu-
ously differentiates early banks from their twentieth-century successors.
Modern banks engage in insider lending to some extent, of course, but
the practice is neither as pervasive nor as fundamental a part of banking
operations as it was then. Indeed, it is my contention that insider lending
is the key to understanding New England's early-nineteenth-century
banking system; it is the crucial piece of the puzzle that enables us to
arrange the banks' other distinctive features in a coherent pattern.

In a developing economy, such as early-nineteenth-century New England's, where capital was scarce and therefore expensive, control of a
bank yielded obvious advantages in gaining access to credit. Once it
became apparent, as one pamphleteer put it, "that *Bank Directors* had
priority of claim in the dispensation of bank favors, . . . then it was that
others, less fortunate, conceived the idea that it was a very happy thing to
participate in the control of a bank."[5] Shrewd entrepreneurs, eager to use
banks as vehicles to accumulate capital for their own ventures, and especially eager for the accommodation loans that banks could extend to their
favorites, put enormous pressure on state legislatures to charter additional banks. The politics of the Jacksonian era made it difficult to resist such
demands for long, and the region was soon inundated by large numbers
of small unit banks – for the most part operated by, and in the interests of,
their directors.

There was nothing underhanded or deceptive about the personal use to
which bank directors put these institutions. The fact that banks lent so
large a proportion of their funds to insiders was common knowledge at
the time: legislators investigated the practice; journalists reported on it;

5. Henry Williams (A Citizen of Boston, pseud.), *Remarks on Banks and Banking; and the Skeleton of a Project for a National Bank* (Boston: Torrey &
   Blair, 1840), 13–14.

and pamphleteers occasionally debated it. Nevertheless, investors willingly bought up large quantities of bank stock during this period, in large measure because insider lending greatly increased the stock's attractiveness. Investors knew that when they bought stock in a bank they were actually investing in the diversified enterprises of that institution's directors. Investment in bank stock, consequently, was a way in which ordinary savers could participate in the activities of the region's most prominent entrepreneurs – and could do so without exposing themselves to serious risk. Although we call these early-nineteenth-century institutions banks, in actuality they functioned more like investment clubs. As such, moreover, they proved to be extraordinarily effective vehicles for channeling savings into economic development.

This in brief is the argument I develop over the course of the first three chapters of the book. Chapter 1 traces the early history of the banking system, documenting the pervasiveness of insider lending and describing the sequence of financial manipulations that allowed groups of men with only limited resources to found banks and turn them into vehicles for accumulating capital. Chapter 2 takes up the subject of attitudes toward the practice of insider lending during the Jacksonian period. I argue that insider lending provoked general opposition only to the extent that banks were defined as public institutions. As the number of banks multiplied during the 1820s and 1830s, they came increasingly to be viewed as private entities with the prerogative of lending to insiders if they so desired. In the aftermath of the Panic of 1837, when public faith in the soundness of the banking system was at a low ebb, there was a flurry of legislation limiting the proportion of capital that banks could lend to their directors. This legislation did little to curb insider lending, however, and the practice continued to be an important aspect of banking operations when the economy emerged from depression during the late 1840s.

Chapter 3 argues that the failure to regulate insider lending had few or no adverse consequences for the economy as a whole, because other aspects of the banking system minimized the potentially pernicious effects of the practice. Insider lending necessarily resulted in discrimination in the credit markets, but the tremendous expansion in the number of banks that occurred during these years largely offset this effect. Similarly, though insider lending could in theory undermine a bank's soundness, the low level of leverage that characterized most early banks (that is, the low ratio of notes and deposits to total liabilities) operated to prevent most failures. Stockholders, of course, bore the brunt of any losses that the practice inflicted, but directors had powerful incentives to keep the level of risk low. Anxious to maintain the unsullied character of their reputations (which were essential for business success during this period) and also to preserve the health of their golden goose, directors carefully monitored each other's borrowing to prevent the kinds of excesses that might damage them all. Reassured by this vigilance and by the high and steady earnings that bank stock typically yielded during these years, investors poured large sums of money into banks, in the process fueling the region's economic growth and development.

The last three chapters of the book analyze the processes that transformed this early-nineteenth-century banking system into something more like the one we are familiar with today. As the century progressed and the region's credit markets continued to evolve, banks came to function less like investment clubs and more like strictly commercial institutions. Economic development was itself a source of change: as the economy expanded and additional banks and other financial institutions were founded, New England was transformed from a capital-scarce region into a capital-rich one. Once credit became more abundant, control of a bank became less necessary for access to loans, and as a result insider lending gradually began to decline. Not that it completely disappeared – some insiders were still monopolizing the bulk of their banks' loans as late as the 1890s – but, in general, the practice was becoming less common.

Chapter 4 documents this shift as well as the downward trend in earnings that afflicted the region's banks beginning in the mid 1870s. Although the drop in earnings was largely a result of an overpopulation of banks in the region, it operated to stimulate further changes in lending behavior. As bankers tried desperately to reduce their losses from bad loans, they developed new standards for evaluating the creditworthiness of borrowers. These standards, in turn, fostered an ethic of professionalism that ran counter to the values that had originally sustained insider lending. At the same time, declining earnings also encouraged bankers to take more aggressive measures to solicit deposits, causing leverage ratios to rise sharply.

As Chapter 5 argues, this rise in deposits increased banks' interdependence and vulnerability to runs, and hence made insider lending appear more dangerous than it had looked earlier in the century. The root of the problem was that depositors had no way of obtaining reliable information concerning the contents of banks' loan portfolios. If one bank collapsed as a result of excessive borrowing by insiders, depositors might rush to withdraw their funds from other institutions as well, fearing that all of them were similarly endangered.

Bankers responded to this potential danger by attempting to eliminate the kinds of excesses that could trigger such episodes in the first place. In particular, they sought to prevent opportunistic behavior on the part of directors by promoting new lending standards that could be monitored easily by conscientious stockholders and directors. In this endeavor they were vigorously assisted by an energetic group of professionals (career bank employees, trade-journal publicists, and government regulators) interested in advancing their own positions within the banking community. The end result of their combined efforts was a much narrower definition of the proper scope of banking operations – a definition that effectively restricted a bank's business to commercial lending pure and simple. To the extent that banks adopted the new standards, then, they came to play a much more limited role in economic development than had been true of their early-nineteenth-century predecessors.

In the meantime, the earnings of the banking sector continued to decline. As Chapter 6 explains, by the end of the century falling profit rates finally instigated a movement to combine many of the region's small banks into much larger agglomerations of capital. Significant numbers of mergers occurred only in Boston and Rhode Island, but there they had dramatic effects, substantially reducing the number of banks while greatly increasing the average size of the remaining institutions. More important, as the new financial giants gravitated toward hitherto unexplored areas of national finance, they applied the new professional lending standards more rigorously in their everyday banking business. The net result was to make it more difficult for entrepreneurs, especially in new manufacturing industries, to obtain access to credit in the region. Banks' conservative lending practices thus had the effect of exacerbating the economy's dependence on the continued profitability of the industries of the first industrial revolution.

Widespread insider lending was not unique to the early-nineteenth-century New England economy. There is substantial evidence that banks in other parts of the United States engaged in similar types of lending behavior during this period. Bray Hammond has pointed out, for example, that merchants throughout the Northeast "clubb[ed] a capital together" in order to supply each other with discounts. Fritz Redlich has observed that favoritism in lending was widespread throughout the early years of the century and that the Bank of North America had been "all but crippled" during the 1790s because a few powerful borrowers had monopolized its funds. Similarly, the recent history of New York's Citibank, compiled by Harold van B. Cleveland and Thomas F. Huertas, recounts the bank's transformation during the 1840s from "a kind of credit union for its merchant-owners" into a "treasury" for Moses Taylor's far-flung business empire. The South Carolina planter James Henry Hammond remarked frequently in his diary that the business interests of

Franklin Harper Elmore and other officers and directors of the Bank of the State of South Carolina were supported by loans from the bank, and similar references to insider lending are sprinkled through Larry Schweikart's voluminous scholarly work on southern banking.[6]

Outside the United States the story was much the same. Recent studies of British banking have uncovered close links between local banks and businessmen resembling those in New England. C. W. Munn has shown that Scottish provincial banks during the late eighteenth century were primarily "self-help" associations for merchants in need of credit, and P. L. Cottrell has discovered that industrialists made similar use of local banks in mid-nineteenth-century England. It hardly seems necessary to refer the reader to the voluminous literature documenting the interrelationships between banks and industrialists in Germany and elsewhere on the European continent. Nor to the equivalent literature on developing countries, with its frequent references to the "group" form of enterprise – that is, to kinship-based networks whose diversified business ventures were and are supported and controlled with the help of captive banks.[7]

6. Bray Hammond, "Long and Short Term Credit in Early American Banking," *Quarterly Journal of Economics,* 49 (November 1935), 79–103; Redlich, *The Molding of American Banking,* 11; Harold van B. Cleveland and Thomas F. Huertas, *Citibank: 1812–1970* (Cambridge: Harvard University Press, 1985), 5–31; Carol Bleser, ed., *Secret and Sacred: The Diaries of James Henry Hammond, a Southern Slaveholder* (New York: Oxford University Press, 1988), 162, 163–4, 220; Larry Schweikart, *Banking in the American South from the Age of Jackson to Reconstruction* (Baton Rouge: Louisiana State University Press, 1987), 190–224, and "Entrepreneurial Aspects of Antebellum Banking," in *American Business History: Case Studies,* ed. Henry C. Dethloff and C. Joseph Pusateri (Arlington Heights, Ill.: Harlan Davidson, 1987), 122–39.

7. C. W. Munn, "Scottish Provincial Banking Companies: An Assessment," *Business History,* 23 (March 1981), 19–41; P. L. Cottrell, *Industrial Finance, 1830–1914: The Finance and Organization of English Manufacturing Industry* (London: Methuen, 1980), 210–36; Richard Tilly, *Financial Institutions and Industrialization in the Rhineland, 1815–1870* (Madison: University of Wisconsin Press, 1966); Rondo Cameron, ed., with the collaboration of Olga Crisp, Hugh T. Patrick, and Richard Tilly, *Banking in the Early Stages of Industrialization: A Study in Comparative Economic History* (New York: Oxford University Press, 1967); Holger L. Engberg, *Mixed Banking and Economic Growth in Germany, 1850–1931* (New York: Arno, 1981); Hans Pohl, "Forms and Phases of Industry Finance up to the Second World War," *German Yearbook on Business History* (1984), 75–94; Nathaniel H. Leff, "Entrepreneurship and Economic Development: The Problem Revisited," *Journal of Economic Literature,* 17 (March 1979), 46–64, and "Industrial

My point in focusing on New England is not to claim that insider lending was uniquely important there but rather that any such phenomenon needs to be understood in the context of the particular social and cultural environment in which it is imbedded. Just as the functions of banks have varied from one time and place to another, so too have the consequences of insider lending. In many developing countries, for example, this type of lending has had pernicious results. Practiced by banks with a substantial degree of monopoly power, it has served to reduce competition and has thus had a constraining effect on economic growth. In still other cases (including certain parts of New England in recent years), large loans to insiders have undermined the soundness of some banks and jeopardized the health of the local financial system.[8]

By contrast, insider lending as practiced in early-nineteenth-century New England seems to have had a much more salutary effect. The purpose of this study is to explore the reasons why, and in the process to develop a general understanding of the conditions under which banks are likely to play a positive role in economic development. It is my contention that whenever banks maintain a strictly arm's-length relationship with their customers they tend to avoid the risks involved in financing entrepreneurial ventures. When entrepreneurs themselves control banks, this reluctance naturally disappears, but insider lending can itself become a potential source of instability in the economy. In New England's case, however, this problem seems to have been minimized by a combination of easy entry into banking and an incentive structure that encouraged insiders to monitor each other's borrowing. Ironically, however, the system's very success in fostering economic development eliminated the conditions that supported it. Insider lending declined, and banks simultaneously retreated from their active role in supporting investment within the region.

New England is a particularly good place to conduct this kind of study,

Organization and Entrepreneurship in the Developing Countries: The Economic Groups," *Economic Development and Cultural Change*, 26 (April 1978), 661–75.

8.   For examples, see Stephen H. Haber, "Industrial Concentration and the Capital Markets: A Comparative Study of Brazil, Mexico, and the United States, 1830–1930," *Journal of Economic History*, 51 (September 1991), 559–80; Nathaniel H. Leff, "'Monopoly Capitalism' and Public Policy in Developing Countries," *Kyklos*, 32 (1979), 718–38; Vartan Gregorian, *"Carved in Sand": A Report on the Collapse of the Rhode Island Share and Deposit Indemnity Corporation* (Providence: Brown University, 1991); Stephen Pizzo, Mary Fricker, and Paul Muolo, *Inside Job: The Looting of America's Savings and Loans* (New York: McGraw-Hill, 1989).

because the combination of rapid industrialization and a well-developed banking system permits us to explore the relationship between the two. Because, moreover, the banking systems of the various regions of the United States differed from one another in other significant respects, there is good reason to confine this study to New England. In the first place, the regulatory environment in which New England banks operated was unlike that of other regions. At a time when states elsewhere, especially in the Mid Atlantic and Old Northwest, were developing general incorporation laws for banking, the New England states continued to charter banks by special legislative act. At a time when many southern and midwestern states were allowing banks to operate branches, New England remained a region of small unit banks. Similarly, at a time when states like New York and Ohio were experimenting with safety funds and coinsurance schemes, New England continued to rely on the Suffolk system, a private system of note redemption enforced by the largest Boston banks, to keep the region's banking system sound. The balance sheets of New England banks also differed in systematic ways from those of banks in other parts of the country. New England banks, for example, raised a larger proportion of their resources from the sale of capital stock than banks elsewhere. The ratio of deposits and currency to capital for New England banks averaged 69 percent in 1860, as opposed to 114 to 149 percent for banks in other regions of the country. Nevertheless, New England banks were able to supply their communities with more bank money (that is, deposits plus banknotes) per capita than were their counterparts elsewhere. They were also more stable than banks in other parts of the United States.[9]

One final point. Because I am interested in the relationship between banks and economic development, I have focused my attention on the industrial parts of the region: the more or less continuous belt of manufacturing that runs from Rhode Island and eastern Massachusetts to southern New Hampshire and southern Maine.

9. Massachusetts and Connecticut passed general incorporation laws for banks in the early 1850s, but very few banks were chartered under them. Hugh T. Rockoff, "Varieties of Banking and Regional Economic Development in the United States, 1840–1860," *Journal of Economic History*, 35 (March 1975), 160–77; Fenstermaker, *The Development of American Commercial Banking*, 13–29, 77–82; Charles W. Calomiris and Larry Schweikart, "Was the South Backward? North–South Differences in Antebellum Banking During Normalcy and Crisis," unpub. paper, 1988; Sylla, *The American Capital Market*, 249–52; Kenneth Ng, "Free Banking Laws and Barriers to Entry in Banking, 1838–1860," *Journal of Economic History*, 48 (December 1988), 877–89.

1

Vehicles for accumulating capital

In nineteen out of twenty cases, banks have been got up for the creation of money facilities and capital. . . . The object has not been to *invest* money, but to *create* it. Hence it has happened that bank charters have been asked for and obtained, where a vast majority of the corporation, instead of being *lenders* of money, were actually *hungry borrowers*.

Henry Williams[1]

I

Commercial banking got its start in New England (as elsewhere in the United States) shortly after the Revolutionary War, when groups of prominent merchants in the region's leading port cities began petitioning their state legislatures for charters of incorporation. Because at that time the grant of a corporate charter conferred special privileges and quasi-governmental authority, legislatures reserved them for projects deemed to be in the public interest. Accordingly, merchants who were seeking charters emphasized the many benefits that banks would bring to their communities. They claimed, for example, that banks would make it possible to obtain credit at reasonable rates of interest, thus ensuring that "the enormous advantages made by the griping Usurer from the Necessities of those who want to borrow Money will be immediately checked & in a great Measure Destroyed." Banks would also provide the surrounding community with a safe and readily convertible supply of paper money, such that "the Benefits of an increased Medium & the Payment of Taxes & the Negotiation of all other Business will be rendered more safe & easy." As an added boon, banks would promote "a general Punctuality" in business transactions.[2]

1. (A Citizen of Boston, pseud.), *Remarks on Banks and Banking; and the Skeleton of a Project for a National Bank* (Boston: Torrey & Blair, 1840), 16.
2. The quotations are from the petition for the Massachusetts Bank; other early requests for charters were similar. See N. S. B. Gras, *The Massachusetts First National Bank of Boston, 1784–1934* (Cambridge: Harvard University

The extent to which successful petitioners actually made good on these promises varied considerably from one case to another. In its early years, for example, the Providence Bank (chartered in Rhode Island in 1791) primarily benefited a group of the bank's own directors, who immediately absorbed most of its lendable funds, leaving little to satisfy the credit needs of the rest of the community. Discount records for 1792 and 1798 show that the bank's directors and their relatives accounted for 75 to 80 percent (by value) of total loans. Although Moses Brown, the directors' self-appointed conscience, sought to limit the indebtedness of the other board members (including his credit-hungry brother John, the bank's first president), his efforts proved ultimately futile. As late as 1811 he was still vainly inveighing against the laxness of his fellow directors both in collecting past-due debts from and in granting overdrafts to themselves. He was also critical of their reluctance to let him inspect the bank's books: "I have calld on the Officers a number of Times Since to know if the Accts were ready for My Examination. the period has never yet Arived, the reason Suggested for the Delay by the Officers was their not having time . . ."3

The case of the Massachusetts Bank, chartered in Boston in 1784, provides a striking contrast. Although some of the original proprietors used their influence to borrow extensively from the bank and to secure the renewal of their loans at will, a reform coalition headed by William Phillips soon forced them to sell their stock and withdraw from the institution. Elected president of the bank in 1786, Phillips initiated a series of policy changes that prohibited renewals of notes and limited the amount of money that any one individual or firm could borrow. The results of these changes can be seen from a list of the bank's discounts for March 1788, by which time only about 17 percent of total loans went to directors or others with the same last name. Similarly, in 1792 the bank

Press, 1937), 212–14. This volume includes transcriptions of the bank's early records. For another example, see Frank Weston and Fred Piggott, *The Passing Years, 1791 to 1966* (Providence: Industrial National Bank, 1966), 11.

3. Letter from Moses Brown to the Board of Directors of the Providence Bank, Sept. 29, 1811, Moses Brown Papers, Rhode Island Historical Society Manuscript Collections. For the actual loan amounts, see Discount Book, 1791–3, and Notes and Bills Discounted, 1798, Providence Bank, Fleet National Bank Archives. Moses Brown's role is suggested in a Nov. 2, 1797, letter from his brother John to Henry Smith, who was disgruntled at getting only part of a loan he had sought from the bank. In attempting to soothe the ruffled feelings of his correspondent, John explained that he had not gotten all the discounts he had wanted either, and that had his brother Moses been at the directors' meeting, things would have gone even worse for them. John Brown Papers, Rhode Island Historical Society Manuscript Collections.

was able to report that its loans to stockholders amounted to a mere 23 percent of capital. Most of its borrowers, the report asserted, were "opulent Merchants of extensive business and credit, but a small part of whose property is in the funds of the Bank."[4]

Even at the Massachusetts Bank, however, the reform impulse seems to have atrophied over time. As early as 1790 the directors in effect voted to repeal the limitation on loans; moreover, minutes of board meetings over the next few years reflected a growing leniency with respect to renewals. The suspicion began to take root, both inside and outside the state legislature, that a handful of wealthy individuals had gained control of the bank and were using it for their own private purposes.[5] Whether this suspicion was actually justified or not is difficult to say, for the relevant records no longer exist. What is certain, however, is that the bank's resources, as well as those of pioneering institutions in other cities, were far too small to meet the region's growing demand for credit. Pressures mounted on the various state legislatures to approve additional charters, and in the anti-monopoly climate of the Jacksonian era they were difficult to resist. As one observer commented, "Under our form of government where monopolies and exclusive privileges are strictly forbidden, an important privilege cannot with any consistency be extended to one, and refused to other(s) of equal claims."[6] As a result, the number of banks in New England rose from 1 in 1784 to 52 in 1810 and to 172 in 1830. By 1837 there were more than 320 banks in the area, with more than 60 in little Rhode Island alone (see Table 1.1).

This proliferation of banks certainly broadened access to credit, but it did not result in any fundamental change in lending practices. Although policies varied from one institution to another, many of the new banks provided ample confirmation of the suspicions that had previously been

4. Gras, *The Massachusetts First National Bank,* 26, 53–4, 78, 263, 268–9, 273–6; Discount Book, 1786–8, Massachusetts Bank, Bank of Boston Archives.
5. Gras, *The Massachusetts First National Bank,* 61–2, 70, 331–2, 349–56; Oscar Handlin and Mary Flug Handlin, *Commonwealth: A Study of the Role of Government in the American Economy: Massachusetts, 1774–1861* (New York: New York University Press, 1947), 121–2.
6. A Citizen of Boston, *A New System of Paper Money* (Boston: I. R. Butts, 1837), 3. By the early 1830s Massachusetts and Rhode Island derived 66% and 35%, respectively, of their revenues from taxes on bank capital. For Maine and New Hampshire the comparable figures were 13% and 25%. Not surprisingly, these tax monies operated as a powerful incentive to charter additional banks. Richard Sylla, John B. Legler, and John J. Wallis, "Banks and State Finance in the New Republic: The United States, 1790–1860," *Journal of Economic History,* 47 (June 1987), 391–403.

Table 1.1. *Number and paid-in capital stock of banks in New England, 1820–1860*[a]

Year	Maine	Mass.	N.H.	R.I.	New England[b]
1820	1.65	10.60	1.00	3.06	16.82
	(15)	(28)	(10)	(31)	(87)
1830	2.45	19.30	2.10	6.07	34.77
	(18)	(63)	(21)	(46)	(172)
1837	5.46	38.28	2.84	9.85	66.44
	(55)	(129)	(27)	(62)	(323)
1850	3.10	34.63	2.19	11.21	62.87
	(32)	(119)	(23)	(61)	(300)
1860	7.53	66.48	4.94	21.15	123.56
	(69)	(178)	(51)	(90)	(505)

[a]Numbers of banks are in parentheses. Capital is denominated in millions of dollars.
[b]Includes Connecticut and Vermont.
Sources: J. Van Fenstermaker, *The Development of American Commercial Banking, 1782–1837* (Kent, Ohio: Bureau of Economic and Business Research, Kent State University, 1965), 186–247; Richard Eugene Sylla, *The American Capital Market, 1846–1914: A Study of the Effects of Public Policy on Economic Development* (New York: Arno, 1975), 249–52; Maine, Bank Commissioners, *Annual Report* (1860), 75–6; Massachusetts, Secretary of the Commonwealth, *Abstracts of the Returns from the Banks* (1860), 78–9; New Hampshire, Bank Commissioners, *Reports* (1860), 92–3; Rhode Island, State Auditor, *Annual Statement Exhibiting the Condition of the Banks* (1860), 35.

raised about the Massachusetts Bank, namely, that they lent the bulk of their resources to insiders. For example, in 1810 Eli Brown, a former director of the Hillsborough (New Hampshire) Bank, submitted a petition to the state legislature in which he complained that the bank's bylaws had enabled its directors "to fix themselves in power beyond a possibility of removal, and in secret conclave, to manage the business of the Bank for their own private emolument." In rebutting this charge, director Samuel Bell claimed that he had actually lost money through his affiliation with the bank, mainly because of the heavy debts that Brown himself had incurred when he was a director, and which he was now seeking to evade by fraudulently conveying his property to other parties.[7] The failure in

7. Samuel Bell, *An Answer to the Petition of Eli Brown, Complaining of Misconduct, &c. &c. of the Directors and Agents of the Hillsborough Bank* (Amherst, N.H.: R. Boylston, ca. 1810).

1829 of the Sutton Bank of Massachusetts revealed a similar pattern of lending activity. The bank had lent nearly 90 percent of its funds to various enterprises owned by the Wilkinson family, which also dominated the bank's board of directors. When the Wilkinsons' textile and machinery empire collapsed during an economic downturn in the late 1820s, so did the bank.[8] Similarly, the Nahant Bank of Lynn, Massachusetts, failed in 1836 as a consequence of large loans made to its president, Henry A. Breed.[9]

Legislative investigations uncovered substantial loans to insiders in the portfolios of virtually every bank that failed during the first half of the nineteenth century. Such lending practices, however, were not confined to banks that ran into financial trouble; they characterized many solvent institutions as well. At the Pawtuxet Bank (chartered in Warwick, Rhode Island, in 1814), a list of discounted notes dating from the early 1840s shows that fully 53 percent of them (by value) belonged to James Rhodes, the partnership J. Rhodes and Sons, or various manufacturing enterprises associated with the partnership of C. and W. Rhodes. James Rhodes was both president and a director of the bank until his death in 1841. His brothers, Christopher and William (the principals of C. and W. Rhodes), also served from time to time as directors, with Christopher succeeding to the presidency after James's death. Other members of the bank's board of directors absorbed an additional 16 percent of the loans.[10] Similarly, at the Wakefield (Rhode Island) Bank, chartered in 1834, the obligations of two local manufacturers, Samuel Rodman (a director) and Isaac P. Hazard (a kinsman of Rodman's and of several other directors), accounted for

8. Applications for Discount, 1828–30, Sutton (Mass.) Bank, Mss. 781, Baker Library, Harvard University Graduate School of Business Administration. On the Wilkinsons' financial collapse, see Peter J. Coleman, *The Transformation of Rhode Island, 1790–1860* (Providence: Brown University Press, 1969), 100–3, 114–15; James Lawson Conrad, "The Evolution of Industrial Capitalism in Rhode Island, 1790–1830: Almy, the Browns, and the Slaters," unpub. Ph.D. diss., University of Connecticut, 1973, 311–13, 316.

9. "Notes Promised by H. A. Breed" and "Notes Considered Doubtful Endorsed by Henry A. Breed," Nahant Bank, Lynn, Mass., Case 1, Mss. 781, Baker Library, Harvard University Graduate School of Business Administration; Massachusetts, General Court, "Report of the Special Joint Committee on the Nahant Bank," Senate Doc. 5, 1837.

10. These totals probably understate the proportion of notes discounted for the benefit of insiders, because they are based on information about promisors only. The names of endorsers were not noted in the records. Directors' and Stockholders' Minute Book, 1815–85, Pawtuxet Bank, Warwick, R.I., Rhode Island Historical Society Manuscript Collections.

54 percent of the discounts outstanding as of March 1, 1845. Notes involving members of the three interrelated families that controlled the bank (Rodmans, Hazards, and Robinsons) accounted altogether for 84 percent of the bank's total loans.[11]

When Rhode Island's banking commissioners investigated the situation in late 1836, they found that insider lending was widespread. "At two of the [Providence] banks lately visited," they reported, "one half of the whole amount respectively loaned by them, was discounted for the accommodation of the directors, and of copartnerships of which they were members. At a third, three-fifths of the aggregate loans went into similar hands." Indeed, as a result of their investigation the commissioners were forced to conclude that the practice of insider lending had become so pervasive that banks were "to a considerable extent mere engines to supply the directors with money."[12]

New Hampshire's bank commissioners arrived at similar conclusions, as did their counterparts in Massachusetts. In 1838, for instance, the Massachusetts state legislature passed a law offering special privileges to any bank that would restrict its loans to directors to 30 percent of its capital unless the stockholders expressly authorized higher limits. Of the state's nearly 120 banks, only 29 accepted this condition. As for the rest, upon examining their books the commissioners commented, "The liabilities of the directors in most of the Banks, which have not accepted the Act, are above the limits established by the law."[13] Nor were the regula-

11. These figures, which include appearances in the records as both principals and endorsers, are probably underestimations, because sloppy (or perhaps deceptive) bookkeeping practices appear to have concealed additional loans to these individuals. Bill Book A, Wakefield (R.I.) Bank, Rhode Island Historical Society Manuscript Collections. See also Directors' and Stockholders' Minute Book, 1834–65, Wakefield Bank, Fleet National Bank Archives; and Caroline E. Robinson, *The Hazard Family of Rhode Island, 1635–1894* (Boston, 1895 [privately printed]). Additional evidence and examples are scattered through this and the next two chapters. See also Andrew A. Beveridge, "Local Lending Practice: Borrowers in a Small Northeastern Industrial City, 1832–1915," *Journal of Economic History*, 45 (June 1985), 393–403; Bray Hammond, "Long and Short Term Credit in Early American Banking," *Quarterly Journal of Economics*, 49 (November 1935), 79–103; Fritz Redlich, *The Molding of American Banking: Men and Ideas* (New York: Hafner, 1947), pt. 1, 11, 31, 43.

12. Rhode Island, General Assembly, Acts and Resolves (January 1837), 89–92.

13. Norman Walker Smith, "A History of Commercial Banking in New Hampshire, 1792–1843," unpub. Ph.D. diss., University of Wisconsin, 1967, 233–4; Massachusetts, General Court, "Report of the Bank Commissioners," Senate Doc. 5, 1839, 12–14. At some point all the New England state legislatures required banks to report the percentage of discounts

tors alone in their assessment; bankers themselves admitted that directors frequently turned to their own banks for loans. Some of them, such as Boston banker Thomas G. Cary, even attempted to justify the practice:

> It would certainly be advisable that bank directors should be men of property, retired from business, who never wish to borrow money. But this cannot be. Such men can but rarely be induced to trouble themselves with engagements of this nature, and the duty of lending from the bank is left to be performed, in most cases, by those who are borrowers themselves.[14]

Not all banks engaged in high levels of insider lending. A few institutions, such as the Concord (Massachusetts) Bank, pursued a more "modern" conception of their business, lending their funds to customers who maintained accounts with them and paying interest to attract deposits.[15]

granted to their own directors, but these figures were typically so understated as to be virtually worthless as indexes of insider lending. In the first place, vague reporting requirements and a lack of standardized accounting procedures allowed banks considerable latitude in compiling their reports. Second, the totals did not include loans made to directors' relatives or business associates. Nor did they include any loans to corporations with which the directors were associated. As a result, there was often a significant discrepancy between the amount of directors' loans a bank officially reported to the legislature and the extent of insider lending actually reflected on its books. In 1828, for example, the Eagle Bank of Bristol reported to the Rhode Island legislature that it had lent 18% of its funds to directors, yet a careful examination of its records shows that this figure included only notes on which directors were the principal signatories. Adding notes on which directors appeared as endorsers raises the total to 33%. Moreover, this revision still excludes nearly $30,000 in bad loans owed by insiders whose businesses had recently failed. Inclusion of these "doubtful notes" would have raised the total to 55%. The Pawtuxet Bank's report to the General Assembly in 1842 indicated that loans to directors amounted merely to 6% of the total, and the Wakefield Bank's report for 1845 showed directors receiving only 14%. Even if the reported amounts for stockholders' notes were added to these percentages, the official figures for the latter two banks would still be only 38% and 23%, respectively. Similarly, at approximately the same time as Rhode Island's bank commissioners were finding extensive evidence of insider lending, the maximum proportion of loans to directors reported in the official bank returns was 35%. Draw Account Book, Eagle Bank, Fleet National Bank Archives; Rhode Island, General Assembly, *Acts and Resolves* (May 1828), 37a; (May 1837), 42a; (June 1842), 16a; (October 1845), 40a.

14. Thomas G. Cary, *A Practical View of the Business of Banking* (Boston, 1845), 13.

15. The records of the Concord Bank, chartered in 1832, have been deposited at the Old Sturbridge Village Research Library. They include a discount book

In other cases, investors with surplus capital established banks to provide themselves with an outlet for their funds.[16] In still other cases, banks were organized in communities that really could not support them. Not only did the directors of such institutions have only modest requirements for loans, but often bank managers had to range far afield in order to keep their resources fully invested.[17]

The practice of granting large loans to insiders seems, however, to have been the rule rather than the exception, and not all observers found the practice as defensible as Cary did. The Honorable Benjamin Hazard of Rhode Island complained in 1826 that "those who have sought after banks have, generally, been those who themselves were in want of capital." He worried that this tendency would undermine the soundness of the banking system, and he attempted to use his power in the legislature to block pending petitions for charters.[18]

II

Hazard's rationale for blocking further expansion of the banking system found a receptive audience among the elite merchants who dominated the region's oldest banks. These merchants had consistently opposed any growth in the number of charters. Like Hazard, they believed that bank charters were being sought by persons "with a view to furnish funds for private speculation, or the private use of the principal stockholders." The result, they feared, would be a flood of insufficiently capitalized banks whose fortunes depended "on the success and solvency of the principal

> as well as directors' and stockholders' minute books from the pre–Civil War period.

16. The Shawmut Bank (originally chartered in 1836 as the Warren Bank of Boston) is a good example. See Asa S. Knowles, *Shawmut: 150 Years of Banking* (Boston: Houghton Mifflin, 1986), 21, 25.

17. Examples include the Strafford Bank of Dover, N.H. (whose records are stored in the Dover branch of the Bank of New Hampshire), and the Mendon (Mass.) Bank (whose records are stored in the Mendon Historical Society Museum). Stockholders in the latter institution decided to close up its affairs in 1831. Such banks were particularly vulnerable to takeovers by out-of-state residents, who often destroyed them and left local stockholders to pick up the pieces. See, for example, accounts of the failures of the Burrillville and Scituate banks in Rhode Island, General Assembly, *Acts and Resolves* (October 1834), 60–1; (October 1836), 49–50.

18. Rhode Island, General Assembly, *Report of the Committee to Inquire into the Expediency of Increasing the Banking Capital* (Providence: Smith & Parmenter, 1826), 24.

stockholders" and whose consequent vulnerability to failure threatened the stability of the entire financial system.[19]

Although their predictions of dire consequences were ultimately proven wrong, these merchants were largely correct in assessing the motives of the men who founded the new institutions. The early nineteenth century was a time of rising economic opportunity, and banks could provide an aspiring entrepreneur with the capital he needed to finance industrial ventures. In fact, in the eyes of many of these entrepreneurs, banks were an alchemist's dream come true. By securing a charter for a bank, they obtained a vehicle that, almost as if by magic, could assist them in raising funds. First, the incorporators subscribed for a controlling interest in the new bank's stock; then, when the payment for the stock came due, they borrowed the requisite sum from another institution. Such loans were not difficult to obtain, because they were essentially riskless. As soon as the state's examiners had satisfied themselves that the new bank's capital had actually been deposited, the investors could borrow back the money they had tendered for their stock (using the stock itself as security for the loan) and repay the original debt.[20]

At this point, of course, the new bank had virtually no resources to lend to its proprietors, because a large proportion of its capital was fictitious. Some money might be raised by issuing currency, but the funds that could be obtained in this way were strictly limited by the so-called Suffolk system (a private system of note redemption enforced by the largest Boston banks), which required each institution to maintain a deposit of specie to redeem its notes. Deposits, moreover, had not yet become an important source of funds for the banking sector. The main source of funding for banks during this era was the sale of bank stock, for which savings institutions, insurance companies, charitable associations, and private individuals proved willing purchasers.[21] Thanks to this mar-

19. Nathan Appleton, *An Examination of the Banking System of Massachusetts, in Reference to the Renewal of the Bank Charters* (Boston: Stimpson & Clapp, 1831), 19–20.

20. Legislative investigations generated detailed information about such financial practices, especially in Massachusetts, where a number of newly chartered banks failed in the aftermath of the Panic of 1837. See, for example, Massachusetts, General Court, "Report Relating to the Kilby Bank," Senate Doc. 34, 1838, 9–14, and "Report of the Bank Commissioners," Senate Doc. 7, 1840, 28–9. See also Rhode Island, General Assembly, *Report into the Expediency of Increasing the Banking Capital*, 30–2; Howard Kemble Stokes, *Chartered Banking in Rhode Island, 1791–1900* (Providence: Preston & Rounds, 1902), 36; and Walter W. Chadbourne, "A History of Banking in Maine, 1799–1930," *Maine Bulletin*, 39 (August 1936), 21.

21. See Chapter 3.

ket, the original investors were usually able to sell off some of their share holdings once their bank had been in operation for a few years. They could then use the proceeds from these sales to repay their stock loans at the bank, or else they could pocket the money and substitute some new form of security (typically the endorsement of one of their associates) in place of the stock, thus perpetuating their lines of credit. Over time, as the bank established a market for its securities, the proprietors could raise additional funds by increasing the bank's capitalization and selling new shares.

Records of the Eagle Bank in Bristol, Rhode Island, show how easy it could be for a bank's organizers to unload their investments. When the bank was chartered in 1818, large blocks of stock were bought by members of the DWolf family, as well as by other prominent citizens of the town, most of whom promptly borrowed back their purchase money on the security of the stock itself. The bank's transfer book shows that over the next few years some of these investors sold off a substantial portion of their holdings. By 1823, for example, Robert Rogers, Jr., had reduced his holdings from 300 shares to 146, Charles DWolf, Jr., from 320 to 143, and George DWolf from 250 to nothing (though he retained liberal borrowing privileges at the bank through the influence of other family members). Minutes of directors' meetings show that these men were usually not required to repay their stock loans when they sold off their holdings but instead were allowed to offer new security in the form of an endorser.[22]

By selling off some of their original stock purchases, bank organizers

22. Directors' and Stockholders' Minute Book, 1818–46, Stock Transfer Book, 1818–84, and Stock Book, 1818–1900, Eagle Bank, Bristol, R.I. The records of the Fleet National Bank of Providence contain a letter dated Aug. 6, 1825, from Amasa Manton, a director of the Mechanics Bank of Providence, to a Dr. J. Williams that illustrates the kind of sales pitch used by bank organizers to dispose of their stock:

> The cheapest stock now to be had in this market in my opinion is the Mechanics Bank stock. This Bank has been under way two years. They began with a capital of 100000 dol—— & this year increased it to 250,000 dol——. They have no real Estate on hand & no incumbrance whatever is on the Bank. They have always divided 7 per cent pr ann & hope and think they will in future. I have the honor to be a director in the Bank, which doubtless adds much to the value of the stock. I have got 150 shares in this Bank & will sell you what you want at 7 pr cent premium. I sold 25 shares to one person at this rate & I sold 12 shares to another one at 8 pr ct. It is to be had however at 7 pr cent, though there is not much to sell. The Roger Wms Bank can be had at 10. & the Eagle at same – Union Ditto. I think the Mechanics will be as high as any of them in a year or two. Nothing prevents it now except that it is a young Bank. . . . Mr. J F Croade & some Misses Croades are stockholders in this Bank.

were able to transform their initial promise to buy stock into real wealth. By this means too, they were able to acquire a line of credit that could significantly exceed the value of the shares they continued to hold. As time went on and the organizers sold off an increasing proportion of their shares, the discrepancy between the amount of stock they actually owned and the extent of their debts to the bank could widen considerably. In 1845, for example, Samuel Rodman owed the Wakefield Bank as principal and endorser nearly $23,000, though he held only $2,000 of the bank's stock. His cousin, Isaac P. Hazard, owned no stock whatsoever, yet his name appeared on notes valued at $14,500. All told, borrowers surnamed Rodman, Hazard, and Robinson (the three interrelated families who dominated the bank) accounted for nearly $40,000 in loans, or 84 percent of the total, even though they owned no more than $23,500 in stock (47 percent of the total).[23]

After selling off as much of their own holdings as they wished, the directors could still augment their credit resources by increasing the bank's capitalization and issuing new shares. The Pawtuxet Bank, for example, rapidly expanded its stock issues between 1823 and 1826, increasing its number of shares from 2,400 to 4,875. Minutes of the bank's board meetings suggest that the directors did not plan to buy much of this stock themselves. In 1823, for example, they voted to offer 600 of the 1,200 new shares they had authorized to the Rhode Island Society for the Encouragement of Domestic Industry (ultimately this society, which was run by the bank's president, wound up buying 825 shares). Then, in 1826, they voted to sell an additional 500 shares at a price of $19 apiece ($1 over par), with the extra dollar per share to be distributed among the existing stockholders.[24] Although the records do not indicate who (other than the society) purchased the Pawtuxet Bank's issues, minutes of stockholders' meetings reveal that by the early 1840s the Rhodes brothers were voting only 10 to 12 percent of the bank's outstanding shares, and even this figure probably included some proxies. Yet, as we have already seen, during the early 1840s the brothers obtained more than 50 percent of the bank's total loans.[25]

23. Family members held $23,500 of stock in 1834, but their holdings probably declined after that. In any event, even including proxies, family members never voted as much as 47% of the stock at any subsequent meeting, and sometimes voted considerably less. Bill Book A and Directors' and Stockholders' Minute Book, 1834–65, Wakefield Bank.

24. See esp. the minutes of the Jan. 11, 1823, and March 16, 1826, meetings. Directors' and Stockholders' Minute Book, 1815–85, Pawtuxet Bank, Warwick, R.I.

25. Ibid. Maintaining a controlling interest was apparently not a serious problem, for stockholders generally displayed little interest in the management of

The histories of other banks reveal how frequently this strategy of accumulation was employed and how lucrative it could be. When the American Bank of Providence was chartered in 1833, it issued only $193,000 of its authorized capital stock of $500,000. Two years later, however, the bank's stockholders voted to increase its capitalization to $300,000. In 1839 they voted to raise it once again, this time to $400,000, and in 1845 to $500,000. Having reached the upper limit of the bank's authorized capital, the stockholders petitioned the General Assembly in 1851 for permission to increase the ceiling to $1,000,000, and state banking records indicate that a mere four years later American's paid-in capital amounted to $983,750. The bank's stockholders thereupon submitted another petition to the legislature – this time to increase the capitalization to $2,000,000. Scattered notations in the minutes of the bank's board of directors indicate that large blocks of stock were purchased by such institutions as the American Insurance Company, the Roger Williams Insurance Company, and the Manufacturers Mutual Fire Insurance Company.[26]

Nor was this an isolated example. In Boston alone eleven banks were able to increase their initial capitalization by at least 50 percent between 1820 and 1850. In the rest of the state, forty-two banks had similar records.[27] All in all, New Englanders displayed an impressive willingness to put their savings into bank stock during this period. The amount of capital invested in the region's banks increased 101 percent during the 1830-to-1837 boom and another 97 percent during the expansionary 1850s. Over the entire period 1819 to 1860, investment in bank stock registered a more than sevenfold increase (see Table 1.1).

III

The financial alchemy that these newly established banks made possible required collective action. In order to secure a charter from the legislature and attract the necessary capital investment, individuals had to band

their banks. They were so apathetic, in fact, that banks had difficulty obtaining quorums at their annual meetings. See, for example, Massachusetts, Bank Commissioners, *Report,* Senate Doc. 5, 1839, 17.

26. Directors' and Stockholders' Minute Book, 1833–59, American Bank, Providence, Rhode Island Historical Society Manuscript Collections; Rhode Island, Secretary of State, *Abstract Exhibiting the Condition of the Banks* (1855), 5.

27. Massachusetts, General Court, "List of Banks Chartered in Massachusetts," House Doc. 93, 1850, 4–19.

together. They formed the requisite alliances in a variety of ways and for a variety of reasons. For example, the men who organized the State Bank of Boston in 1811 were active Democratic-Republican politicians who sought to undermine the Federalist monopoly of financial institutions. In other cases, men with common economic interests organized banks. The founders of the Shawmut Bank in Boston (originally the Warren Bank) were mainly merchants whose businesses were located on the Central and Long wharfs and who had previously associated with each other in various insurance ventures. Several of them, moreover, were active in the Whig Young Men of Boston, a group of up-and-coming merchants in their early thirties. Similarly, the Bath Bank of Bath, Maine, was the creation of a group of local shipbuilders and owners. In still other cases, the leading citizens of a town simply got together and organized a bank. The founders of the Indian Head Bank of Nashua, New Hampshire, for example, included six merchants, a doctor actively involved in town affairs, an engineer, the owner of a machine shop, and a lawyer who served as town moderator.[28]

Although many similar examples could be listed, by far the most common bond that tied a bank's directors together during these years was kinship. The Massachusetts Bank in Boston was founded by the Cabot–Lowell–Higginson clan, and the Providence Bank in Rhode Island by the interconnected Brown and Ives families.[29] These two cases, involving the region's oldest banks and wealthiest merchants, are well-known examples of the phenomenon. What is less generally recognized, however, is that the multiplication of banks during the early nineteenth century extended this pattern by enabling less prominent kinship groups to organize their own institutions as well. The American Bank of Providence, for example, was dominated by a group of merchant-manufacturers related in one way or another to Henry P. Franklin, a textile producer who served for many years as the bank's president and director. Other long-term directors included Franklin's son-in-law, Amos D. Smith, who joined with Franklin and his son in a series of textile-mill ventures; John Waterman, Franklin's

---

28. Amos W. Stetson, *Eighty Years: An Historical Sketch of the State Bank, 1811–1865 [and] the State National Bank, 1865–1891* (Boston, 1891 [privately printed]); Knowles, *Shawmut,* 25; *Our First Hundred Years: The Story of the Bath National Bank, 1855–1955* (Bath, Me., 1955 [privately printed]), 6–12; *Indian Head National Bank: Seventy-fifth Anniversary, 1851–1926* (Nashua, N.H., 1926 [privately printed]).

29. Peter Dobkin Hall, *The Organization of American Culture, 1700–1900: Private Institutions, Elites, and the Origins of American Nationality* (New York: New York University Press, 1984), 294; Weston and Piggot, *The Passing Years,* 48.

nephew and occasional business partner; and Shubael Hutchins, a merchant whose partner, Edward A. Green, was Amos D. Smith's son-in-law.[30] As mentioned earlier, the Pawtuxet Bank was dominated by James, William, and Christopher Rhodes. Additional directors (at various times) included James's son-in-law, William's son, and Christopher's son's father-in-law, as well as a nephew, grand-nephew, niece's husband, and numerous cousins of various degrees of closeness.[31]

Not only were the directors of these early banks frequently related to one another, but their families often retained positions of influence at these institutions for extremely long periods of time. The Phillips family gained a controlling interest in the Massachusetts Bank shortly after its founding and dominated its presidency for much of the next century. The Brown and Ives group maintained control of the Providence Bank for over 125 years. The Franklin and Rhodes clans ran the American and Pawtuxet banks, respectively, until at least the time of the Civil War.[32] Nor is there any lack of further examples. The Suffolk Bank in Boston was dominated for more than seventy years by the families composing the Boston Associates, and members of the Sprague family controlled the Globe Bank of Providence from the 1830s until their manufacturing empire collapsed during the Panic of 1873. The Richmond, Chapin, and Taft families presided over the Merchants Bank of Providence from 1818 to 1926; the Abbott and Tapley families exerted similar influence at the City Bank of Lynn, Massachusetts, during the half-century after its founding in 1854. The Robinson family continued to supply the Wakefield Bank with its presidents until at least the 1920s, and the Beal family dominated the presidency of the Granite Bank (later Second National) in Boston until the 1950s. The Blake and Stetson families were so closely identified with the management of the Merchants Bank in Bangor, Maine, that for

30. Directors' and Stockholders' Minute Book, 1833–59, American Bank, Providence, R.I.; *The Biographical Cyclopedia of Representative Men of Rhode Island* (Providence: National Biographical Publishing Co., 1881), vol. 1, 213–14; vol. 2, 311–12; Rhode Island vol. 9, 128–9, 136, R. G. Dun & Co. Collection, Baker Library, Harvard University Graduate School of Business Administration.

31. I am indebted for this information to my research assistant Ellie ⌐ ⌐ddard, who painstakingly reconstructed the genealogy of this kinship group from records at the Rhode Island Historical Society Library.

32. Gras, *The Massachusetts First National Bank*, 17–1°; Weston and Piggot, *The Passing Years*, 47–8; Directors' and Stockholders' Minute Book, 1833–59, American Bank, Providence; Directors' and Stockholders' Minute Book, 1815–85, Pawtuxet Bank, Warwick, R.I.; Redlich, *The Molding of American Banking*, pt. 1, 17, 20.

many years the institution was known informally as the Blake and Stetson Bank. Similarly, the Baylies and Williamses were long synonymous with the Taunton Bank of Taunton, Massachusetts.[33]

All this evidence of continuing family domination of banks runs counter to the claims of modernization theorists, who argue that kinship connections lost much of their economic significance during the first half of the nineteenth century because the spread of banks and other types of corporations enabled businessmen to raise investment funds without turning to their relatives for help.[34] Although it is certainly true that banks and corporations could tap the savings of a broad spectrum of the population, the appearance of these institutions did not necessarily reduce the importance of family ties. A firm that borrowed from a bank, for example, normally had to find an endorser for its notes – someone who was not directly involved in the enterprise but who was willing to guarantee repayment of the loan. Because of the risks involved, only a kinsman or close business associate could typically be counted upon to perform this service.

What modernization theorists fail to realize is that kinship ties served

33. D. R. Whitney, *The Suffolk Bank* (Cambridge, Mass., 1878 [privately printed]), 67–73; Stokes, *Chartered Banking in Rhode Island,* 56–7; Weston and Piggot, *The Passing Years,* 47–8; Arthur W. Pinkham and Frank E. Bruce, *Men and Money at the National City Bank of Lynn, Massachusetts, During the Past Seventy-five Years* (Lynn: Nichols Press, 1929), 22, 33, 37; "Wakefield Trust Company, Wakefield, Rhode Island," undated clipping from a 1928 issue of the *Narragansett Times,* in Wakefield Bank Collection, Rhode Island Historical Society Manuscript Collections; Alexander S. Wheeler, *The History of the Second National Bank of Boston from 1860 to 1896* (Boston, 1932 [privately printed]); Thomas P. Beal, *The Second National Bank of Boston* (Boston, 1958 [privately printed]); *Three Quarters of a Century, 1850–1925: Commemorating the Seventy-fifth Anniversary of the Founding of the Merchants National Bank of Bangor* (Bangor, 1925 [privately printed]); *Looking Backward: One Hundred and Twenty-five Years of Progress* (Taunton, Mass.: Bristol County Trust Co., 1937).

34. For the New England case, see esp. Peter Dobkin Hall, "Marital Selection and Business in Massachusetts Merchant Families, 1700–1900," in *The Family: Its Structures and Functions,* ed. Rose Laub Coser, 2d ed. (New York: St. Martin's, 1974), 226–40; "The Model of Boston Charity: A Theory of Charitable Benevolence and Class Development," *Science and Society,* 38 (Winter 1974–5), 464–77; "Family Structure and Economic Organization: Massachusetts Merchants, 1700–1850," in *Family and Kin in Urban Communities, 1700–1930,* ed. Tamara K. Hareven (New York: Franklin Watts, 1977), 38–61; *The Organization of American Culture,* 55–75, 91–124.

vital economic functions in a developing economy such as that of early-nineteenth-century New England. Information systems were still primitive, data about potential business dealings was difficult and costly to obtain, and people were not sure whom they could trust. As Robert A. Pollak has pointed out, in such an environment family enterprises are typically the preferred form of economic organization. Family members are in close contact with each other for personal as well as business reasons and therefore can monitor each other's activities. More important, relations among family members are structured by obligations of affection and loyalty that are backed up by real economic incentives. Transgressors face penalties that are much more serious than the loss of a job or a contract: they risk ostracism from the kinship group and the loss of both their claim on family resources and the connections vital to business success.[35]

Kinship enterprises had their drawbacks, of course, but, contrary to modernization theory, banks and other corporations could actually help them overcome some of the most restrictive ones. For example, by founding banks and other kinds of corporations, kinship groups could transcend the limited resources of their members. Banks, as we have already seen, were particularly useful devices for collecting investments from the larger community. In addition, banks could provide kinship groups with a permanent institutional base – a structure that helped to compensate for the transitory nature of the many partnerships into which their members were divided. Any time a firm dissolved – whether through failure, the withdrawal or death of a partner, or some other reason – its accounts had to be completely settled. As a result, endorsing notes – even for one's relatives – was a risky business. If it turned out that the maker of a note had overextended himself and was unable to make good on his obligations, the endorser was liable for the full amount of the debt. But even if the makers did not overextended themselves, the dissolution process was still often fraught with problems. During periods of tight money, for example, nonliquid assets might need to be converted at a loss into cash to satisfy a debt, and if in the process the firm ended up insolvent, its endorsers were liable for any deficiency.

Banks could help remedy this problem by clothing kinship networks in corporate form, thereby giving them a life independent of their constituent economic units. Among other things, banks could prevent the distress sales of assets by accepting notes to settle accounts. For example, in 1799 the Providence Bank allowed the firm of Samuel G. Arnold and Company

---

35. "A Transaction Cost Approach to Families and Households," *Journal of Economic Literature*, 23 (June 1985), 581–608.

to substitute its own notes for a debt due from the estate of Welcome Arnold, a former director. Similarly, the bank made special arrangements with the endorsers and heirs of John Brown, the bank's deceased president, allowing Brown's large loans to "lay without Renewing" until it was more "Convenient for the Heirs or Executors" to pay them off.[36]

To give another example, when Samuel Rodman's textile business failed in 1863, a committee of the Wakefield Bank's directors approached Isaac P. Hazard, Rodman's endorser, "to ascertain what [he] will do in regard to taking up said obligations." Rodman and Hazard were both members of the kinship group that controlled the bank, and the directors readily agreed to accept in settlement Hazard's personal notes, endorsed by his brother, payable at intervals over the next two years. At the end of this period some of the debt apparently still remained unpaid, for the bank's officers again approached Hazard. From that point on, however, there is no further mention of problems in the bank's minutes.[37] Although Hazard lost a total of about $140,000 as a result of the Rodman failure, his affiliation with the Wakefield Bank permitted him to pay off his obligations gradually without sacrificing productive assets. According to the R. G. Dun credit records, the Hazard firm was once more accumulating "heavy surplus capital" and was in good financial standing by 1867, a mere four years after the Rodman debacle.[38]

IV

As more and more kinship groups formed banks during the expansion of the 1820s and 1830s, the expectation that these institutions would serve a public function diminished. The grant of a corporate charter had originally carried with it the presumption of monopoly (the grantees obtaining an exclusive right to engage in a particular economic activity in return for performing some vital public task), but as the number of charters increased, the monopoly element necessarily declined, making it more difficult to conceive of the grant as a reward for public service. As Oscar and Mary Flug Handlin have pointed out, once banks increased to the point

36. Directors' meetings of Feb. 15, 1799, Oct. 7, 1803, July 16, 1804, and Oct. 29, 1804, Directors' Minute Book, 1796–1805, and letter from Brown & Ives to the President and Directors of the Providence Bank, Oct. 17, 1803, Providence (R.I.) Bank, Fleet National Bank Archives.
37. Directors' and Stockholders' Minute Book, 1834–65, and Directors' and Stockholders' Minute Book, 1865–90, Wakefield Bank. See esp. the records of meetings held on Sept. 29 and Dec. 29, 1863, and July 8, 1865.
38. Rhode Island vol. 15, 26, 87, R. G. Dun & Co. Collection.

where several of them competed in a given locality, the public found it difficult to conceive of them as community agents.[39]

This shift in the popular perception of banks is apparent in the documents that successful petitioners drafted to support their proposals for charters. Whereas in the late eighteenth century petitioners had uniformly invoked the general public interest in their requests, by the 1820s and 1830s it was common for them to cite the needs of specific groups in their communities. In 1823, for example, the incorporators of the Mechanics Bank of Providence argued "that the mechanics compose a large portion of the citizens of the town, and that the great & growing importance of the business in which they are engaged require the facilities and accommodations of a bank."[40] In similar fashion, Boston's leading Democratic newspaper, the *Morning Post,* applauded an attempt by "some of our North-end traders and Mechanics" to secure "a bank of moderate capital becoming men of moderate means."[41]

Other petitioners did not even bother appealing to the needs of a particular class but frankly admitted that they were seeking to establish a bank for their personal benefit. Incorporators of the Smithfield (Rhode Island) Exchange Bank, for instance, wanted an institution in which "they can become stockholders, and particularly if they can have one located and established in their own vicinity or neighborhood; in order to share or participate with their fellow Statesmen in equal privileges."[42] There were also by the 1820s a significant number of petitioners who secured banks without making any attempt whatsoever to justify their formation. Their applications consisted solely of a list of participants and a brief statement explaining that the undersigned wished to organize a bank. There was not much official resistance to this trend; indeed, by the mid 1830s Maine's legislators went so far as to announce that, since "no evil consequences can result to the community from an excess of Banking Capital, due regard being had to the competency of the individuals incorporated," they would approve any and all applications submitted by reputable individuals.[43]

The increasingly private nature of the banking system can also be seen in the evolving relationship between banks and the state. Every charter granted in Massachusetts during the first half of the nineteenth century

39. *Commonwealth,* 162–72.
40. Rhode Island, General Assembly, "Charters," 8 (1823–5), 15. These are manuscript records stored in the state archives.
41. *Boston Morning Post,* April 23, 1836, 1.
42. Rhode Island, General Assembly, "Charters," 7 (1820–3), 52.
43. Maine, Legislature, "Report of the Joint Standing Committee on Banks and Banking," Senate Doc. 28, 1836, 6.

reserved for the Commonwealth the right of subscribing to the bank's stock; it also permitted the state to appoint a director in order to safeguard its financial interest and to requisition loans up to a fixed percentage of the bank's capital. As time went on, however, these provisions increasingly fell into disuse. Before the War of 1812, for instance, the Commonwealth had supplied as much as one-eighth of the banking capital in the state, but during the 1820s it ceased to invest in banking enterprises altogether. By then, too, at least some of the banks had begun to treat the state as just another borrower whose demands could be refused if its terms were not regarded as desirable or if the bank was not "in funds" – that is, if discounts for private individuals had absorbed all its lendable resources.[44]

Although the bond between the banks and the state had weakened, however, it had by no means completely dissolved. Provisions requiring banks to lend to the government on demand remained on the books of most New England states, and occasionally they were activated. As late as 1834, for example, Maine was still requisitioning loans, and when the state treasurer discovered in 1836 that he could make some money for the state by borrowing from banks at the legally mandated rate of 5 percent and investing the money in bank stock, the legislature voted him authority to borrow $15,000 for this purpose.[45]

As a result of their special legislative charters, moreover, banks still obtained privileges from the state not granted to most other firms. Like other corporations by the 1820s, banks typically had the right to confer limited liability on their stockholders.[46] Unlike other corporations, however, banks also received the right to issue currency in the form of non-interest-bearing notes. By the early nineteenth century these notes constituted the bulk of the region's circulating media. Because a stable money supply was so vital to the well-being of the entire community, legislatures continued to play an active role in regulating the affairs of banking corporations. In contrast to their laissez-faire attitude with respect to the financial health of most of the other corporations they chartered, they required

44. Handlin and Handlin, *Commonwealth*, 129–30, 174–5.
45. Maine, Treasurer, "Report on the Finances," *Documents Printed by Order of the Legislature* (1835), pt. F and Schedule 26; (1836), 6–7; Maine, Legislature, "Resolve for Investing Money in Bank Stock, and Receiving Dividends," Senate Doc. 49, 1836.
46. Rhode Island banks chartered after the early 1830s were an exception. See, for example, Rhode Island, General Assembly, *Acts and Resolves* (January 1834), 76; (October 1834), 35. Massachusetts diluted the privilege by extending it to partnerships in 1835. Handlin and Handlin, *Commonwealth*, 234–5.

banks to file periodic statements of assets and liabilities. Whenever a bank failed, moreover, the government appointed a special commission to take control of its affairs with the aim of minimizing losses to note holders.[47]

As a result, then, of these two interrelated trends – the multiplication of banks and the community's increasing dependence upon banks for a circulating medium – there was growing confusion as to whether banks were public or private institutions. This basic confusion over the role of banks was to become especially troublesome by the end of the 1830s. On the one hand, because of their importance in supplying the region's money stock, banks were regarded by many citizens as institutions that performed a vital public function. On the other hand, the groups of businessmen who controlled the banks saw them as vehicles to accumulate capital for their private enterprises. These two very different perspectives had contradictory implications for the way banks functioned and for the role they played in the larger economy, contradictions that would come to a head in the aftermath of the Panic of 1837.

47. For examples of such legislative activities in Massachusetts, see Wilfred Stanley Lake, "The History of Banking Regulation in Massachusetts, 1784–1860," unpub. Ph.D. diss., Harvard University, 1932.

2

Insider lending
and Jacksonian hostility
toward banks

The democracy aim to protect the banks and bankers in all their legal and just franchises, and equal rights, as they do the merchant, mechanic, and farmer, but they will consent to no more exclusive, onesided legislation in favor of MAMMON.

The Lowell Advertiser[1]

I

It is tempting to conclude that the insider lending practiced by so many of the early banks explains the Jacksonians' well-known hostility toward those institutions. And to some extent such an inference would be valid. Critics of the banking system repeatedly charged that banks were "the partial instruments of the favored few," got up "for the advancement of their private interests, rather than great public blessings, of universal participation." Democratic newspapers in particular were filled with this sort of commentary, as, for instance, "the franchises of Banks are valuable to their stockholders much more than to the public. – They have, in fact, the fabled power of Midas" or "Banks are always got up by great speculators, who want to use all the money they can get."[2]

But these complaints about insider lending were only one aspect of a complex set of attitudes that might also manifest itself as indifference to, or even outright acceptance of, the practice. Take, for example, Rhode Island's response to the failure of the Farmers and Mechanics Bank in Pawtucket in 1829. The collapse was triggered by the financial embar-

1. April 16, 1838, p. 2.
2. Henry Williams (A Citizen of Boston, pseud.), *Remarks on Banks and Banking; and the Skeleton of a Project for a National Bank* (Boston: Torrey & Blair, 1840), 12; *Boston Daily Advocate,* Jan. 7, 1836, p. 2, and March 29, 1836, p. 2.

rassment of the Wilkinson family, whose members dominated the bank's board of directors and who at the same time were deeply indebted to the bank. The fact that heavy borrowing by its directors was at the root of the bank's troubles was well known; the General Assembly had commissioned reports on the matter, and local newspapers had broadcast the details. Nevertheless, the incident seems to have excited little adverse comment. The General Assembly appointed a commission to take control of the bank and settle its affairs, but nothing in the charge to the commissioners suggests that legislators regarded the Wilkinsons' behavior as particularly disturbing or that they were determined to prevent similar occurrences in the future. Had contemporaries viewed such insider lending as a breach of the public trust embodied in the bank's charter, some comment to this effect would surely have found its way into the legislature's deliberations, the commission's reports, or contemporary newspaper accounts. Yet nothing of the sort appeared. On the contrary, the *Manufacturers and Farmers Journal* noted that, although the stockholders of the bank were individually liable for its debts if the directors' actions violated the General Bank Act, such liability "can only arise in case of fraud on the part of Directors, which is not pretended in this case." The newspaper never made an issue of the fact that A. and I. Wilkinson alone owed the bank more than $150,000, or about half its outstanding loans, though it did report the figure. Admittedly, the *Journal* might be dismissed as a probank newspaper, but the Jacksonian *Republican Herald,* which also reported on the failure, treated the Wilkinsons no more harshly.[3]

A similarly blasé response greeted the 1837 Rhode Island bank commissioners' report, which concluded that banks had become "mere engines to supply the directors with money." Though the commissioners were not regarded as friends of the banking establishment (they had recently issued a tough report on usurious interest charges and pushed for legislation that the banking community vehemently opposed), they did not use their findings to criticize the directors' behavior. Instead they concluded that extensive insider lending was more or less inevitable: "Certain it is, that at present, a person who is a director in one bank, can

---

3. Rhode Island, General Assembly, *Acts and Resolves* (June 1829), 29; (October 1829), 54–6; (January 1830), 45; (May 1830), 46; (June 1830), 29; (October 1830), 24–6; (January 1831), 29; (May 1831), 36; (June 1831), 57–9; (October 1831), 75–6; (Providence) *Manufacturers and Farmers Journal,* June 25, 1829, p. 2; (Providence) *Republican Herald,* June 27, 1829, p. 2.

rarely obtain any accommodation at another." It was no wonder, they decided, that directors turned to their own institutions for funds.[4]

The commissioners recognized that heavy borrowing by directors meant that outsiders might find it difficult to obtain loans: "If the wants of [a director] and his associate directors are large, there will be of course but little left for those without the board." But though they doubted that "it was originally intended or expected that banks would be devoted chiefly to supplying the wants of those who managed them," they refrained from suggesting that such favoritism constituted "an abuse of the chartered privileges requiring the correction of law" and did not recommend any remedial legislation.[5]

One might expect this conclusion to have generated some controversy, but in contrast to the uproar that greeted the commissioners' earlier report on usury, the press scarcely took notice of it.[6] The major Providence newspapers, the *Manufacturers and Farmers Journal* and the *Republican Herald,* printed similar one-paragraph synopses of the report. They offered no comment at all on the commissioners' main conclusion, remarking only upon a secondary finding that certain directors of the Merchants Bank had lent out money they had borrowed from their own institution at rates in excess of the usury ceiling.[7]

Additional evidence of a lack of concern about insider lending comes from the various state investigations of usury sparked by the tight-money conditions of the mid to late 1830s. Called upon to justify interest charges that legislators claimed were excessive, bank officers cited their own practice of insider lending by way of defense. The public, they argued, had the mistaken notion that the purpose of banks was to help rich capitalists lend their surplus funds at the highest possible rates. In fact, nothing could be farther from the truth. The greater part of the region's stock of banking capital, they pointed out, was held by savings banks,

---

4. Rhode Island, General Assembly, *Acts and Resolves* (January 1837), 89–92. One of the bank commissioners, Thomas W. Dorr, would later lead the violent rebellion that bears his name.

5. Ibid.

6. The commissioners' 1836 finding that banks were surreptitiously charging usurious interest rates generated a storm of controversy. See the long exchange of letters by "Ricardo" and his various critics and supporters in the *Manufacturers and Farmers Journal* in July and August 1836. See also John Whipple (A Rhode Islander, pseud.), *Jeremy Bentham and the Usury Law* (n.p., 1836).

7. *Republican Herald,* Jan. 25, 1837, p. 2; *Manufacturers and Farmers Journal,* Jan. 23, 1837, p. 2.

charitable associations, trusts and estates, and widows and orphans. The men who controlled the banks' lending operations, on the other hand, usually had only a minor financial stake in the institutions they managed. They were not so much moneylenders as money borrowers, so *they* were the ones who paid most of the excess rates on loans. Representatives of the Merchants Bank of Providence pointed out that "the amount deducted from notes discounted for persons out of the Bank has generally been less than from those discounted for the Directors. . . . The principal part of the notes discounted is for the board of Directors." Similarly, the officers of the People's Bank of Roxbury, Massachusetts, asserted that "in charging such [extra] exchange no distinction has ever been made between the directors and other customers of the bank, excepting indeed, that a principal portion of such exchange has been paid by directors, so that no ground can exist for imputing to them the slightest intent of personal gain or advantage, independently of the trifling interests they respectively had in common with the other stock-holders." Spokesmen for the State Bank of Boston summarized the bankers' defense succinctly: "All of them [the bank's directors] borrow money, why should they raise its price or increase the hardship of its terms?"[8]

Unlike their interest charges, the bankers' defense elicited no negative comments from the press – not even from the *Boston Daily Advocate,* one of the region's most avowedly antibank newspapers. (The *Advocate* turned its venom entirely on the banks' alleged violation of the usury laws.)[9] This absence of any apparent interest in the subject of insider lending is particularly surprising, considering the tight-money conditions that plagued the close of Jackson's presidency. Given the existence of a usury ceiling (and the banks' limited ability to evade it), one would expect monetary stringency to have resulted in credit rationing; logically, tight

8. Rhode Island, General Assembly, *Report of the Committee Appointed to Visit and Examine the Banks in This State* (Providence: William Simons, Jr., 1836), 15; Massachusetts, General Court, "Second Report of the Bank Investigating Committee," House Doc. 62, 1836, 69–70, 82. See also the testimony of other bank officers in these same investigations and in Massachusetts, General Court, "Report Relative to Investigation of Banks," Senate Doc. 47, 1836.

9. Feb. 5, 1837, p. 2. I have searched for responses in a number of rural newspapers associated with both parties, as well as in the major Boston dailies. Democratic papers showed a marked lack of interest in the investigation – not surprising, given that the worst violations were found in banks controlled by members of that party. The *Boston Daily Advocate* did not hesitate to criticize the banks under investigation, but it was attacked by other Democratic papers for doing so.

money should have combined with the usury laws to make the practice of insider lending more apparent and more objectionable than ever. As we shall see, however, it was not until the Panic of 1837 that the connection was widely made.[10] Until that time it was usury – not insider lending – that generated the most concern.

II

At the root of people's ambivalent attitude toward insider lending was confusion about whether banks were public or private enterprises. To the extent that banks were considered private ventures, insider lending was not a matter of concern. Because family ties still formed the basis for most economic relationships, businessmen routinely favored kinsmen and other close personal associates in their dealings, and there was no reason to expect that bankers would behave any differently. To the extent that banks were considered public entities, however, insider lending had potentially serious implications. Jacksonian Americans were acutely sensitive to the abuse of power by those in positions of governmental authority, and favoritism in the dispensation of privileges was prima facie evidence of such abuse. Thus in 1832 a congressional committee hostile to the Second Bank of the United States made much of the fact that the bank had granted large and seemingly irregular loans to the firm of Thomas Biddle, a relative of the bank's president. This information was so potentially damaging to the credibility of the bank's administration that supporters rushed to explain the circumstances of the loans. Once made, however, the charge of favoritism proved difficult to dislodge. It was the only portion of the committee's report that Boston's Democratic newspapers picked up, and it resurfaced in 1834 during the controversy over the removal of federal deposits from the bank, serving to confirm the existence of a "system of favoritism" perpetrated by this "monstrous monopoly" at the public's expense.[11]

The multiplication of banks during the first third of the nineteenth century made it increasingly difficult for New Englanders to conceive of

10. One exception was a Fourth of July oration by Robert Rantoul, Jr., who argued that "by the combined operation of the banking system and the usury laws, it has become very difficult for anyone not belonging to the party of bankers to obtain money on loans." See his *Memoirs, Speeches and Writings,* ed. Luther Hamilton (Boston: John P. Jewett & Co., 1854), 569–70.

11. See *Boston Morning Post,* May 9, 1832, p. 2; Jan. 10, 1834, p. 2; and Feb. 28, 1834, p. 2; *Boston Daily Advocate,* May 7, 1832, p. 2.

these institutions as public entities. Banks still retained important public functions, however – most important, responsibility for the region's currency. Some financial writers attempted to resolve the confusion inherent in this situation by distinguishing banks' private business dealings from their public duties. Nathan Appleton, for example, argued in 1831 that "the public have a deep interest in the solidity and good management of a bank of circulation; whilst they have comparatively none in the management of a bank employing their own funds, in making discounts only, or in buying and selling bills of exchange."[12] Few contemporaries went so far as to accept Appleton's recommendation that the power to issue currency be restricted to a small number of very large banks whose policies would be closely monitored by the government, but most seemed to have accepted the division of function that he laid out. Hence the general preoccupation with usury and the relative lack of concern with insider lending.

Standing outside this consensus, however, were the radicals who occupied the extreme left of the Jacksonian party – the so-called hards, or advocates of a metallic currency.[13] Banks provided these disaffected politicians with a potent issue that could be used to focus both the anxieties produced by rapid economic growth and the inchoate resentment that many New Englanders felt toward the rich and powerful.[14] No charge during this period was more potentially damaging, nor more politically explosive, than the claim that persons with access to government had secured advantages that others did not possess – advantages that gave them power to harm the public. Such was the case the hards attempted to make against banks.

It was nonsense, they claimed, to argue that mere multiplication had stripped banks of their monopoly power and hence of their public charac-

---

12. *An Examination of the Banking System of Massachusetts, in Reference to the Renewal of the Bank Charters* (Boston: Stimpson & Clapp, 1831), 7.
13. James Roger Sharp, *The Jacksonians Versus the Banks: Politics in the States After the Panic of 1837* (New York: Columbia University Press, 1970), 14–18. See also Ronald P. Formisano, *The Transformation of Political Culture: Massachusetts Parties, 1790s-1840s* (New York: Oxford University Press, 1983), 272–3; Arthur B. Darling, "Jacksonian Democracy in Massachusetts, 1824–1848," *American Historical Review*, 29 (October 1923), 286; Donald B. Cole, *Jacksonian Democracy in New Hampshire, 1800–1851* (Cambridge: Harvard University Press, 1970), 186–7; David A. Martin, "Metallism, Small Notes, and Jackson's War with the B.U.S.," *Explorations in Economic History*, 11 (Spring 1974), 227–47.
14. On this point see Marvin Meyers, *The Jacksonian Persuasion: Politics and Belief* (New York: Random House, 1960).

ter. As one legislator put it, "Perhaps by the definition of the word *monopoly* in Queen Elizabeth's time, or by Coke's or Blackstone's definition, banks are not monopolies. But the meaning of the word changes with time." He then proceeded to redefine the term as "an *exclusive privilege,* conferred by law on any person or persons." "Now, if banks are tried by this definition," he asserted, "it will be hard to show, that banks are not monopolies."[15]

Foremost among the privileges that banks had obtained from government was the right to issue money – a right, the *Boston Advocate* claimed, that "increases nine times the value of [the banker's] actual property, thus allowing him to receive for $11\frac{1}{9}$ cents the same interest which the law allows every other citizen to receive for one hundred cents."[16] Although the *Advocate*'s arithmetic exaggerated the advantage that banks received with their charters, the right to issue currency was unquestionably a valuable privilege. Moreover, as the hards claimed, it was a privilege that gave those who obtained it a decided edge over their competitors. Because the legislature "collected from the many the whole monied capital of the state . . . and placed it under the management of the *few,*" everyone in business "is obliged to apply [to them] for the means to manage his concerns." Bank insiders could borrow from their own institutions at the legally mandated discount rate of 6 percent and then relend the proceeds to outsiders at the higher market rate of interest.[17] Even worse, "the monopoly which the banks enjoy . . . enables the favorites of those institutions to take advantage of the state of the markets, which others, not so favored, cannot do." In times of monetary stringency, "the directors and their friends are naturally accommodated before strangers. . . . With scarce money they buy at low prices." Then, as monetary conditions ease and prices once again begin to rise, "the favorites" are able to sell off their holdings at a profit and repay their loans at the bank. For the hards, these manipulations had alarming implications: "those who have the management of the Banks have individually advantages in trade which can not be enjoyed by others. They are enabled to facilitate their operation in various ways, to the almost entire monopoly of all the business of any magnitude."[18]

15. *Boston Daily Advocate,* March 28, 1836, p. 2.
16. Ibid., Feb. 13, 1836, p. 2.
17. *Republican Herald,* Aug. 17, 1836, p. 2; *New-Hampshire Gazette,* Dec. 27, 1836, p. 3. It was this sort of complaint that spurred Rhode Island's bank commissioners to investigate insider lending.
18. Rantoul, *Memoirs, Speeches and Writings,* 569–70, 576; *Lowell Patriot,* Jan. 22, 1836, p. 2; *Boston Daily Advocate,* March 29, 1836, p. 2; *Republican Herald,* Aug. 17, 1836, p. 2.

Even for the hards, however, the issue was not whether banks were controlled by those who used their resources for their own private ends but rather whether the state had intervened in the economy by granting certain individuals special privileges not possessed by others. The crucial point was government intervention, for by singling out a few such enterprises for special treatment, the state had transformed otherwise ordinary private businesses into instruments of exploitation. "If an association of individuals wish to loan money, let them; no one wishes to prevent it," asserted Massachusetts Democrat Robert Rantoul. "But it is wrong and unjust that a set of individuals who make it a business to let money, should be allowed to enjoy privileges which would be denied to men in other business."[19] An editorialist writing under the pseudonym Equal Laws expanded Rantoul's point:

> Banking is, *in itself,* a trade useful to society; and therefore *the manner in which it is regulated,* is the source of evil and the object of reform. . . . Does not the State – by the conditions it imposes on us in consequence of its policy of granting to banking corporations the exclusive privilege of issuing notes, as currency, of limiting at its own discretion the number of such corporations, the amount of capital and credit to be employed by them, the number of persons concerned in them, and of receiving to itself the power of deciding who shall be favored with charters, at the same time that it imposes the further conditions that none shall enjoy the privilege or become a corporation other than those it may choose to favor – does it not by these conditions cut off proper and wholesome competition in the trade? . . . We . . . firmly believe that corruption (or partiality, if you please,) and tyranny are the *necessary effects.*[20]

The hards' primary aim was to strip banks of their state-accorded privileges while returning to a purely private system of banking – to "Banks unconnected with the Government," as the *New-Hampshire Gazette* put it.[21] To this end, they proposed two fundamental reforms. First, state legislatures must eliminate the element of privilege inherent in banks' special charters, either by passing general incorporation laws that would open up banking to the populace at large or, conversely, by taking away from banking corporations their right of limited liability.[22] Second, the legislatures must eliminate banks' power over the currency. Although

19. Rantoul, *Memoirs, Speeches and Writings,* 351.
20. *Boston Morning Post,* Dec. 29, 1835, p. 1.
21. Dec. 13, 1836, p. 3.
22. The former proposal was popular in Massachusetts, whereas the latter was favored by radicals in New Hampshire. See, for examples, *Boston Morning Post,* April 7, 1836, p. 1; Massachusetts, General Court, "Address of His Excellency Marcus Morton to the Two Branches of the Legislature," House Doc. 9, 1840, 11; Oscar Handlin and Mary Flug Handlin, *Commonwealth:*

a number of different solutions to the money-supply problem was proposed, including the creation of a single state bank with exclusive responsibility for the currency, the remedy that New England's hard-money Jacksonians most frequently advocated was the suppression of all bank-notes of small denomination. Because bills larger than $10 or $20 rarely circulated among the general population, the suppression of small bills would effectively end banks' role as suppliers of money for routine tasks. The large notes that remained would function similarly to bills of exchange; deprived of their character as everyday money, they would still serve a useful purpose in the pursuit of trade.[23]

Contrary to the charges often leveled against them, the hards claimed their reforms would in no way lead to the destruction of the region's banking system. Most of them steadfastly insisted they had no desire for such an outcome, and their protestations on this point should be taken seriously. They intended rather to reconstitute banks as purely private businesses whose proprietors neither benefited from nor owed anything to the state. Over such a system government oversight would no longer be needed, except for measures necessary "to protect those who hold [banks'] promises . . . [by insuring] the enforcement of their contracts."[24] Even the usury laws could be repealed. As one writer explained, if the

A Study of the Role of Government in the American Economy: Massachusetts, 1774–1861 (New York: New York University Press, 1947), 232, 234–5; Henry Hubbard, Message of His Excellency the Governor to Both Branches of the General Court of New-Hampshire (Concord: Barton & Carroll, 1842); Cole, Jacksonian Democracy in New Hampshire, 192–4, 201–11; Norman Walker Smith, "A History of Commercial Banking in New Hampshire, 1792–1843," unpub. Ph.D. diss., University of Wisconsin, 1967, 226–7.

23. See, for examples, Boston Morning Post, Dec. 29, 1835, p. 1; March 12, 1836, p. 2; Boston Daily Advocate, March 29, 1836, p. 2; Lowell Patriot, Jan. 22, 1836, p. 2; Feb. 19, 1836, p. 2; Massachusetts, General Court, "Address of His Excellency Marcus Morton," 1840, 16; Rantoul, Memoirs, Speeches and Writings, 530; Maine, Legislature, "Report of the Special Committee on the Currency," House Doc. 77, 1836; Maine, Legislature, "Message of Governor [John] Fairfield to Both Branches of the Legislature," Documents Printed by Order of the Legislature (1840). See also Robert DeGroff Bulkley, Jr., "Robert Rantoul, Jr., 1805–1852: Politics and Reform in Antebellum Massachusetts," unpub. Ph.D. diss., Princeton University, 1971, 200, 205; Cole, Jacksonian Democracy in New Hampshire, 192–4; Walter W. Chadbourne, "A History of Banking in Maine, 1799–1930," Maine Bulletin, 39 (August 1936), 56–7; Martin, "Metallism, Small Notes, and Jackson's War with the B.U.S.," 242–3.

24. Massachusetts, General Court, "Address of His Excellency Marcus Morton," 1840, 11.

legislature were to end the practice of granting special charters and prohibit the issuance of small bills, then the state could "open free trade in Banking as in other trades, and abolish the Usury laws, not only with safety, but with immense benefit to the whole community."[25]

Nor would insider lending any longer present a problem. If bankers obtained no special privileges from the state, if anyone who wished to enter the banking business could do so in a free and open manner, then it hardly mattered to whom a bank lent its money. Not only was it assumed that banks would operate primarily in the interests of their own proprietors (publicists from both parties generally agreed that the desire for access to credit was the main reason for founding a bank in the first place), but such an arrangement could now be conceived as a positive good, as a means of transmitting the benefits of economic development to every element of the population. Thus one pamphleteer, who decried special charters as "mere instrument[s] of selfishness and despotism," proposed an alternative system whereby those needing access to credit could organize their own branches of a state bank.

> The mechanics and men of small trade, whose wants are moderate and who in a great measure have hitherto been excluded from bank favors, can if necessary, and they see fit, form companies by themselves for the establishment of branch banks, with small capitals, which will give them access to the principal bank for an equitable share of its loanable means.[26]

25. *Boston Morning Post,* April 7, 1836, pp. 1–2. Most Democrats thought the usury laws were necessary as long as banks retained their special privileges, but a few thought they should be repealed regardless. See, for example, William Kendrick, "Interest of Money – Pernicious Laws – Farming," *Boston Daily Advocate,* Jan. 30, 1836, p. 2. See also *Lowell Patriot,* Jan. 22, 1836, p. 2. The *Patriot* also reprinted Kendrick's article on Feb. 5, 1836, p. 2.

26. A Citizen of Boston, *A New System of Paper Money* (Boston: I. R. Butts, 1837), 5, 17–18. At the central bank, however, borrowing by officers and directors would be strictly prohibited. This shift in attitudes toward insider lending, depending on whether banks were perceived as public or private enterprises, is also reflected in William B. Greene's radical agrarian pamphlet, *Mutual Banking* (West Brookfield, Mass.: O. S. Cooke & Co., 1850). Greene criticized Pierre Joseph Proudhon's proposal for a central bank on the ground that it did not adequately guard against favoritism, yet proceeded to construct an alternative based on the principle of insider lending. Greene proposed the formation of what he called Real Estate Mutual Banks, which farmers could join by pledging their land. Membership brought with it the right to borrow paper money from the bank in an amount equal to three-quarters of the property pledged; no money would be lent to nonmem-

III

Although the reconstruction of the banking sector on a purely private basis was the hards' major goal, their program was by no means free of the ambiguities that plagued the subject of banking generally. In the hards' case, the trouble was that political and economic realities combined to defeat their proposed reforms. In a state such as Massachusetts, which was dominated by the Whig party, the hards had little or no chance of success. But even in Democratic states like New Hampshire they faced the opposition of conservatives within their own party, who were often as heavily involved in banking as their Whig counterparts.[27] Moreover, in those cases where the hards did manage to secure at least partial passage of their program, their measures often proved unworkable in practice. Maine's attempt to prohibit banks from issuing bills in denominations of less than $5 only resulted in the influx of currency from surrounding states. Similarly, when Maine's legislators effectively instituted free banking by declaring that they would approve all applications for charters, they discovered there was insufficient capital to organize all the institutions. Only 14 of the 26 banks chartered in the state between 1820 and 1831 actually went into operation. Between 1831 and 1837 the number of banks expanded as 39 of 47 new charters were effectuated, but only 36 of the state's 56 banks had sufficient resources to survive the Panic of 1837.[28]

bers. According to Greene, insider lending by Real Estate Banks, unlike that practiced by existing "aristocratic organizations," would not be a source of evil, for it would be predicated on the free and mutual association of ordinary landowners, not on special governmental favors.

27. For example, Isaac Hill was a director of the Merrimack County Bank in Concord and subsequently president of the Mechanicks Bank of the same city, Levi Woodbury had investments in both the Piscataqua and Portsmouth Banks of Portsmouth, and Franklin Pierce was actively involved with Portsmouth's Commercial Bank, the first federal depository in New Hampshire. Democratic politicians in other states had important banking connections as well. Most of the federal depositories in New England were controlled by prominent Jacksonians, and there were also many smaller "Democratic banks." When Robert Rantoul resolved to devote a Fourth of July speech in Worcester to an attack on banks, he found he had to tone down his remarks so as not to offend local party officials, all of whom were either bank officers or stockholders. Cole, *Jacksonian Democracy in New Hampshire,* 130–4; Frank Otto Gatell, "Spoils of the Bank War: Political Bias in the Selection of Pet Banks," *American Historical Review,* 70 (October 1964), 50–3; Bulkley, "Robert Rantoul, Jr.," 201.

28. Maine, Legislature, "Report of the Joint Standing Committee on Banks and

Faced with this lack of success – and with the entrenchment of the existing banking system – hard-money Jacksonians began to pursue a second set of reforms. These policies implicitly accepted the banking system as a given and aimed to extend the state's regulatory authority over it. Because these policies seemed to contradict the laissez-faire thrust of their campaign against state-created banks, they have given historians a great deal of difficulty.[29] In actuality, however, the one set of proposals was merely the flip side of the other. If the hards could have succeeded in eliminating the special privileges that banks obtained through their legis-lative charters, then banks would function as private enterprises no more in need of government oversight than any other business. But if these privileges could not be eliminated, then banks were indisputably public in character, and government regulation was needed to insure that they performed their duties in a responsible manner: "Being public Institu-tions, clothed with the high power of furnishing the currency of the State, [they] should, at all times, be watched with a jealous eye."[30]

Thus the same hard-money Jacksonians who supported the privatiza-tion of the banking system also proposed numerous pieces of regulatory legislation: laws that specified the amount of gold and silver that banks were required to keep in their vaults, that limited loans to a fixed propor-tion of capital, and that created boards of bank commissioners with the power to inquire into transactions with customers. Similarly, the same hards who showed little concern about favoritism when practiced by banks that were truly private in nature took steps to prevent insider lending by chartered corporations that benefited from special legislative privileges, introducing bills that restricted loans to directors to a small fraction of the banks' total capital.[31]

Banking," Senate Doc. 29, 1835; Senate Doc. 11, 1836; Senate Doc. 28, 1836; "Message of Governor [Robert P.] Dunlap to Both Branches of the Legislature," *Documents Printed by Order of the Legislature* (1836), 15; "Report of the Bank Commissioners," Senate Doc. 13, 1836; Chadbourne, "A History of Banking in Maine," 33, 38, 54–7; Sharp, *The Jacksonians Versus the Banks,* 309–12.

29.   John M. McFaul, for one, has attributed this assortment of policies to political expediency. Although there is certainly some measure of truth to his position, there was also a higher consistency at work. See McFaul, *The Politics of Jacksonian Finance* (Ithaca, N.Y.: Cornell University Press, 1972).

30.   Maine, Legislature, "Report of the Joint Standing Committee on Banks and Banking," House Doc. 38, 1835, 2.

31.   For surveys of reform proposals and legislation, see Chadbourne, "A Histo-ry of Banking in Maine," 35–7, 56–8; Cole, *Jacksonian Democracy in New Hampshire,* 192–4, 201–6; Wilfred Stanley Lake, "The History of Banking

These alternative proposals actually met with some success in a couple of states. When a Democratic–Antimasonic alliance came to power in Rhode Island in 1836, the legislature passed a bill that tightened the usury laws and other statutes governing banks and, more important, created a board of bank commissioners to enforce the regulations. Maine, which was normally a Democratic state, created a board of bank commissioners during the early 1830s. In addition, the Maine legislature passed a law restricting the amount of money any one bank could lend its directors to 33 percent of its paid-in capital stock.[32]

The hards' program would probably not have gotten much further, however, had it not been for the Panic of 1837. Originating overseas in an attempt by the Bank of England to staunch an outflow of specie, the crisis initially had little to do with problems confronting the region's banking system. American firms involved in international trade, however, suddenly found it difficult to obtain credit. Several important concerns failed, and the resulting pressure on the financial system forced banks in New York and New Orleans to suspend specie payments. New England banks followed suit a few days later. Even though most of them still had plenty of specie in their vaults, they had to suspend payments or else face the prospect of watching their specie drain rapidly out of the region.[33]

Although the suspension of specie payments was provoked by events external to the region, and though it actually helped to ease the monetary stringency rather than exacerbate it, people at the time had difficulty disentangling cause and effect. The suspension was the most visible aspect of a crisis that caused prices to decline sharply and many businesses to fail, and it seemed dramatically to confirm the charge that problems with the banking system were at the heart of the region's economic woes. So too did a series of bank failures that erupted in early 1838. The most spectacular of these collapses involved the Commonwealth Bank in Boston. This bank had been one of the earliest recipients of government funds removed from the Second Bank of the United States, and it had used the money to increase its loans – mainly to its president, its cashier, and a few other insiders, all of whom were prominently associated with the Demo-

Regulation in Massachusetts, 1784–1860," unpub. Ph.D. diss., Harvard University, 1932; Smith, "A History of Commercial Banking in New Hampshire," 159–60, 209–10, 224–34; Howard Kemble Stokes, *Chartered Banking in Rhode Island, 1791–1900* (Providence: Preston & Rounds, 1902), 39–45.

32. Stokes, *Chartered Banking in Rhode Island,* 42–3; Chadbourne, "A History of Banking in Maine," 34–7.

33. For a detailed account of events leading to the Panic, see Peter Temin, *The Jacksonian Economy* (New York: Norton, 1969), 113–47.

cratic party. When the president died with outstanding debts of more than $250,000, the bank could not meet its demands and was forced to close. The failure of the Commonwealth was quickly followed by the collapse of several other banks dominated by Democratic politicians. Subsequent investigations showed that in each case the bank's troubles had resulted from the financial manipulations of insiders.[34]

As one might expect, the Whig press had a field day, pointing out that Jacksonian political leaders had used the charge of monopoly power and favoritism to remove public deposits from the Second Bank of the United States, only to funnel the money into their own less reputable pockets. Conveniently ignoring the failure of a number of banks unconnected with the Jacksonians – failures that also involved substantial loans to insiders – they harped on the abuse of public power exposed by the collapse of the pet banks, denouncing "the system of partisan reward, plunder and speculation" that enabled Jacksonian bosses to "seize the public money, and then to squander and misapply it, converting it into an instrument for their own aggrandizement."[35] The problem, the Whig editors implied, lay not with the banking system itself but with the private use to which the Jacksonians had put public funds. Family connections between Jackson's secretary of the treasury, Levi Woodbury, and officers of two of the failed banks helped the Whigs to underscore this point. According to the Boston *Atlas*, the principal officers of the Franklin and Lafayette banks were selected "from among the immediate connections of Mr Woodbury" in a scheme "to obtain from the Secretary of the Treasury a portion of the public booty." The editor could hardly contain his outrage: "Here is the Secretary of the Treasury himself . . . lending the PEOPLE'S MONEY on the most flimsy security to his IMMEDIATE RELATIVES and DEPENDENTS."[36]

Although hard-money Jacksonians were embarrassed by the revelations that followed upon the failure of the pet banks, they benefited from the much greater discomfiture of their conservative enemies within the Democratic party – even as they attempted to deflect criticism away from the party by claiming that the problems afflicting these Democratic institutions were endemic to the banking system as a whole. Each and every

34. Massachusetts, General Court, "Report Respecting the Franklin Bank," Senate Doc. 25, 1838; "Report and Bill Relating to the Middlesex Bank," Senate Doc. 27, 1838; "Report Relating to the Commonwealth Bank," Senate Doc. 35, 1838; "Report Respecting the Lafayette Bank," Senate Doc. 51, 1838; (Boston) *Atlas*, Jan. 26, 1838, p. 2; *Springfield Weekly Republican*, Feb. 24, 1838, p. 1; March 3, 1838, p. 1.

35. *Atlas*, Jan. 13, 1838, p. 2; Jan. 15, 1838, p. 2. See also (Worcester) *National Aegis*, Jan. 24, 1838, p. 2; *Springfield Weekly Republican*, Feb. 24, 1838, p. 2.

36. *Atlas*, Feb. 2, 1838, p. 2.

legislative charter, they insisted, placed the power of the government in the hands of a privileged few. Robert Rantoul, the most articulate spokesman for the hards in the Massachusetts House and a member of the select committee appointed to examine the affairs of the Commonwealth Bank, claimed on the floor of the legislature that he had not seen anything in the management of this particular bank that was "essentially at variance with the practice of all the other banking institutions, with which he was acquainted."[37] Legislative investigations of additional failures – of banks controlled by Whigs as well as Jacksonians – provided considerable evidence in support of his contention.[38]

The hards proceeded to develop this point into a full-blown explanation for the Panic. Not only were the excesses that brought down the Commonwealth Bank epidemic in the region, but they had made the entire banking system prone to crisis. The root of the problem, according to this line of thought, was the directors' habit of lending money to themselves, which "has contributed more to the multiplication of banks than every thing else."[39] Once it had become apparent that bank directors had privileged access to credit, everyone needing capital clamored to form banks: "The excluded become the applicants for new charters which they may control. But others and others are wanted for the same reason, and to be used for the same purposes." The result was a twofold evil: banking institutions that were individually weak, "without any money or capital whatever," and a banking system that was overextended, doomed to "fall under its own weight." The Panic of 1837 was "the necessary result."[40]

As the crisis dramatically illustrated, it made no sense at all to distin-

---

37. Ibid., Jan. 19, 1838, p. 2. See also *Boston Daily Advocate*, Jan. 15, 1838, p. 2; Feb. 15, 1838, p. 2; *Boston Morning Post*, Jan. 15, 1838, p. 2; Jan. 29, 1838, p. 2; *Barnstable Patriot and Commercial Advertiser*, Jan. 17, 1838, p. 2; *Lowell Advertiser*, Jan. 15, 1838, p. 2; Jan. 31, 1838, p. 2; *Lynn Record*, Feb. 7, 1838, p. 2.

38. See, for examples, Massachusetts, General Court, "Report Relating to the Kilby Bank," Senate Doc. 34, 1838; "Report and Bill Repealing the Charter of the Fulton Bank," Senate Doc. 88, 1838; "Report and Bill Repealing the Charter of the Commercial Bank," Senate Doc. 89, 1838; "Final Report Respecting the American Bank," Senate Doc. 99, 1838; New Hampshire, Bank Commissioners, *Report in Relation to the Concord Bank* (1840); *New Hampshire Patriot*, June 15, 1840, p. 2; Maine, Legislature, "Bank Commissioners' Report," House Doc. 8, 1838, 33–4.

39. *Lowell Advertiser*, Jan. 31, 1838, p. 2. See also Williams, *Remarks on Banks and Banking*, 13–14.

40. A Citizen of Boston, *A New System of Paper Money*, 3, 7; (Providence) *Republican Herald*, Oct. 4, 1837, p. 2.

guish banks' private lending activity from their public functions. As long as banks had responsibility for providing the region with a circulating medium, the decisions they made in the lending part of their business affected the stability of the economy as a whole. As long as "bank bills constitute the currency of the country," therefore, insider lending was a dangerous practice that had to be curbed. As Marcus Morton told the Massachusetts legislature after narrowly winning the governorship in 1842, "The aggravating cause of the failure of so many of our banking institutions has been the abuse of the power of bank officers in making extravagant loans to themselves, and swallowing up the capitals of the banks in their private speculations."[41] Either banks had to be made truly private concerns or they had to be restored "to the legitimate objects for which they were granted, the public good, and not for the private emolument of one man or any set of them."[42]

Many New Englanders apparently agreed with this view, for the hards experienced a sudden surge in their popularity, winning an unprecedented number of electoral victories. Rhode Island's politics were complicated by the events leading up to the Dorr Rebellion of 1842, but in New Hampshire and Maine, both strongly Democratic states, the hards were able to wrest control of the party from the conservatives who had dominated state government before the Panic. Even in Massachusetts the hards made some headway. Voters turned against the Whigs in the aftermath of the Panic, and at the same time the Commonwealth Bank failure brought an end to the conservatives' dominance of the Democratic party. As a result, the hards were able to elect Marcus Morton as governor both in 1839 and 1842, though they never managed to secure control of the state legislature.[43]

Energized by these victories, the hards pushed forward with their legislative agenda, though the responsibilities of power necessarily limited their options. As Morton observed upon assuming the governorship for the first time, "It is the worst feature of unequal legislation, that while it

41. Massachusetts, General Court, "Address of His Excellency Marcus Morton to the Two Branches of the Legislature of Massachusetts," House Doc. 3, 1843, 19–20. See also Hubbard, *Message of His Excellency,* 23; Maine, Legislature, "Message of Governor Fairfield," 10–11.
42. *Boston Daily Advocate,* Jan. 3, 1838, p. 2.
43. Sharp, *The Jacksonians Versus the Banks,* 309–18; Cole, *Jacksonian Democracy in New Hampshire,* 186–7; Steven P. McGiffen, "Ideology and the Failure of the Whig Party in New Hampshire, 1834–1841," *New England Quarterly,* 59 (September 1986), 387–401; Darling, "Jacksonian Democracy in Massachusetts," 271–87; Formisano, *The Transformation of Political Culture,* 262–301.

creates separate interests, eager for its preservation and defence, it so infuses itself into the affairs of the community, that reform itself becomes painful."[44] Nevertheless, the hards argued, "if it is thought necessary to continue the banks, in order to avoid the shock of suddenly winding them up," the regulatory authority of the state must be asserted. "We must change the system; and so change it, that banks may have something of the character of public institutions, which hitherto they have not had."[45]

In this endeavor, the hards were aided, especially in Massachusetts, by conservative Whigs, who had long opposed granting bank charters to "those who themselves were in want of capital." The result was a wave of new legislation. Massachusetts and New Hampshire passed laws creating boards of bank commissioners, and Maine strengthened the authority of its existing board. More important, the hards took direct aim at the practice of insider lending. Both the Massachusetts and New Hampshire legislatures passed bills limiting the proportion of a bank's resources that directors could legally borrow. Maine Democrats had already obtained passage of such legislation in 1831; they now made the limits more restrictive. As Marcus Morton cautioned the Massachusetts legislature on the occasion of his second election as governor, "the relations of borrower and lender, like those of buyer and seller, are so incompatible, that they can never be safely joined in the same persons."[46] By thus appropriating a conflict-of-interest model previously applied only to government officials, the hards were aggressively asserting the public nature of chartered banks. Once banks were redefined as public institutions, insider lending became, as a matter of course, a problem of serious concern.[47]

---

44. Massachusetts, General Court, "Address of His Excellency Marcus Morton," 1840, p. 9. See also *Boston Morning Post*, Feb. 7, 1838, p. 2; *Barnstable Patriot and Commercial Advertiser*, Feb. 11, 1838, p. 1; *New-Hampshire Gazette*, June 22, 1841, p. 2.

45. Rantoul, *Memoirs, Speeches and Writings*, 531; A Citizen of Boston, *A New System of Paper Money*, 9–10.

46. Massachusetts, General Court, "Address of His Excellency Marcus Morton," 1843, 19–20.

47. *Atlas*, April 27, 1838, p. 2; Bulkley, "Robert Rantoul, Jr.," 221; Smith, "A History of Commercial Banking in New Hampshire," 209–10, 224–7; Cole, *Jacksonian Democracy in New Hampshire*, 192–4; Chadbourne, "A History of Banking in Maine," 57. Unlike their counterparts in New Hampshire and Maine, Massachusetts Democrats ultimately opposed the creation of a board of bank commissioners, because they feared that the commission would be controlled by Whigs. See *Franklin Democrat*, Feb. 7, 1843, p. 2; *Lowell Advertiser*, Jan. 22, 1838, p. 2; Bulkley, "Robert Rantoul, Jr.," 219–23.

IV

As a result of the Panic, then, there was a marked shift in emphasis in the program of the hard-money Jacksonians in favor of government regulation, and also a much greater degree of practical success. The new regulatory laws passed in the Panic's aftermath, however, did not ultimately have much effect on banks' behavior. For one thing, some of these statutes proved extraordinarily weak. Because the Massachusetts legislature was reluctant unilaterally to alter the terms of any preexisting bank charter, for example, compliance with the law restricting the amount of money banks could lend to their directors was required only from those institutions that voluntarily accepted the provisions of the Act. Even then the banks' stockholders were permitted to modify the agreement by authorizing higher limits. As an inducement to accept the Act, the legislature offered banks the right to levy additional charges for exchange – otherwise regarded as usurious – on IOUs payable outside Boston. Nevertheless, only a handful of banks – fewer than one-sixth of them – complied, and only two of those that did were located in the city of Boston. Subsequent reports by the state's banking commissioners indicate that most banks simply ignored the law until 1851, when all their charters expired simultaneously. At that point they were forced to accept the modification, but internal records that have survived from several banks during this period indicate that stockholders often responded by authorizing higher borrowing ceilings for their directors.[48]

Even in those states, such as New Hampshire and Maine, where the regulatory statutes were much stricter, insider lending remained widespread. Limits on loans to directors were easily circumvented by placing close relatives on the boards of directors or simply by incorporating the family's businesses. Those entrusted with enforcing the law lamented the pervasiveness of such tactics. According to Maine bank commissioner William D. Williamson, although loans to bank directors were legally

---

48.   See, for example, the stockholders' meetings of Oct. 20, 1852, Nov. 1, 1853, Nov. 1, 1854, Nov. 2, 1855, Nov. 8, 1856, Nov. 6, 1857, Nov. 5, 1858, Nov. 4, 1859, Stockholders' Minute Book, 1836–64, Shoe and Leather Dealers Bank, Bank of Boston Archives. For additional examples see Chapter 3. See also Massachusetts, General Court, "Report of the Bank Commissioners," Senate Doc. 5, 1839, 12–14, 47; "Report of the Bank Commissioners," Senate Doc. 7, 1840, 20; "Third Annual Report of the Bank Commissioners," House Doc. 4, 1841, 10; "Fifth Annual Report of the Bank Commissioners," Senate Doc. 20, 1843, 8; "Final Report of the Bank Commissioners," Senate Doc. 11, 1851, 9–11; Massachusetts, Bank Commissioners, *Annual Report* (1851), 7–8.

restricted to one-third of paid-in capital, "yet it is found by aggravated experience, that this is not a sufficient preventive of the apprehended evil." He went on to explain that "most of the limited sum is borrowed by a part of the Directors – perhaps by those least able to pay; or if a sum large as one's desires cannot otherwise be obtained, he can resign his place at the Board, and then there will be no legal restriction to the amount of a loan."[49]

Similar evasions seem to have vitiated New Hampshire's laws. Despite officially reported low levels of borrowing by directors, the loan portfolios of New Hampshire banks remained highly concentrated. In 1852, for instance, commissioner James M. Rix found that over $1.2 million (or more than 55 percent) of the bank loans in his district had been made to just forty-seven corporations, firms, or individuals.[50] It is likely that many of these enterprises were associated with bank insiders. Such, at any rate, was the pattern that Andrew A. Beveridge discovered when he studied the loan records of the Cheshire Provident Institution for Savings in Keene, New Hampshire. The bank's officers were involved in a variety of manufacturing, railroad, and utility enterprises. All told, loans to these men, their relatives, and the firms with which they were affiliated accounted for 49 percent of the institution's portfolio between the years 1853 and 1862.[51]

Nor was any serious attempt made to strengthen the laws governing the practice of insider lending. In 1858 New Hampshire passed a law prohibiting loans to any individual, firm, or corporation in excess of one-quarter of a bank's capital stock, but stockholders were authorized to override the ceiling – and frequently did.[52] None of the other New England states passed any additional legislation of this type.[53]

In essence, public attitudes toward banks reverted to the pre-Panic pattern of ambivalence and expressed itself once again in political inertia. Although Democratic politicians still occasionally inveighed against the banks' control of the money supply, and though conservative Whigs still sometimes grumbled about directors who were money borrowers rather

49. Maine, Legislature, "Report of the Bank Commissioners," House Doc. 7, 1840, 10.
50. New Hampshire, Bank Commissioners, *Reports* (1852), 33–8.
51. "Local Lending Practice: Borrowers in a Small Northeastern Industrial City, 1832–1915," *Journal of Economic History*, 45 (June 1985), 393–403.
52. New Hampshire, Bank Commissioners, *Reports* (1859) and (1860).
53. See Chadbourne, "A History of Banking in Maine," 58, 76–7; Lake, "The History of Banking Regulation in Massachusetts'; Stokes, *Chartered Banking in Rhode Island,* 49.

than lenders, the issue lost much of its political significance as the depression of the early 1840s lifted and the number of banks once more began to multiply. At the same time, the habit of regarding banks as private businesses – as enterprises that operated primarily in the interests of their proprietors – reasserted itself. By 1854 the Joint Standing Committee on Banks and Banking of the Massachusetts General Court could justify granting additional charters on the ground that new banks were needed to accommodate those without access to credit, because existing institutions were for all practical purposes closed to new borrowers: "The old circle of customers use the existing banks to the extent of their capacity and keep their doors shut against new men."[54]

Even borrowers who were outsiders seem to have accepted the practice of insider lending without complaint. In 1854, for instance, John Foster, a disgruntled customer of Boston's Tremont Bank, wrote a pamphlet objecting to the way his firm was treated by the bank. He mentioned only in passing that the institution had temporarily ceased discounting paper for him and other outsiders: "[Foster and Taylor's] paper was taken by the Bank in amounts *entirely* satisfactory, up to January 10, 1853. From that date to November 1st we believe few of the regular outside customers of the Bank have had anything like the usual line of paper passed."[55] Foster was not complaining here about the favoritism habitually shown insiders. Nothing in his pamphlet implies that he objected to the bank's lending practices per se, and indeed his casual use of the term "regular outside customers" suggests that he considered such favoritism the normal state of affairs. His grievance against the bank was that, in the process of trying to conserve its own resources, it had refused to cash one of his firm's checks, even though (he claimed) the firm had adequate deposits to cover it. Worse, the bank had rushed with indecent haste to cash another check which his firm had drawn on a second institution, thus implicitly impugning his credit. Foster mentioned the lack of discounts only to bolster his contention that the bank – not his firm – had gotten itself into financial trouble; it was the bank's credit, therefore, and not his firm's, that deserved to be impugned.

> The President, during this period, has frequently volunteered to apologise for the poverty of the Bank, and their inability to do much of anything for their customers to what they should do, with which explanation we were entirely satisfied, although a good deal of sur-

---

54. Massachusetts, General Court, "Report of the Joint Standing Committee on Banks and Banking," Senate Doc. 65, 1854, 9–10.
55. John Foster, *A Plain Statement of Facts, Touching the Dealings of the Tremont Bank with One of Its Customers* (Boston: J. S. Potter & Co., 1854), 5.

prise has been expressed by a large number of the regular depositors
of the Bank, that it should get into *such* a *situation* as to require *so
long* a time to get into "good trim."[56]

Insider lending was not something worth troubling about; it was part of
the natural order of things.

56.   Ibid.

3

Engines of economic development

Whatever tends to aid the operations of mechanical labour, must necessarily contribute to the wealth & prosperity of the whole community.

Petition for the Mechanics Bank[1]

Despite the burst of regulatory legislation that followed the Panic of 1837, the banking system in the 1840s and 50s continued to operate much as it had during the 1820s and early 30s. Many institutions were still managed by and for the groups that controlled them, and there was little the newly created boards of bank commissioners could do to change this behavior.

But were the banking practices of the period actually in need of reform? Was insider lending a genuinely serious problem? The purpose of this chapter is to explore these issues by assessing the extent to which insider lending led to discrimination in the credit markets, undermined the soundness of the banking system, and slowed the pace of industrialization. It is my contention that the detrimental consequences of the practice were minimal in the context of the early-nineteenth-century economy, and that insider lending contributed in a positive way to the economic development of the region. Because the practice of insider lending was common knowledge, purchasers of bank stock knew that they were for all practical purposes investing in the enterprises of the institution's directors. As a result, early-nineteenth-century banks functioned more like investment clubs than like modern commercial institutions. They provided a relatively safe way for ordinary savers to invest in the economic development of their communities.

I

The extent to which insider lending led to discrimination in the credit markets is difficult to ascertain. Certainly where bank directors and their

1. Rhode Island, General Assembly, "Petitions," 8 (1823–5), 15. These are manuscript records stored in the Rhode Island State Archives.

associates drew heavily on their own institutions for loans, there was likely to be "but little left for those without the board," as Rhode Island's bank commissioners observed.[2] A good example was the Sutton Bank of southern Massachusetts, whose resources were almost completely monopolized by members of the Wilkinson family. In March of 1829, for instance, the bank received applications for discounts totaling $10,210.36 but approved only a quarter of that amount. Notations to the records indicate that most applications were denied not on grounds of creditworthiness but instead were "laid over" for lack of funds. At the same time, the Wilkinsons and their business associates owed the bank more than $80,000, or nearly 90 percent of its outstanding loans.[3]

The Sutton Bank may have been a special case. It had only recently been chartered, and its resources were consequently still largely fictitious. The Wilkinsons owned about 90 percent of the bank's stock, and their loans consisted mainly of stock notes – that is, money tendered as payment for stock and then immediately borrowed back using the stock itself as security for the debt.[4] On the other hand, there were certainly examples of well-established banks that channeled virtually all their resources to insiders. The Wakefield (Rhode Island) Bank, the reader will recall, in 1845 lent as much as 84 percent of its funds to members of the three interrelated families that controlled the institution.

It is unlikely, however, that outsiders would have been so completely excluded from credit at most other institutions. John Foster's pamphlet protesting his treatment by the Tremont Bank of Boston indicated that it was common for banks to discount notes for "outside" customers who maintained deposits with them, and most banks had loans on their books to people unconnected with the institution. Some banks, indeed, had

2. Rhode Island, General Assembly, *Acts and Resolves* (January 1837), 89–92.
3. Applications for Discount, 1828–30, and Bills Receivable, Sept. 30, 1829, Folder 9, Mss. 781, Sutton (Mass.) Bank, 1828–31, Baker Library, Harvard University Graduate School of Business Administration.
4. The Wilkinsons were in serious financial trouble at the time and desperately in need of credit. Several months later, in fact, their entire textile empire would collapse, bringing down with it the Sutton Bank as well as several other financial institutions with which they were closely connected. "List of Original Subscribers," May 13, 1828, Folder 2, and "Memorandum of Debts Due to the Sutton Bank Secured by Pledge of Stock," Aug. 1, 1829, Folder 9, Sutton Bank; Peter J. Coleman, *The Transformation of Rhode Island, 1790–1860* (Providence: Brown University Press, 1969), 100–3, 114–15; James Lawson Conrad, "The Evolution of Industrial Capitalism in Rhode Island, 1790–1830: Almy, the Browns, and the Slaters," unpub. Ph.D. diss., University of Connecticut, 1973, 311–13, 316.

more funds to lend than insiders and other borrowers in their communities could absorb. During the early 1850s, for example, the Strafford Bank of Dover, New Hampshire, repeatedly sent one of its directors to Boston to invest its surplus funds "in good Boston paper."[5] Most institutions, moreover, were eager to accommodate outsiders if it would help them increase the circulation of their banknotes. James Brown, for example, obtained a loan from the Phoenix Bank of Charlestown, Massachusetts, after he promised its president "a good circulation." The bank's records indicate that other loans were recommended on similar grounds.[6] Borrowers understood banks' need for circulation and framed their appeals accordingly. When Edward Little of Danville, Maine, sought a loan from Portland's Canal Bank, he promised that "the only use we shall make of the loan is to purchase wool of our neighbours in the Country about us. It will therefore be distributed in small lots to many people."[7]

Outsiders who found it difficult to obtain bank loans themselves, moreover, could still benefit from the expansion of credit made possible by the growth of the banking system. The loans that insiders received from their banks enabled them in turn to extend credit in the form of mercantile loans to their customers and suppliers, many of whom may not have had direct access to a bank. Furthermore, established merchants with important banking connections might also make loans for investment purposes. Nicholas Brown, for instance, whose family controlled the venerable Providence Bank, was known for granting credit to young

5.　See, for examples, directors' meetings of Feb. 2, 1852, and March 14, March 28, May 2, and Oct. 3, 1853, Directors' and Stockholders' Minute Book, 1846–65, Strafford Bank, Dover, N.H., Bank of New Hampshire (Dover branch) Archives. At two banks with low levels of insider lending, the great majority of applications for discount were approved. The Mendon (Mass.) Bank approved 65% of all applications in October 1827, and the Concord (Mass.) Bank approved 77% in the first quarter of 1850. Discount Book, 1825–31, and Applications for Discount, 1827–31, Mendon Bank, Mendon Historical Society Museum; Discount Book, Concord Bank, Mss. 1965.29, Old Sturbridge Village Research Library.

6.　Letter from James Brown to William Wyman, Nov. 21, 1833, Phoenix Bank, Charlestown, Mass., 1832–57, Box 1, Folder 10, Massachusetts Historical Society. For other examples, see letter from Isaac Fiske to William Wyman, Oct. 2, 1834, ibid., Box 1, Folder 17; and letter from Isaac Fiske to William Wyman, Nov. 13, 1834, Box 1, Folder 18.

7.　Letter from Edward Little to the Canal Bank, Portland, Me., June 27, 1836, John Fox Papers, 1811–39, Coll. 37, Mss. 70–90, Box 1, Folder 8, Maine Historical Society. See also letter from Frederic Tudor to William Wyman, Jan. 10, 1839, Phoenix Bank, Charlestown, Mass., Box 3, Folder 11.

men just getting started in business.[8] Loans of this type had been an important source of credit before banks had appeared on the scene, and they continued to play a role in the early-nineteenth-century economy. Men looking for discounts might appeal to the bank's officers as well as to the institution itself. When Henry F. McGee applied for a discount at the Phoenix Bank of Charlestown, Massachusetts, for example, he also wrote the bank's president, "If you Sir are inclined to do them yourself for me I shall be much obliged."[9]

Even if outsiders did have difficulty obtaining credit at particular points in time, however, they may not have faced a serious problem in the long run. To the extent that entry into the banking sector was approximately free, one would anticipate the appearance of new banks to serve those excluded by the favoritism of existing institutions. Of course entry into banking was not completely free, but such barriers as did exist were not very high. One limitation on entry, for instance, was the legal requirement that banks had to pay in a certain amount of capital in specie before they were allowed to operate. The amount required, however, varied from state to state and from town to country. Moreover, there is evidence that legislators responded to political pressures to lower capital requirements for banks in capital-poor areas and to allow less wealthy citizens to found their own banks. During the 1830s, for example, Democratic agitation in Massachusetts for "a bank of moderate capital becoming men of moderate means" forced legislators to abandon their unwritten rule not to charter banks in the city of Boston with less than $500,000 capital.[10] For country banks in Massachusetts, the minimum capital was usually $100,000, though there were a number of important exceptions. In New Hampshire and Maine capitalizations were often as low as $50,000, and in Rhode Island banks went into operation with as little as $20,000 in paid-up stock.[11]

A large number of the banks chartered in Maine between 1820 and 1838 (20 out of a total of 71) never actually opened, suggesting that in the

8. Obituary for William Foster, "Dorr's Obituaries," vol. 7, 34. This volume is part of a collection of newspaper clippings at the Rhode Island Historical Society Library.

9. Letter from Henry F. McGee to Isaac Fiske, April 3, 1835, Phoenix Bank, Charlestown, Mass., Box 1, Folder 21.

10. *Boston Morning Post,* April 23, 1836, p. 1.

11. Massachusetts, General Court, "List of Banks Chartered in Massachusetts," House Doc. 93, 1850; New Hampshire, Bank Commissioners, *Reports* (1844); Maine, Legislature, "Report of the Bank Commissioners," House Doc. 7, 1840; Rhode Island, General Assembly, *Acts and Resolves* (October 1830), 72a; (May 1837), 48a.

least developed areas of New England, capital requirements could be an important barrier to entry. The problem, however, seems to have been less significant in the rest of the region. In Massachusetts only 4 of the 130 banks chartered during this period failed to go into operation, in Rhode Island only 2 out of 33, and in New Hampshire, none out of 18.[12] Moreover, as already discussed, banks could easily evade minimum capital requirements by borrowing from other institutions, and they often went into operation with little of their own specie in their vaults.

Another possible barrier to entry was the requirement, enforced by the associated banks of Boston, that country institutions maintain deposits of specie with the Suffolk Bank to insure the redemption of their note issues. The amount of the deposit varied with the capitalization of the bank and the amount of currency issued, but small country bankers nevertheless bitterly resented the imposition. The Maine legislature, for example, periodically received memorials complaining that the Suffolk system artificially restrained the amount of currency in circulation and demanding the passage of laws that would stem the outflow of specie from the state.[13] The vehemence of these protests might lead one to conclude that the deposit requirement had a restrictive effect on banking, but it is more likely that the Suffolk system actually lowered entry barriers rather than raising them. If it had not existed, bankers would nonetheless have had to maintain reserves against the redemption of their note issues, and it is well known that the Suffolk system actually lowered the level of reserves required for safe banking.[14]

12.   J. Van Fenstermaker, *The Development of American Commercial Banking, 1782–1837* (Kent, Ohio: Bureau of Economic and Business Research, Kent State University, 1965), 130–5, 139–49, 154–5, 174–7.

13.   See, for example, Maine, Legislature, "Memorial from Fellow Citizens and Constituents," House Doc. 9, 1835. See also Bray Hammond, *Banks and Politics in America from the Revolution to the Civil War* (Princeton, N.J.: Princeton University Press, 1957), 551–5.

14.   Peter Temin, *The Jacksonian Economy* (New York: Norton, 1969), 75; Charles W. Calomiris and Charles M. Kahn, "The Efficiency of Cooperative Interbank Relations: The Suffolk System," unpub. paper, 1990. By the 1830s, moreover, it had become common for country banks to overdraw their accounts, and the Suffolk began to function more like a bankers' bank, providing substantial amounts of credit to institutions from which it had previously demanded deposits. In April 1836, for example, 44 banks had overdrafts with the Suffolk amounting collectively to $664,000, an average of approximately $15,000 per bank. In April of the next year, most of the banks in Portland, Me., had overdrawn their accounts. See letter from J. M. Boyd to John Fox, April 28, 1837, and letter from William Swan to John Fox, April 28, 1837, John Fox Papers, Box 1, Folder 10. See also D. R.

Another potentially significant barrier to entry was the need to secure a special charter from the state legislature. All the states included in this study either prohibited unincorporated banking entirely or else forbade banks without charters to issue currency.[15] Because there were no general incorporation laws for banking during this period (Massachusetts passed the first such law in the region in 1851), the only way to found a bank was to obtain a special charter from the legislature, where political affiliation and personal connections (as well as the dominant party's attitude toward banks) might well affect an application's fate. New Hampshire was the most restrictive of the New England states in this regard. As late as 1838 it had granted a total of just twenty-eight charters for banks, a mere seven of them during the expansionary 1830s. Over the next two decades, however, the legislature gradually modified its policy, and by 1860 there were fifty-one banks in the state. Maine's legislators, on the other hand, were the most lenient in the region. As already discussed, by the mid 1830s they had begun to approve all legitimate applications for charters, granting fifty of them in that decade alone. The legislatures of Massachusetts and Rhode Island fell somewhere between these two extremes, at times refusing all applications for charters, at others freely granting them.[16] In the end, the periods of leniency seem to have carried the day, for there was a tremendous expansion in the number of banks in the region. As Table 3.1 shows, by 1860 New England led the nation in the number of banks and the amount of banking capital per capita. On a world scale, only Scotland (with its 4,600 persons per banking office in 1865) was more densely served by banks, and Rhode Island considerably exceeded even this figure.[17]

Whitney, *The Suffolk Bank* (Cambridge, Mass., 1878 [privately printed]), 21–2, 23–6.

15. Fenstermaker, *The Development of American Commercial Banking*, 22.

16. Ibid., 130–5, 139–49, 154–57, 174–7; Maine, Legislature, "Report of the Joint Standing Committee on Banks and Banking," Senate Doc. 28, 1836.

17. Rondo Cameron, "Scotland, 1750–1840," in *Banking in the Early Stages of Industrialization: A Study in Comparative Economic History*, ed. Rondo Cameron with the collaboration of Olga Crisp, Hugh T. Patrick, and Richard Tilly (New York: Oxford University Press, 1967), 66. For additional comparisons, see the other essays in this volume, as well as those in Rondo Cameron, ed., *Banking and Economic Development: Some Lessons of History* (New York: Oxford University Press, 1972).

The early passage of general incorporation laws would probably not have increased the number of banks in New England by any significant amount. As Kenneth Ng has shown, when Massachusetts finally did pass such a law in 1851, no new banks were chartered under it. Although this result was

Table 3.1. *Density of banks and bank capital in 1860*

Area	No. of banks	Capital in banking ($000)	Population (000)	Persons per bank	Capital per person ($)
Maine	69	7,533	628	9,100	12
Mass.[a]	178	66,482	1,231	6,900	54
Boston	40	37,732	178	4,500	212
N.H.	51	4,941	326	6,400	15
R.I.	90	21,152	175	1,900	121
New England[b]	505	123,560	3,313	6,600	37
U.S.A.	1,579	422,540	31,443	19,900	13

[a]Includes Boston.
[b]Includes Connecticut and Vermont.
Sources: Maine, Bank Commissioners, *Annual Report* (1860), 75–6; Massachusetts, Secretary of the Commonwealth, *Abstracts of the Returns from the Banks* (1860), 78–9; New Hampshire, Bank Commissioners, *Reports* (1860), 92–3; Rhode Island, State Auditor, *Annual Statement Exhibiting the Condition of the Banks* (1860), 35; Richard Eugene Sylla, *The American Capital Market, 1846–1914: A Study of the Effects of Public Policy on Economic Development* (New York: Arno, 1975), 251–2.

It is possible, of course, that the effectiveness of this long-run market mechanism in meeting the credit needs of excluded groups may have been weakened by difficulties new banks experienced in accumulating capital. It stands to reason that established banks whose directors were leading merchants and respected public figures would have found it easier to attract investment than those whose directors were less widely known, because the former were better positioned to inspire small savers with confidence. More important, directors who sat on the boards of insurance companies and other capital-accumulating institutions, such as charitable associations, could use their connections to gain access to funds. For example, the Providence Insurance Company, controlled by the Browns, was by 1814 the largest stockholder in the Providence Bank, also

> partly a consequence of barriers to entry created by the statute itself (in particular the need to deposit securities with the state that were equivalent in value to the bank's note issues), it also indicates that barriers to entry under the existing system of special charters were not especially high. "Free Banking Laws and Barriers to Entry in Banking, 1838–1860," *Journal of Economic History*, 48 (December 1988), 877–89.

controlled by the Browns. The Rhode Island Insurance Company, chartered in 1803 in association with the Newport Bank, owned half the latter's stock. Similarly, James Rhodes was able to use his position as president of the Rhode Island Society for the Encouragement of Domestic Industry to secure investments in his Pawtuxet Bank's stock.[18]

The difficulty small banks might experience in raising capital is evident from the investments of savings institutions in bank stock. Rhode Island records indicate that by 1855 savings institutions accounted for 4 percent of the banking capital in the state. Yet the top 10 percent of banks (measured by total liabilities) obtained 60 percent of this investment, whereas forty-seven banks (out of a total of ninety-two) received nothing at all. This skewed distribution of investment, moreover, cannot be explained by the superior performance of the big banks' stock. Their dividends over the preceding ten years averaged about 7 percent, the same as other banks in the state.[19]

Notwithstanding their advantage in attracting investment from large institutional sources, the top 10 percent of banks controlled only 34 percent of the state's banking capital in 1855 – the same percentage the largest 10 percent had controlled twenty years earlier, despite a 114 percent growth of investment in banking in the meantime. Moreover, as Table 3.2 makes clear, the position of some of the oldest and most prestigious banks in the state had actually declined relative to newer, more

18. Howard Kemble Stokes, *Chartered Banking in Rhode Island, 1791–1900* (Providence: Preston & Rounds, 1902), 15–16; Directors' and Stockholders' Minute Book, 1815–85, Pawtuxet Bank, Warwick, R.I., Rhode Island Historical Society Manuscript Collections. For a discussion of the interlocking directorates employed by the Boston Associates to raise capital for their businesses, see Peter Dobkin Hall, "The Model of Boston Charity: A Theory of Charitable Benevolence and Class Development," *Science and Society,* 38 (Winter 1974–5), 464–77.

    Small banks responded to the situation by seeking to charter capital-accumulating institutions themselves. For example, "friends" of the Mechanics and Traders Bank in New Hampshire petitioned to form a new savings bank on the ground that the existing institution was "managed by the Piscataqua Exchange Bank and on this & other accounts is not popular with certain classes, or rather, does not draw within its influence all who might wish to avail themselves of the benefits of such an institution." Letter from Richard Jenness to James Madison Rix, Nov. 21, 1848, James Madison Rix Papers, Correspondence, 1836–56, New Hampshire Historical Society, Manuscript Collections.

19. Rhode Island, Secretary of State, *Abstract Exhibiting the Condition of the Banks* (1855). See also the reports for the preceding ten years. (Before 1849 these were published in the General Assembly's *Acts and Resolves.*)

Table 3.2. *Top ten percent of banks in Rhode Island in 1835
and 1855 (measured in terms of total liabilities)*

	1835		1855	
Rank	Bank	Capital ($000)	Bank	Capital ($000)
1	Merchants	500	Arcade	785
2	Providence	500	Commerce	1,062
3	Roger Williams	500	American	1,984
4	Exchange	500	North America	780
5	Union	500	Providence	500
6	Blackstone Canal	454	Merchants	500
7			Blackstone Canal	500
8			Commercial	696
9			Manufacturers	500

Sources: Rhode Island, General Assembly, *Acts and Resolves* (October 1835), 76a; Rhode Island, Secretary of State, *Abstract Exhibiting the Condition of the Banks* (1855).

aggressive institutions. Only three of the six banks in the top 10 percent in 1835 remained among the nine banks that made up the top 10 percent in 1855, and these ranked fifth, sixth, and seventh rather than second, first, and sixth, respectively. In Massachusetts the situation was much the same (see Table 3.3). The concentration of capital increased only slightly between 1835 and 1855, as the share of the top 10 percent of banks rose from 34 to 37 percent. More significant, by 1855 the third, fifth, sixth, seventh, eighth, and eleventh largest banks had not numbered among the eleven banks making up the top 10 percent twenty years earlier. Indeed, four of them had not even existed in 1835.

These figures indicate that the banking system was sufficiently open so that resourceful entrepreneurs could build financial empires rivaling those of the oldest and most established merchant families in the region. This conclusion was confirmed, at least for the case of Providence, Rhode Island, by a study I conducted with Christopher Glaisek comparing the taxable wealth in 1830 and 1845 of directors of new banks formed during the great expansion of the 1830s with that of directors of more established institutions. (We also compared both groups with a random sample drawn from the city's taxpaying population as a whole.) Although the future directors of new banks were considerably less wealthy in 1830

Table 3.3. *Top ten percent of banks in Massachusetts in 1835
and 1855 (measured in terms of total liabilities)*

Rank	1835		1855	
	Bank	Capital ($000)	Bank	Capital ($000)
1	Suffolk	2,480	Merchants	7,129
2	State	2,393	Suffolk	3,782
3	Globe	2,239	Commerce	3,720
4	Merchants	2,132	State	3,247
5	City	1,973	Webster	2,856
6	New England	1,443	Tremont	2,621
7	Oriental	1,340	Exchange	2,270
8	Boston	1,316	Shoe & Leather	2,100
9	Eagle	1,247	Boston	2,035
10	Commonwealth	1,225	Globe	1,990
11	Massachusetts	1,148	Union	1,840
12			Grocers	1,795
13			City	1,625
14			New England	1,607
15			Blackstone	1,605
16			Granite	1,572
17			Eagle	1,498

Source: Massachusetts, Secretary of the Commonwealth, *Abstract from the Returns from the Banks* (1835) and (1855).

than their old-bank counterparts, by 1845 their relative position had improved dramatically (see Tables 3.4, 3.5, and 3.6). The average tax liability of new-bank directors was still lower in 1845 than that of old-bank directors, but it had risen to 60 percent of the latter's liability, as compared with 30 percent in 1830. Seventy percent of the new-bank directors now ranked in the top quintile of the city's taxpayers, whereas fewer than a third had achieved that level in 1830. The younger members of the new-bank group did especially well. The average tax liability in 1845 of those born after 1800 actually exceeded that of old-bank directors of comparable age: $119.77 versus $104.26.[20]

20.   For a full description of our sources and methods, see Naomi R. Lamoreaux and Christopher Glaisek, "Vehicles of Privilege or Mobility? Banks in Provi-

Table 3.4. *Average tax liability of Providence bank directors*
in 1830 and 1845

Group	1830 ($)	1845 ($)
Old-bank directors[a]	83.08	188.55
New-bank directors[b]	25.13	111.54
Sample of taxpayers	15.97	39.46

[a] 1838 directors of banks chartered before 1830.
[b] 1838 directors of banks chartered in or after 1830.
Source: Lamoreaux and Glaisek, "Vehicles of Privilege or Mobility?" 515.

This sort of evidence lends considerable support to the view that the expansion of the banking system benefited men without much capital who were seeking to make their way in the world of business. The great majority of directors of banks established in the city after 1830 were men of modest means. Control of banks enabled them to tap the savings of their community and invest the funds in a variety of enterprises – expanding their existing businesses and diversifying into other profitable activities. Although the practice of insider lending undoubtedly resulted in some degree of favoritism in the credit markets, the situation was remarkably fluid, enabling aspiring entrepreneurs to challenge the economic hegemony of their social betters. Indeed, more than half the new-bank directors whose business interests we were able to trace became heavily involved in either textile manufacturing or long-distance trade or both – activities previously dominated by the old elite.[21]

II

Little wonder, then, that directors of established banks felt threatened by these newcomers and opposed any further expansion of the banking system. Whatever their real reason for opposing new banks, however, elite merchants always articulated their objections by invoking their concern for the safety of the banking system as a whole. Because bank

dence, Rhode Island, during the Age of Jackson," *Business History Review*, 65 (Autumn 1991), 502–27. As the article shows, the improvement in the relative position of the new-bank directors was not an artifact of the way bank stock was taxed or the different age structures of the two groups.
21. Ibid.

Table 3.5. *Tax quintiles for directors of new and old banks in Providence in 1830*

	Quintile	% of directors	
		New banks[a]	Old banks[b]
1	(> $15.25)	31	73
2	($7.63 - $15.25)	19	13
3	($3.97 - $7.62)	20	5
4	($2.13 - $3.96)	11	5
5	(< $2.13)	8	1
No property		11	4

Note: 27 of the 91 new-bank directors and 4 of the 114 old-bank directors could not be located on the tax rolls or in the city directory for 1830.
[a]1838 directors of banks chartered in or after 1830.
[b]1838 directors of banks chartered before 1830.
Source: Lamoreaux and Glaisek, "Vehicles of Privilege or Mobility?" 516.

charters were often sought by entrepreneurs with little in the way of financial resources, and because, they claimed, the cause of most bank failures "is easily traceable to one source – the original want of capital," it was folly to continue chartering new banks.[22]

These worries about safety proved greatly overblown. Although there were some spectacular examples of banks that collapsed as a result of excessive loans to their own directors, all told there were relatively few bank failures in the region. The records of the Rhode Island General Assembly for the years 1831 to 1845 – a period that included the contraction of 1834, the Panic of 1837, and the long depression that began in 1839 – indicate that only 3 of the state's 62 banks collapsed. New Hampshire banks had an even better record; only 1 out of 27 failed. In Massachusetts a rash of failures after the Panic of 1837 brought down 17 out of the more than 120 banks in the state. But half these failures involved banks that had been chartered in the year before the panic and had not had time to put their operations on a sound financial footing before the monetary system collapsed. Moreover, a number of the others involved pet banks that had used their share of federal deposits to overextend their

22. Nathan Appleton, *An Examination of the Banking System of Massachusetts, in Reference to the Renewal of the Bank Charters* (Boston: Stimpson & Clapp, 1831), 19.

Table 3.6. *Tax quintiles for directors of new and old banks in Providence in 1845*

		% of directors	
	Quintile	New banks[a]	Old banks[b]
1	(> $32.29)	70	86
2	($11.40 - $32.39)	21	07
3	($4.94 - $11.39)	4	3
4	($1.91 - $4.93)	0	2
5	(< $1.91)	0	1
	No property	4	1

Note: 24 of the 91 new-bank directors and 16 of the 114 old-bank directors could not be located on the tax rolls or in the city directory for 1845.
[a]1838 directors of banks chartered in or after 1830.
[b]1838 directors of banks chartered before 1830.
Source: Lamoreaux and Glaisek, "Vehicles of Privilege or Mobility?" 518.

outstanding loans. The unusual character of this wave of failures is confirmed by the fact that over the entire period 1784 to 1850, there were just 3 other bank failures in the state. Only in Maine was the banking system relatively unstable, probably as a result of local scarcities of capital. Of the state's 56 banks, 7 failed during the period 1830 to 1845, and there had been 5 failures during the 1820s.[23]

Low failure rates, however, do not in themselves provide evidence for the safety of insider lending, because New England banks were not highly leveraged during this period. As Table 3.7 shows, the average ratio of capital to total liabilities in 1835 ranged from 48 percent for banks in Maine to 69 percent for banks in Rhode Island. Note issues averaged between 13 and 30 percent of total liabilities, and deposits between 13 and 21 percent. Even in Boston, capital stock constituted on average fully 54 percent of total liabilities. Banks in the region could therefore afford to lose as much as half their assets without affecting their ability to reimburse note holders and depositors. (The major exception was new banks

23. Rhode Island, General Assembly, *Acts and Resolves* (1831–45); Norman Walker Smith, "A History of Commercial Banking in New Hampshire, 1792–1843," unpub. Ph.D. diss., University of Wisconsin, 1967, 157–219; Massachusetts, General Court, "List of Banks Chartered in Massachusetts," 4–19; Walter W. Chadbourne, "A History of Banking in Maine, 1799–1930," *Maine Bulletin*, 39 (August 1936), 69, 181–2.

Table 3.7. *Ratios of capital, banknotes, and deposits*
to total liabilities for 1835 and 1860

State	1835			1860		
	Capital	Notes	Deposits	Capital	Notes	Deposits
Maine	0.48	0.30	0.18	0.47	0.27	0.21
Mass.	0.54	0.17	0.21	0.49	0.18	0.22
N.H.	0.59	0.31	0.10	0.53	0.34	0.13
R.I.	0.69	0.13	0.13	0.67	0.12	0.12

Note: In most cases the proportions do not sum to 1.0, because there are other minor elements of liability on the banks' balance sheets.

Sources: Fenstermaker, *The Development of American Commercial Banking,* 203–4, 207–8, 214–15, 226–7; Maine, Bank Commissioners, *Annual Report* (1860), 75–6; Massachusetts, Secretary of the Commonwealth, *Abstracts of the Returns from the Banks* (1860), 78–9; New Hampshire, Bank Commissioners, *Reports* (1860), 92–3; Rhode Island, State Auditor, *Annual Statement Exhibiting the Condition of the Banks* (1860), 35.

whose capital stock was still mostly fictitious – hence the large number of newly chartered banks that failed after the Panic of 1837.)

In order, then, to assess the safety of this kind of banking system, it is necessary to understand why leverage ratios were so low, and also the extent to which this pattern was connected with the practice of insider lending. One way to approach the problem is to compare the desirability of various types of bank liabilities from the standpoint of both a bank's investors and its managers. For example, note issues and non-interest-bearing deposits subject to check were the most desirable way for bank managers to raise funds, because they bore no interest charges. But there were limits to the amount of funds that could be raised in this manner. For one thing, all the New England states restricted currency issues to a fixed proportion of each bank's capital stock. These regulations, however, do not seem to have been particularly constricting, for actual note issues typically fell far shy of the legal limits. In Massachusetts in 1835, for example, banks were allowed to issue bills up to 100 percent of the value of their paid-in capital, but, as Table 3.7 shows, on average they issued only 31 percent of that amount.[24]

24. Massachusetts, General Court, *The Revised Statutes of the Commonwealth of Massachusetts Passed November 4, 1835* (Boston: Dutton & Wentworth, 1836), 310.

Cost may have been a more important factor limiting the use of these two types of bank liabilities. Although New England state governments did not impose reserve requirements on deposits during this period, prudent bankers had to set funds aside in anticipation of unexpected withdrawals. Moreover, banks had to maintain deposits with the Suffolk Bank in Boston to guarantee the redemption of their note issues. According to a recent econometric study by J. Van Fenstermaker and John E. Filer, however, the Suffolk's deposit requirement had no significant restrictive effect. Using time-series intervention analysis, Fenstermaker and Filer found that the Suffolk system did not retard the growth of bank money (including deposits) in the region, and actually operated to increase the ratio of banknotes in the total.[25] These results suggest that the costs imposed by the Suffolk system were not out of line with the costs of maintaining reserves against deposits. They also indicate that, by insuring that note issues were adequately backed with specie, the Suffolk system increased the public's willingness to hold money in the form of banknotes as opposed to deposits, which were not subject to similar regulation.

It is likely that the ultimate limit on these two forms of bank money – currency and deposits subject to check – was the public's need for cash for transaction purposes. Bank customers wanted to hold only a limited amount of their funds in the form of money, because they earned no interest this way. In order to tap funds not immediately needed for transaction purposes, banks offered their customers two financial instruments: deposits in interest-bearing accounts and shares of stock. These alternatives had very different characteristics. Deposits, on the one hand, earned a fixed rate of return that was contracted for in advance for a set period of time. A customer could withdraw his or her funds at will, though there might be some loss of interest for early withdrawals. Stock, on the other hand, earned a variable rate of return that was determined twice yearly by the directors on the basis of the bank's current earnings. Although shareholders could not withdraw their investments from the bank, the market for bank stock was well developed by the 1830s, and holdings could always be disposed of at current market prices. The existence of a market for bank stock also meant that shareholders could potentially earn capital gains (or sustain losses).

Investments in bank stock differed from deposits in another way as well: they entailed greater risk. In the event of a bank failure, depositors risked losing their funds, although their claims (and those of note holders

25. "Impact of the First and Second Banks of the United States and the Suffolk System on New England Bank Money, 1791–1837," *Journal of Money, Credit, and Banking,* 18 (February 1986), 28–40.

as well) took precedence over those of stockholders. Stockholders were in effect residual claimants on the assets of the bank. Only after all the other creditors had been paid would the bank's remaining assets be divided among them. Moreover, stockholders could also be liable for amounts in excess of their investments. In Massachusetts, for example, if a failure resulted from mismanagement by the bank's officers, and if the bank's assets were not sufficient to pay off its creditors in full, stockholders could be assessed an amount equal to the par value of their holdings to make up for any deficiency. Upon the expiration of a bank's charter, stockholders were also personally liable for its outstanding notes. In Rhode Island the stockholders of banks chartered in the 1830s had no limited liability. They were collectively responsible for the full value of the corporation's debts.[26]

Common sense would seem to indicate that, all things being equal, savers would prefer to invest their money in deposits than in shares of bank stock, because of the higher risk the latter entailed. This choice, moreover, was also encouraged by the presence of what economists call "asymmetric information" in relations between bank managers and investors. Because small investors find it difficult and expensive to monitor what managers do with their money, they are better off when they place their funds in deposits than when they purchase stock. In the first place, because depositors can withdraw their funds at will, such short-term debt contracts force bankers to create reserves against emergencies and encourage them to avoid investments that might jeopardize their ability to repay depositors. Second, because depositors are reimbursed on a first-come, first-served basis, this kind of debt contract creates an incentive for large depositors to spend the resources necessary to monitor bankers' activities so that they can be first in line to withdraw their funds in the event of trouble. Although small savers are likely to lose out in the event of a run, the monitoring activities of large depositors improve the overall safety of the bank and consequently reduce the chance of default.[27]

If one accepts this line of argument and concludes that savers were likely to prefer short-term debt instruments, such as deposits, over stock, how can the relative unimportance of deposits during this period be explained? The answer that emerges from a study of early-nineteenth-century bank records is that managers deliberately restricted the avail-

---

26. Massachusetts, General Court, *Revised Statutes*, 312; Rhode Island, General Assembly, *Acts and Resolves* (1832–5).

27. Charles W. Calomiris and Charles M. Kahn, "The Role of Demandable Debt in Structuring Optimal Banking Arrangements," *American Economic Review*, 81 (June 1991), 497–513.

ability of deposits because of the risk of withdrawal that they entailed. During the early nineteenth century, in fact, bankers argued that lending on deposits was equivalent to lending on borrowed money, a practice generally regarded as unsafe. Following this line of reasoning, the Massachusetts legislature during the 1830s actually forbade banks to issue any security or enter into any contract to pay interest on money due at a future date.[28]

Relying on deposits seemed risky to directors because most early-nineteenth-century banks lent a large proportion of their funds long term. Although bank loans usually took the form of discounts of short-term notes, it was understood that accommodation notes were subject to renewal, making them in effect long-term obligations. The exact form of the arrangement varied from one institution to the next. Some banks required borrowers to pay off a proportion of their debt at each renewal; others merely collected another set of interest charges.[29] Regardless of the form

28. Massachusetts, General Court, *Revised Statutes*, 315. Some banks got around the restriction by interpreting the law as forbidding only "the making of contracts to pay money, at a future day certain, with interest" and continued to pay interest on accounts where depositors had "the right to draw their money, when they please, losing the interest, if they draw it out, contrary to the understanding between the parties." As will be seen below, however, most Massachusetts banks did not pay interest on deposits. Massachusetts, General Court, "Report of the Bank Commissioners," Senate Doc. 5, 1839, 20.

29. That there was indeed a wide range of practice is suggested by an application for discount from the firm Kidder and Simmons to the Phoenix Bank of Charlestown, Mass. Kidder and Simmons offered to "pay 25 or 50 pr ct upon [its notes] as they become due, the balance being renewed – or we will consider it if you prefer a permanent Loan." Letter from Kidder and Simmons to William Wyman, April 4, 1834, Phoenix Bank Papers, 1832–57, Box 1, Folder 14.

   It is difficult to get an estimate of the proportion of bank loans that were subject to renewal. Eighty-two percent (by value) of the loans approved by the directors of the Mendon (Mass.) Bank in October 1827 were renewals of previously discounted notes. Unfortunately, similar records are not available for other banks during this period. Although in theory one should be able to measure the rate of renewal by tracing notes through banks' discount books, in practice variations in transaction dates and in the proportion of a note the directors were willing to renew make it impossible to distinguish renewals from new obligations discounted for the same borrowers. Nonetheless, the high proportion of accommodation paper that characterized early banks' portfolios is an indication that the proportion of notes subject to renewal was also likely to be high. Discount Book, 1825–31, and Applications for Discount, 1827–31, Mendon Bank, Mendon Historical Society Museum.

the arrangement took, however, the tradition of renewing accommodation paper put bank directors in a bind. In the event of a run by depositors, they could theoretically refuse to renew notes as they came due, but such a decision could cause borrowers who depended on the funds to fail, in turn jeopardizing the condition of the bank.

Because bank directors were themselves large recipients of such accommodation loans, moreover, they felt particularly threatened by the risk of unanticipated withdrawals. A sudden run by depositors might force them to repay their debts to the bank immediately or else risk the failure of the institution and the loss of their personal vehicle of capital accumulation. The cost of such repayment could be very high, moreover, if directors were forced to liquidate assets to raise the necessary cash. Not surprisingly, the one institution I have found that routinely offered to pay interest on deposits during the early nineteenth century also had low levels of insider lending.[30]

Most banks did not make interest-bearing accounts routinely available but instead negotiated them individually with a few large depositors (primarily savings institutions and governments). These agreements often included restrictions designed to prevent unanticipated withdrawals. The Suffolk Bank's 1819 contract with the Provident Institution for Savings specified, for example, that withdrawals could be made only during the third week of January, April, July, and October. The agreement was altered in 1820 to permit withdrawals at other times, but the bank now required six months' advance notice.[31] In other cases, the anticipation of corollary benefits induced banks to pay interest on specially negotiated accounts. When the American Bank of Providence agreed to accept the deposits of the Providence and Worcester Railroad, for example, it stipulated that "the Bank shall have the benefit of Circulation as can be given by the officers and agent of the Rail Road Company."[32]

Many institutions, however, were completely unwilling to pay interest

30. The Concord (Mass.) Bank paid 4 percent on all deposits in excess of $100 that remained in the bank for at least six months. See directors' meeting of Dec. 17, 1832, Directors' Minute Book, 1832–1901, Concord Bank.

31. The agreement also allowed the Suffolk Bank to demand, with only sixty days' notice, that the Provident Institution withdraw its funds. This provision was exercised in August of 1820. See directors' meetings of Jan. 16, 1819, and Jan. 29 and Aug. 2, 1820, Directors' Minute Book, 1818–31, Suffolk Bank, Boston, 1818–1904, Vol. 4, Mss. 781, Baker Library, Harvard Graduate School of Business Administration.

32. Directors' meeting of July 6, 1846, Directors' and Stockholders' Minute Book, 1833–59, American Bank, Providence, R.I., Rhode Island Historical Society Manuscript Collections.

on deposits. In New Hampshire, for instance, one of the bank commissioners collected information for his district on the number of banks that held interest-bearing deposits in 1856. Of the fourteen banks for which he reported this information, nine paid no interest at all. One of the remaining five banks paid interest on three-quarters of its deposit accounts. A second paid interest on a total of only $2,100 in deposits, and a third on just $1,000. The other two banks did not report any information about the proportion or value of their accounts bearing interest. In Rhode Island in 1860, only 22 percent of deposits bore interest. In the same year, Massachusetts banks (now freed from legal restrictions) paid interest on only 7 percent of their deposits. The figure for Boston banks was the same as for the state as a whole.[33]

Directors' preference for stock issues over deposits is also apparent from the manner in which banks expanded in size. In Rhode Island, for example, the twenty banks operating within the city of Providence in 1835 increased their total resources by 90 percent over the next twenty years. Six of these banks raised more than 70 percent of their funds by adding to their capital stock, and an additional four raised more than 50 percent of their funds in this way. The average increase in resources for banks that achieved more than 50 percent of their growth by selling stock was 81 percent (weighting each bank equally). For banks that depended on deposits for their growth, the average increase was only 44 percent. These numbers suggest not only that banks preferred to raise funds by issuing new stock but that this was also an easy way to grow.[34] Between 1835 and 1860, banks in Massachusetts, Rhode Island, New Hampshire, and Maine raised more than $52 million by selling stock but less than $20 million by increasing deposits.[35]

33. New Hampshire, Bank Commissioners, *Reports* (1856), 49–82; Rhode Island, State Auditor, *Annual Statement Exhibiting the Condition of the Banks* (1860), 35; Massachusetts, Secretary of the Commonwealth, *Abstract of the Returns from the Banks* (1860), 78–9.

34. Rhode Island, *Acts and Resolves* (October 1835), 76a, and Secretary of State, *Abstract Exhibiting the Condition of the Banks* (1855). The choice to raise funds by soliciting deposits was not always a purely voluntary one. For example, the Providence Bank had several valuable privileges included in its charter that it did not wish to relinquish. Each time it applied for an increase in capital, the legislature made its permission contingent on repeal of these special privileges. The bank was never willing to pay this price for the right to raise more capital.

35. Fenstermaker, *The Development of American Commercial Banking*, 204, 208, 215, 227; Richard Eugene Sylla, *The American Capital Market, 1846–1914: A Study of the Effects of Public Policy on Economic Development* (New York: Arno, 1975), 251–2.

III

The ease with which capital flowed into bank stock during this period poses an intriguing puzzle, given the risks that stockholders bore, the problem of asymmetric information, and particularly the extent to which banks engaged in insider lending. We know the practice was common knowledge. Why then were potential investors not scared away? Why the apparent lack of concern that bank directors would allow their judgment to be clouded by their own need for funds and channel excessive amounts of money into their personal enterprises?

One reason why reports of insider lending had so little effect on the flow of capital into banking was that many large purchases of bank stock were made by insurance companies, savings banks, and other institutions whose investment decisions were controlled by the same groups of men who dominated the banks. Legislatures often deliberately chartered insurance companies in conjunction with particular banks. They also frequently granted charters for savings institutions to groups that had already founded banks, with the two organizations sharing a building, clerical staff, and, more important, many of the same officers and directors. These arrangements were so common by the 1850s that the banking commissioners of Massachusetts expressed reservations about them. In Rhode Island, as late as 1870, nine of the eleven savings institutions in the city of Providence shared at least four directors with an affiliated commercial bank; for these nine, the average number of common directors was seven.[36]

But interlocking directorates between banks and these other institutions cannot completely explain the flow of capital into banking, because many individuals and institutions without such connections were also heavy purchasers of bank stock. In 1840, for example, bank regulators in Maine published complete lists of the stockholders of each bank in the state. Analysis of these lists shows that on average only 35 percent of a bank's stock was owned by its directors, other individuals with the same last name, or local institutions whose boards of directors might overlap with those of the bank. Although some individuals whose last names differed from those of the directors might also have been closely affiliated

36. Massachusetts, Bank Commissioners, *Annual Report* (1853), 55; *Bankers' Magazine*, 3 (May 1854), 871. Lists of directors were taken from selected issues of the *Providence Journal* for 1870, the *Providence City Directory* (1870), and the *Rhode Island Business Directory* (1872). See also Stokes, *Chartered Banking in Rhode Island*, 15–16; Fritz Redlich, *The Molding of American Banking: Men and Ideas* (New York: Hafner, 1947), pt. I, 32–3.

with the board, a large proportion of each bank's capital stock seems to have been held by outsiders.[37]

Banks, of course, could compensate investors for any risks that might be associated with insider lending by offering them a higher rate of return. Bank stock did pay good dividends, especially during the late 1840s and 1850s, but the pace of investment does not seem to have been very sensitive to the yield compared with other assets. As Table 1.1 showed, the two periods of greatest growth of investment in banking capital were the 1830s (until the Panic of 1837) and the 1850s (until the Panic of 1857). Although the yield on Boston bank stock (including capital gains) during the first seven years of the 1850s exceeded the rate of return on New England municipal bonds by nearly four percentage points, during the first seven years of the 1830s the returns on the two types of securities were approximately the same, with municipals leading in three years and bank stock in four.[38]

The existence during the 1830s of an active market for bank stock at prices that reduced yields to the level of comparatively riskless securities suggests that, insider lending notwithstanding, bank stock was perceived as a safe repository for funds.[39] Other evidence confirms this perception. Bank stock was one of the few securities in which Massachusetts savings institutions were allowed to invest their deposits during this period. In addition, so routinely was bank stock purchased with the intention of providing for the future needs of women and children that by 1851 about a quarter of all the stock in Massachusetts was held by women, guardians, and trustees and administrators of estates. Bankers, moreover, seem deliberately to have invested their stock with an image of soundness.

37. Maine, Legislature, "List of Stockholders in the Banks of Maine," State Documents, 1840; "Report of the Bank Commissioners," House Doc. 7, 1840. I have not found any comparable records for Rhode Island or New Hampshire. Massachusetts collected information on investments in bank stock for tax purposes during the late 1860s. In Boston in 1867 the average proportion of a bank's stock held by its directors and others with the same last name (including shares held as trustee or guardian) was 11%. Massachusetts, Tax Commissioner, *A List of Shareholders in the National Banks in the Commonwealth* (Boston: Wright & Potter, 1867). That outsiders held a large proportion of bank stock is also confirmed by the scattered lists of stockholders extant in the records of individual banks that I have examined.

38. J. Van Fenstermaker, R. Phil Malone, and Stanley R. Stansell, "An Analysis of Commercial Bank Common Stock Returns, 1802–97," *Applied Economics*, 20 (1988), 820–1.

39. Preferential access to credit may have been another incentive to buy stock, but bank records show that most small shareholders rarely if ever borrowed from their banks.

During periods of low earnings they were reluctant to cut their dividend rates, sometimes, as the Massachusetts bank commissioners repeatedly complained, dipping into surplus resources in order to sustain dividends at a level in excess of current earnings.[40]

If insider lending was really perceived as a danger, moreover, stock-holders were in a position to do something about it. Virtually all bank charters during this period gave disproportionate power to small inves-tors by limiting the number of votes that could be exercised by those holding large numbers of shares. In addition, as time went on, the rights of stockholders who were not directors received more specific protection. In 1840, for instance, a Massachusetts statute limited to ten the number of proxy votes a director or bank officer could cast; other stockholders were permitted as many as fifty. Three years later the legislature also granted stockholders the right, upon the vote of at least one-eighth of their membership, to investigate their bank's soundness. Finally, in 1851, the legislature put the state's bank commissioners squarely at the stock-holders' service. Whereas previously only the commissioners themselves (or the governor) could trigger a bank examination, a request from five stockholders was now sufficient to compel the commissioners to "make a full investigation of the affairs of such corporation."[41]

Occasionally stockholders did make use of their powers to regulate insider lending by directors. At the Atlantic Bank of Boston, for example, they passed bylaws specifying that "no loan shall be made to, nor any money deposited with, any Director, under any colour or pretence what-ever, free of interest, or at less rate of interest than is required of other persons generally." They also prohibited loans to directors "without oth-er security, than the obligation or responsibility of any one Director and his partner or partners in trade" and forbade directors to overdraw their accounts. After the Panic of 1837, the bank's stockholders responded to a rash of bank failures in the state by voting to limit loans to any one individual or firm to 15 percent of capital. They also voted to appoint annually a committee of "Stockholders who are not Directors" to exam-ine the books of the bank.[42]

40. Massachusetts, General Court, *Revised Statutes*, 319, and "Final Report of the Bank Commissioners," Senate Doc. 11, 1851, 94; Wilfred Stanley Lake, "The History of Banking Regulation in Massachusetts, 1784–1860," un-pub. Ph.D. diss., Harvard University, 1932, 168–70.

41. Massachusetts, General Court, *Revised Statutes*, 308–20; *Laws*, vol. 14, 302–6, 515–17; *Acts and Resolves* (1839–42), 208, (1843–5), 56–8, (1849–51), 625–8.

42. Stockholders' bylaws, March 18, 1828, and stockholders' meetings of Oct. 1, 1838, and Oct. 5, 1840, Stockholders' Minute Book, 1828–64, Atlantic Bank, Boston, Bank of Boston Archives.

Such activism was relatively rare, however. Minutes of annual meetings make clear that stockholders almost never challenged their directors' decisions about lending policy or, for that matter, anything else. Meetings, in fact, were generally poorly attended, and quorums were sometimes difficult to secure. In the 1830s, for example, the Pawtuxet (Rhode Island) Bank lacked a quorum at its 1830, 1832, 1835, 1836, and 1838 annual meetings. Nor was this an isolated case. The Massachusetts bank commissioners reported in 1839 that "not infrequently . . . Directors are obliged to go out into the streets, and compel such luckless stockholders, as they may chance to meet, to come in and vote for them."[43]

Stockholders' apathy is itself evidence of a lack of concern about insider lending, particularly because the issue was on the agenda from time to time. Massachusetts law after 1851 required stockholders to ratify by formal vote any loans to directors in excess of the statutory limit of 30 percent of a bank's capital stock. Surviving records of annual meetings show that such stockholders as bothered to attend willingly granted their approval. Even at the Atlantic Bank they voted repeatedly to raise the limit to 50 percent of capital.[44]

The indulgence with which stockholders treated insider lending is easier to understand once the importance of reputation in this information-scarce economy is appreciated. A glance at the credit reports collected by R. G. Dun and Company, for example, shows that character could be as important as net worth in eliciting a favorable rating. Men who were considered good credit risks were typically described in these reports as "honorable," "trustworthy," and "prompt" in their payment of debts. Conversely, those who got into financial difficulties and defaulted on their obligations might never regain the trust of the business community. Credit reports sometimes concluded with an individual's failure, the ab-

43. Directors' and Stockholders' Minute Book, 1815–85, Pawtuxet Bank, Warwick, R.I.; Massachusetts, General Court, "Report of the Bank Commissioners," Senate Doc. 5, 1839, 17.

44. Stockholders' meetings, Oct. 4, 1852, Oct. 3, 1853, and Oct. 2, 1854, Stockholders' Minute Book, 1828–64, Atlantic Bank, Boston. See also the annual October meetings of the Shoe and Leather Dealers Bank, Boston, from 1852 to 1859, Stockholders' Minute Book, 1836–64, Bank of Boston Archives; the annual November meetings beginning in 1851 of the Suffolk Bank of Boston, Stockholders' Minute Book, 1818–64, vol. 1; N. S. B. Gras, *The Massachusetts First National Bank of Boston, 1784–1934* (Cambridge: Harvard University Press, 1937), 122; Caleb H. Warner, *The National Bank of Commerce of Boston* (Cambridge, Mass., 1892 [privately printed]), 13–14; *Semi-Centennial of the National City Bank of Lynn* (Lynn, Mass., 1904 [privately printed]), 36.

sence of any subsequent entry symbolically recording the borrower's financial oblivion. In those relatively rare instances where the listings continued, they were typically full of warnings, such as "unsafe," "careless of credit," and "improvident," and the resulting inability to raise funds led almost inevitably to a second failure.[45]

Where credit was concerned, even a minor infraction could ruin a man's reputation. When Edmund Dwight referred to Suffolk Bank president Ebenezer Francis as "a damned scoundrel, damn his soul" for charging his firm a premium on a bill of exchange, the bank's board of directors responded to the insult as a body. They demanded that Dwight apologize, and when he refused, voted unanimously that "the conduct of Edmund Dwight Esqr. . . . has been derogatory to his character as a gentleman" and sent copies of the resolution to all the banking institutions in Boston.[46]

Not surprisingly, businessmen went to great lengths to safeguard their reputations, sometimes taking on debts they had no real legal obligation to repay. John James Dixwell, president of the Massachusetts Bank, is a case in point. He had encouraged the bank to loan substantial sums of money to the Boston Brick Manufacturing Company, of which he was also president. When the company failed in 1855, Dixwell felt it incumbent upon himself to assume its obligations to the bank even though he was not a signatory on any of its notes. The other directors gratefully accepted the payment, expressing "the highest respect for that delicate sense of honor" which their president had displayed. Dixwell's reputation survived the incident intact, and he continued to serve as the bank's president for almost two more decades.[47]

As Dixwell's case suggests, the extraordinary regard these bankers had for their reputations operated to protect the interests of stockholders. In addition, bankers had a strong personal interest in safeguarding the reputations of their institutions. Precisely because insider lending was so important, banks were valuable vehicles of capital accumulation for their directors. Endangering the health or reputation of a bank, therefore, was like killing the goose that laid the golden eggs. Harm to the bank's reputation might close off this avenue of accumulation. Worse still, a

45. For examples, see Rhode Island vol. 2, 63; vol. 9, 121, 176, 393, 403; vol. 15, 51, 53, R. G. Dun and Co. Collection, Baker Library, Harvard Graduate School of Business Administration.

46. Directors' meetings of Feb. 25, Feb. 28, March 3, and March 4, 1824, Directors' Minute Book, 1818–31, Suffolk Bank, vol. 4.

47. Gras, *The Massachusetts First National Bank of Boston*, 128, 494–5, 502–4.

failure might force bankers to liquidate assets in order to repay their own outstanding loans.

The fact, moreover, that banks during this period were for all practical purposes group-managed enterprises, whose directors collectively assumed responsibility for allocating loans, enhanced the effectiveness of this mechanism. Directors knew that they could not protect themselves and the health of their institution unless they monitored each other's borrowing. If one of their number overextended himself and endangered the institution by lending excessive sums of money to his own enterprises, all the others stood to suffer. On the line were their reputations, their access to capital, and even the wealth they had already accumulated.[48]

The strategies directors devised to protect themselves against excessive borrowing by one of their number are detailed in the minutes of their board meetings. During the early years of the century, banks generally granted discounts only once or twice per week, when the board as a whole met to pass on the notes submitted in application. Votes typically were taken by secret ballot, and one or two negatives usually were sufficient to reject an offering. As the pace of economic activity increased, however, pressures mounted to do business on a daily basis, and the boards reluctantly began to delegate the authority to make discounts to subcommittees of their membership. In 1825, for example, the directors of the Massachusetts Bank of Boston voted to permit two of their number to discount notes between regular meetings of the board, although a few months later they apparently had second thoughts and rescinded this power. In 1827 they reversed themselves again, this time voting to create a three-member committee with authority to grant discounts, subject to the approval of the board at its next regularly scheduled meeting. Even this procedure proved cumbersome, however; in 1831 the bank reduced the size of its discount committee to two directors, and finally, in 1840, permitted the president to make discounts by himself. Most other banks adopted similar policies, delegating the power to make discounts to subcommittees of directors; to special finance committees consisting of the president, the cashier, and at least one other director; or sometimes (as in the case of the Massachusetts Bank) to the president himself.[49]

48. Although the directors of a bank were often members of the same kinship group, they usually had distinguishable business interests. Most partnerships based on family ties were limited either to fathers and sons or to brothers.

49. Gras, *The Massachusetts First National Bank of Boston*, 46–7, 79, 232–7, 400–3, 432, 436–7, 446, 452–3, 471. For other examples, see directors' bylaws, Oct. 8, 1825, Directors' Minute Book, 1825–53, Bunker Hill Bank,

Despite this delegation of authority, the boards maintained their monitoring function by insisting that all discounts granted by the president or committees be considered provisional until they were voted on by the directors as a group at one of their regularly scheduled weekly (or biweekly) meetings. From the few surviving records that permit counts of those present, the meetings appear to have been well attended. At the Suffolk Bank in Boston, for example, seven out of ten directors attended at least 85 percent of the meetings in 1840, and at the Shoe and Leather Dealers Bank in Boston, directors had a similar attendance record during that same year.[50]

In addition, directors sometimes passed special regulations to help guard against excessive insider lending. These regulations, which could be overridden only by a vote of the entire board, usually consisted of restrictions on the amount of loans that could be granted to any one individual, firm, or corporation, but they could take other forms as well. The directors of the People's Bank of Roxbury, Massachusetts, for example, passed a regulation directed exclusively at themselves: "Voted, that no director shall be indebted to the Bank at any one time, as promisor, or endorser, or both, in a sum exceeding $5000 . . . [excepting] loans on collateral security." At the Bunker Hill Bank of Charlestown, Massachusetts, the directors voted "that the ballot box shall be passed whenever any note is offered for discount by a Director of this board," thus

Charlestown, Mass., Mss. 781, Baker Library, Harvard Graduate School of Business Administration; directors' bylaws, 1833, Directors' and Stockholders' Minute Book, 1833–62, People's Bank, Roxbury, Mass., Bank of Boston Archives; "Rules and Regulations," Directors' Minute Book, 1836–43, Shoe and Leather Dealers Bank, Boston; directors' meeting, July 3, 1854, Directors' and Stockholders' Minute Book, 1851–94, Bank of America, Providence, R.I., Fleet National Bank Archives; directors' meetings of Sept. 11, 1823, Oct. 16, 1833, and June 26, 1837, Directors' and Stockholders' Minute Book, 1823–58, Mechanics Bank, Providence, Fleet National Bank Archives; directors' meetings of March 19, 1827, Sept. 21, 1829, and July 5, 1830, Directors' Minute Book, 1825–49, Merrimack County (N.H.) Bank, Mss. no. 1941–1, vol. 1, New Hampshire Historical Society, Manuscript Collections.

50. Directors' Minute Book, 1831–43, Suffolk Bank, Boston, vol. 5; Directors' Minute Book, 1836–43, Shoe and Leather Dealers Bank, Boston. Attendance was much worse at the Strafford Bank in Dover, N.H. Only three out of seven directors attended meetings at least 80% of the time. The Strafford, however, had low levels of insider lending, so directors may not have found it so necessary to monitor their colleagues. Directors' and Stockholders' Minute Book, 1846–65, Strafford Bank, Dover, N.H.

giving themselves the cloak of secrecy to reject one another's loans – "In all cases of passing the ballot box, two black balls shall prevent the discounting of the note." According to the bylaws of the Granite Bank in Pascoag, Rhode Island, directors had to leave the room whenever notes on which they appeared as either principal or endorser were being discussed.[51]

The effectiveness with which directors monitored each other is difficult to determine. Bank records certainly reveal instances where large loans to insiders resulted in substantial losses. The Eagle Bank of Bristol, Rhode Island, for example, lost about a third of its capital in 1826 as a result of the failure of a member of the bank's controlling family. A quarter of a century later the bank sustained heavy losses once again, this time through the default of the president's son. Similarly, the Atlantic Bank of Boston found itself holding more than $100,000 worth of bad paper in 1829 as a result of the failure of a firm that was part owned by one of its directors.[52]

51. Directors' meeting, July 23, 1833, Directors' and Stockholders' Minute Book, 1833–62, People's Bank, Roxbury, Mass.; directors' meeting, March 7, 1826, Directors' Minute Book, 1825–53, Bunker Hill Bank, Charlestown, Mass.; bylaws, March 22, 1852, Directors' and Stockholders' Minute Book, 1851–1901, Granite Bank, Pascoag, R.I., Fleet National Bank Archives. For other examples, see directors' bylaws, Dec. 3, 1833, Directors' and Stockholders' Minute Book, 1833–59, American Bank, Providence, R.I.; charter, 1851, Directors' and Stockholders' Minute Book, 1851–94, Bank of America, Providence; directors' bylaws, Nov. 4, 1818, Directors' Minute Book, 1818–39, Merchants Bank, Providence, Fleet National Bank Archives; directors' meeting, Aug. 31, 1827, Directors' Minute Book, 1825–31, Mendon (Mass.) Bank.

52. Directors' meetings, June 22, 1826, and April 18, 1827, Directors' and Stockholders' Minute Book, 1818–46, and letters from J. E. French to C. S. LeBaron, June 5, June 14, and June 16, 1851, letter from French to Robert Rogers, July 12, 1851, letter from Rogers to D. D. Lord, Oct. 12, 1852, Letter Book, 1848–53, Eagle Bank, Bristol, R.I., Fleet National Bank Archives; Rhode Island, General Assembly, "Petitions," 54 (1825–6), 68, 80; directors' meeting, Dec. 11, 1829, and "Schedule of Notes for Which the Saco Manufacturing Co. is Liable, Held by Atlantic Bank," Dec. 16, 1829, Directors' Minute Book, 1828–67, Atlantic Bank, Boston.

   Sometimes a director's death could also entail heavy losses if his business was overextended. In 1838 the Pawtuxet Bank of Warwick, R.I., was forced to petition the General Assembly to reduce its capital stock from $87,750 to $78,000 after one of its directors had died insolvent with notes worth $8,800 outstanding at the bank, as well as an additional $1,500 in endorsements. Five years later this same bank faced even heavier losses as a result of

But it is important to realize that loans to outsiders might also lead to heavy losses, because it was difficult during this period to obtain accurate information about the creditworthiness of strangers. Indeed, given the generally poor quality of information, the monitoring of insiders by insiders may actually have been less risky than extending credit to outsiders. Though bank directors may occasionally have succumbed to temptation and lent too much of their funds to themselves, they also knew much more about the businesses of those with whom they were personally connected, enabling them to make more informed decisions about loan amounts than would have been possible in dealing with strangers. Over the long run, this advantage in information could lower losses from bad debts, as Andrew Beveridge found when he studied insider lending at the Cheshire Provident Institution for Savings in Keene, New Hampshire. Over the period 1833 to 1897, Beveridge calculated, 98 percent of all funds lent to anyone personally connected with the bank were repaid, as opposed to 90 percent of all other loans.[53]

Perhaps the most important point to make, however, is that insider lending also gave investors important information about the contents of banks' portfolios, thus solving the problem of asymmetric information that theoretically caused savers to prefer deposits in the first place. Purchasers of bank stock knew that they were investing in the diversified enterprises of the particular group that controlled the bank, not in some anonymously diversified portfolio. In other words, as a result of the practice of insider lending, investors had the information they needed to make important choices – to decide, for example, whether to pursue the less risky option of entrusting their funds to members of the established elite or to take their chances with up-and-coming entrepreneurs.

That investors did indeed make use of such information can be seen from the widely different prices commanded by the stock of each bank in the year immediately following its organization – that is, before it could

the death of its president, who owed the bank more than $25,000. See directors' meetings of Dec. 27, 1838, Feb. 17 and June 22, 1840, Nov. 9, 1843, and Nov. 5, 1846; "Situation on Loss and Doubtful Paper," June 1, 1840; and "List of Notes," Dec. 20, 1842, Directors' and Stockholders' Minute Book, 1815–85, Pawtuxet Bank, Warwick, R.I.

53. "Local Lending Practice: Borrowers in a Small Northeastern Industrial City, 1832–1915," *Journal of Economic History*, 45 (June 1985), 402. Banks could not compensate for the greater risk of loans to outsiders by charging them a higher rate of interest. During the first half of the nineteenth century, banks charged a uniform 6% rate of discount for all notes, probably as a result of the usury ceiling. It was not until the post–Civil War period that banks began to charge more risky customers higher rates of interest.

establish its own earnings record. For instance, the initial selling price of the stock issued by the seven banks chartered in Boston during the year 1836 (par value $100) ranged from $75 to $100 (using each bank's lowest quotation) or from $94 to $100 (using each bank's highest). Over time, of course, the price commanded by a bank's stock reflected its actual record of earnings, but investors' overall assessment of the character of a bank's directors remained important. For Boston banks in 1854, for example, dividends from the preceding ten years and the ratio of retained earnings to capital explained from 48 to 62 percent of the cross-sectional variation in stock prices (depending on whether one uses the year's highest or lowest quotations). It is likely that much of the remaining variance can be explained by differences in the public's assessment of the character of the banks' directors and their business interests.[54]

The low leverage rates that characterized early-nineteenth-century banks thus appear to be directly connected with the practice of insider lending. Because runs on deposits might force insiders with large outstanding loans to liquidate their own assets, directors preferred to raise funds by selling shares of stock. They were able to find a market for this stock because insider lending reduced problems of asymmetric information that might otherwise have discouraged such investment. Because everyone assumed that banks lent large proportions of their resources to insiders, investors obtained a great deal of information about the contents of a bank's portfolio simply by knowing the identity of its directors.

IV

The years 1820 to 1860 encompassed a period of extraordinarily rapid growth and development for the New England economy. According to the conventional historical wisdom, however, banks played at most an insignificant role in financing this development. Sidney Pollard and others have argued that the amount of fixed capital required for manufacturing ventures in the early nineteenth century was not large and that entrepreneurs could raise the necessary sums first by tapping family savings and

54. Stock prices were based on a par value of $100 per share. Joseph G. Martin, *A Century of Finance: Martin's History of the Boston Stock and Money Markets* (Boston, 1898 [privately printed]), 97–101. Martin reported only the highest and lowest quotations for each year. He provided no information about the quantities sold at each price, nor did he calculate an average price for the year. Data on retained earnings and capital are from Massachusetts, Secretary of the Commonwealth, *Abstract of the Returns from the Banks* (1854–5).

then by plowing back the firm's earnings. These scholars recognize that obtaining working capital was a much more serious problem for early manufacturing firms, but they argue that much of the necessary credit was provided by merchants who sold the firms supplies. As evidence of the minor role that banks played in providing manufacturers with capital, they point to the absence of references to bank loans in firms' internal records.[55]

In order to understand the role that banks played in financing economic development, however, one must remember that banks discounted two types of paper during this period: commercial paper and accommodation paper. Manufacturers certainly benefited from the former type of loan, both indirectly, because the ability to discount notes at a bank was what enabled merchants to extend them credit in the first place, and directly, because they in turn could discount the notes they received from wholesalers and retailers. Just as manufacturers rarely could afford to pay cash for their supplies, so their customers rarely could afford to pay cash for goods. Manufacturers were forced to extend credit to customers in order to secure their business, but they could discount the resulting notes at a bank in order to raise funds to cover operating expenses. The Lowell Bleachery, for example, routinely discounted its bills receivable at the Phoenix Bank of Charlestown, Massachusetts, to get the funds it needed to pay its workers.[56]

The role of accommodation paper was somewhat different. These potentially long-term obligations typically were discounted for the benefit of individuals, not firms. Much of this money undoubtedly found its way into manufacturing ventures (where it appeared on the books as a contribution from an individual, not a bank). But some of it undoubtedly was used for other types of investments.

What scholars like Pollard failed to realize, however, was that these other types of investments also played an important role in economic development. The shallow markets and high risks associated with manufacturing during the early industrial period led many entrepreneurs to diversify their investments. It is well known that important merchant

55. For an excellent survey of this literature, see François Crouzet, Editor's Introduction, in *Capital Formation in the Industrial Revolution,* ed. Crouzet (London: Methuen, 1972), 1–69. See also Sidney Pollard, "Fixed Capital in the Industrial Revolution in Britain," *Journal of Economic History,* 24 (September 1964), 299–314; Glenn Porter and Harold C. Livesay, *Merchants and Manufacturers: Studies in the Changing Structure of Nineteenth-Century Marketing* (Baltimore: Johns Hopkins Press, 1971), 62–78.
56. Letter from John Clark to William Wyman, Dec. 3, 1833, Phoenix Bank, Charlestown, Mass., Box 1, Folder 11.

groups, such as the Boston Associates in Massachusetts and the Brown family in Rhode Island, adopted a strategy of diversification. What is less commonly recognized, however, is that many lesser entrepreneurs pursued similar strategies. To give just a few examples, Samuel Weston and Abner Coburn, who founded the Somerset Bank in Maine in 1825, had extensive investments in local mills, timberlands, lumbering, and railroads. Stephen Harris, one of the organizers of the Centreville Bank in Warwick, Rhode Island, had a medical practice, a pharmaceutical dispensary and grocery business, large textile-mill investments, a farm, and a limestone quarry. Similarly, the men who controlled the Cheshire Provident Institution for Savings in Keene, New Hampshire, were involved in a variety of enterprises ranging from textile mills to railroads to local utilities.[57]

The problem with such a strategy of diversification, of course, was that it required considerable amounts of capital – sums that were typically beyond the reach of all but the wealthiest merchant families. Banks helped solve this problem for less affluent groups by providing them with the wherewithal to diversify their interests. At the same time, they enabled the individuals and institutions that purchased their stock to achieve a similar level of diversification by buying what was in essence a share of the group's total investments. Because bank loans during this period were usually secured by the endorsements of respected businessmen rather than by specific items of collateral, they were backed by all the resources (the diversified portfolios) of both the maker of the loan and the endorser(s).

What banks in effect did was enable ordinary savers to invest in the gains from economic development without exposing themselves to serious risk. It is important to recognize that early-nineteenth-century banks were not really commercial banks in the modern sense of the term but instead were essentially investment clubs. The sale of bank stock enabled small savers to buy shares in a diversified portfolio of investments, a portfolio whose character differed in important and known ways from one institution to the next. It thereby enabled small investors to participate in the activities of the local entrepreneurs they most admired. At the same time, banks provided these entrepreneurs with a mechanism they

---

57. *A Century of Service, 1825–1925: The First National Bank of Skowhegan, Maine* (Skowhegan, 1925 [privately printed]), 57, 65–9; Susan M. Basham, "The Greene Manufacturing Company: A Case Study of Cotton Manufacturing in Warwick, Rhode Island During the Early Nineteenth Century," unpub. manuscript, 1973, Rhode Island Historical Society Library, 2–3, 21–3; Beveridge, "Local Lending Practice," 396.

could use to tap the community's savings and channel the proceeds into economic development. The amounts that could be raised in this manner were indeed substantial. By 1860 the banking sector's total resources were approximately equivalent to the *accumulated* stock of manufacturing capital in the region.[58]

58. Sylla, *The American Capital Market,* 249–52; U.S., Census Office, *Compendium of the Ninth Census* (Washington, D.C.: Government Printing Office, 1872), 798.

Most urban banks during the early nineteenth century occupied modest quarters on the second stories of commercial buildings. They could leave desirable ground-floor locations to retailers because their customer base consisted largely of people personally connected with members of their boards. Here two institutions, the Globe Bank and the Grocers and Producers Bank, share the second story of the Lyceum Building in Providence, Rhode Island. (Rhode Island Historical Society, neg. no. RHi X3 5876)

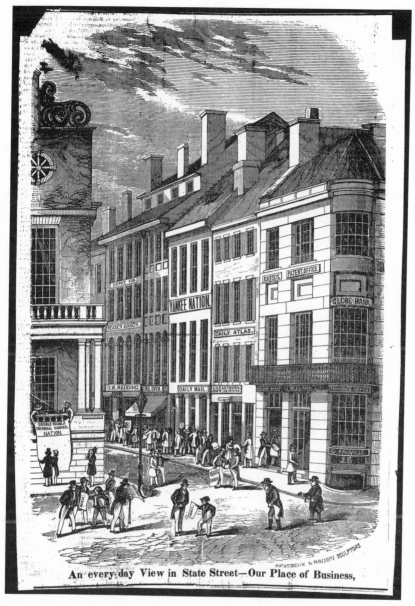

An every day View in State Street—Our Place of Business,

Even in Boston, the region's financial center, early-nineteenth-century banks occupied second-story offices. Virtually all of the banks in the city were crowded together with other businesses on State Street. (Boston Athenaeum)

Country banks often built detached structures, but they were typically of modest proportions. Researchers at Old Sturbridge Village, searching for a typical example of regional bank architecture, moved the Thompson Bank from a small village in Connecticut to their historical museum. (Photograph by Henry E. Peach, reproduced courtesy of Old Sturbridge Village, neg. no. B23977)

The layout of the interior of the Thompson Bank shows that bank officers in the early nineteenth century made little attempt to differentiate the space they occupied from that used by the relatives and friends who constituted their main customers. Note the low counter, the open passage to the vault, and the low wall that separated the directors' room on the left from the rest of the bank. (Photograph by Henry E. Peach, reproduced courtesy of Old Sturbridge Village, neg. no. B21391)

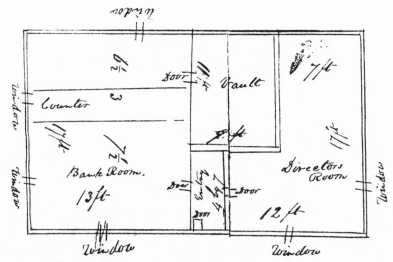

A floor plan drawn up in 1825 for the directors of the Mendon Bank, a country bank in southern Massachusetts, shows clearly how little space banking operations required in the early nineteenth century. The building that was actually constructed deviated from the plan in several ways. Most significantly, there were no interior walls to divide the directors' room from the banking area. (Mendon Historical Society)

The imposing presence of the Boston branch of the Second Bank of the United States, an institution with an avowedly public purpose, contrasts dramatically with the more modest appearance of other banks in the city, which, though state-chartered institutions, mainly served private interests. (Lithograph by John Henry Bufford for Pendleton's Lithographers, reproduced courtesy of the Boston Athenaeum)

By mid century a few prominent banks in the region's largest cities had begun to build monumental buildings, as this 1856 photograph of the new Merchants Bank Building in Boston shows. Even in this building, however, the bank occupied second-story office space. The president of the Merchants Bank was Franklin Haven, an early leader of the conservative banking movement. (Massachusetts Historical Society)

The Merchants Bank's ornate interior matched its grand façade. The architecture sharply differentiated public from work space, symbolically communicating the distance that now existed between the bank's officers and its customers. The high counter extended the complete length of the banking room and prevented the public from coming into direct contact with bank employees. (Image taken from *Boston Massachusetts* by Geo. W. Engelhardt (Boston: Boston Chamber of Commerce, 1897); reproduced courtesy of the Society for the Preservation of New England Antiquities, neg. no. 15878-B)

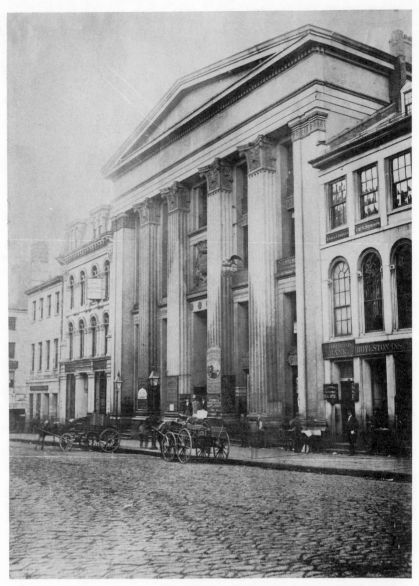

Most Boston banks continued in the late nineteenth century to occupy second-story offices that appeared externally to be very similar to their early-nineteenth-century quarters. Very few as yet used architecture to distinguish themselves from competitors or to create an image of soundness. The imposing structure in this photograph is the Merchants Exchange on State Street. The small sign in the foreground for the Washington National Bank is dwarfed by that of the Boylston Insurance Company. Banks also occupied second-story offices on the other side of the Exchange. (Boston Athenaeum)

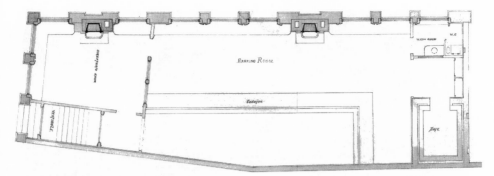

In their interiors late-nineteenth-century banks followed the trend (evident in the photograph of the Merchants Bank) of differentiating public space from work space. This floor plan for the new Continental National Bank in Boston provides a sharp contrast to the earlier plan for the Mendon Bank. The drawing shows the extent to which public space (the Banking Room) had been proportionally reduced and separated from the space occupied by employees (the area behind the counter, the Directors' Room, and a second floor that was off limits to the public). (Drawing by architect Nathaniel J. Bradlee, 1873, reproduced courtesy of the Boston Athenaeum)

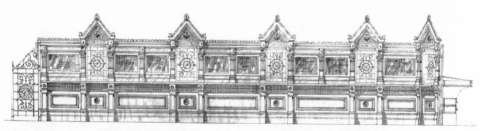

This elevation shows the counter planned for Continental's banking room. The fancy detail only heightened the significance of the barrier to be erected between the bank's customers and its tellers. (Drawing by architect Nathaniel J. Bradlee, 1873, reproduced courtesy of the Boston Athenaeum)

The same differentiation of space came to characterize outlying banks, as this 1890s photograph of the Merchants National Bank in Lawrence, Massachusetts, shows. (Society for the Preservation of New England Antiquities, neg. no. 15877-B)

Before (and immediately after) its 1898 merger, the National Shawmut Bank occupied a second-story office similar to those of other Boston banks. (Boston Athenaeum)

Shortly after the merger, Shawmut's officers began planning construction of a building with proportions commensurate with the bank's new prominence in the city. The building was finally completed in 1907. (Boston Athenaeum)

4

The decline of insider lending and the problem of determining creditworthiness

Many bank officers have no careful system of investigating the credit of those who borrow money, and simply rely on their intuition, so to speak, or some evidence which has descended to them from the past record of the customer.

James G. Cannon[1]

I

However well the banking system based on insider lending functioned, it was not destined to last very long. By the post–Civil War period, economic development and the tremendous expansion that occurred in the number and size of banks had transformed New England from a capital-scarce into a capital-rich economy. Development also reduced the risks involved in specialization, making it easier for firms to raise funds for their ventures without the assistance of financial intermediaries. Both these changes operated in turn to reduce the incidence of insider lending. Because funds were now more widely available, bank directors had less need to draw on their own institutions for loans. Although it was still common for directors to obtain substantial loans from their banks, and although some banks continued to operate primarily in the interests of their managers, the proportion of loans that were granted to insiders seems generally to have declined. For example, reports from national bank examiners to the Comptroller of the Currency indicate that Boston bank directors accounted on average for only about 9 percent of their banks' loans during the early 1890s, with a range of between 1 and 22 percent. For a scattered sample of more than fifty banks elsewhere in the region, the average proportion of loans to directors reported by the bank examiners was 15 percent. In only seven of these banks did directors

1. *An Ideal Bank* (New York, 1891 [privately printed]), 6–7.

84

account for more than 25 percent of total loans, the highest proportion being 46 percent.[2]

Few actual loan records have survived from the latter part of the nineteenth century, but such information as does exist confirms the view that it had become far less common for banks to lend large sums of money to insiders. At the First National Bank of Pawtucket, Rhode Island, for example, the liabilities of officers and directors, both as principals and endorsers, totaled $158,000 in 1895, but this figure constituted only about 17 percent of the bank's outstanding loans.[3] Lists of loans recorded in the minutes of the Shoe and Leather National Bank of Boston in early 1887 show that directors obtained only 11 percent of the total.[4] Much less complete listings in the minutes of the First National Bank of Warren, Rhode Island, for 1886, Newport's National Bank of Rhode Island for 1888, and the National Niantic Bank of Westerly, Rhode Island, for 1893 suggest that, even on the most generous assumptions, insiders received at most about a quarter of total loans.[5]

Accounts of large business failures provide additional evidence of a decline in insider lending. When an important concern failed during the

2. These figures include directors' appearances in the records as both principals and endorsers but exclude loans to relatives or to corporations with which the directors were affiliated. The numbers are highly reliable because they were compiled by federal examiners based on direct inspection of the banks' books. See U.S., Comptroller of the Currency, Records of the Examination Division, National Archives, Washington, D.C., Record Group 101. The collection of bank examiners' reports from outside Boston is not a true random sample but was chosen to match up with other collections of bank records and to plug gaps in coverage.

3. This figure assumes that there was no double counting. If the directors had endorsed each other's notes, the percentage would be even lower. Statement of Condition, July 11, 1895, Directors' and Stockholders' Minute Book, 1879–1900, First National Bank of Pawtucket, R.I., Fleet National Bank Archives.

4. For a brief period in 1887 the bank's new president recorded in the minutes all loans and discounts, except for one group of loans worth $22,500. Even if all the missing loans went to directors, their proportion of the total would still be only 16%. See Directors' and Stockholders' Minute Book, 1885–93, Shoe and Leather National Bank, Boston, Bank of Boston Archives.

5. Directors' and Stockholders' Minute Book, 1864–89, First National Bank of Warren, R.I.; Directors' Minute Book, 1862–1902, National Bank of Rhode Island, Newport, R.I.; and Directors' and Stockholders' Minute Book, 1865–1905, National Niantic Bank, Westerly, R.I. These records are all in the Fleet National Bank Archives.

early nineteenth century, only the bank (or banks) with which it was closely affiliated usually experienced a serious loss. Some such cases also occurred during the second half of the century, but it was far less common for large firms to tie themselves so closely to a particular bank, and far more common for them to borrow from a variety of institutions. Hence when Paine and Sackett, woolen manufacturers, failed in 1882, eight Providence banks each held $10,000 or more of the firm's paper, and four banks held $25,000 or more. Similarly, when the Wauregan Mills failed in 1889, twelve Providence banks held at least $10,000 of the firm's paper, and seven at least $25,000.[6] The notations of overdue loans that appear in many banks' minute books also confirm a decline in insider lending. During the early nineteenth century most of the failed paper held by banks involved their own directors. By the end of the century, however, outsiders were more commonly responsible for unpaid debts. For example, only about ten of the approximately two hundred problem loans noted in the minutes of six Boston banks during the 1890s seem to have involved directors.[7]

The drop in insider lending that the records reveal did not generally result from a decline in the power of the groups that controlled the banks. As we saw in Chapter 1, many families retained positions of dominance in their institutions well into the twentieth century. They simply changed the purposes for which they managed their banks. A good example is the Providence Bank, which was dominated for more than a century after its founding in 1791 by the interrelated Brown, Ives, and Goddard families. As we have already seen, in the years immediately following its organization the bank's lendable funds were largely absorbed by insiders. Over time, however, as the region's credit markets matured and the family's textile ventures became important generators of capital, the Browns

6. Goddard Bros. Diaries, vol. 5, Nov. 13, 1882, and vol. 12, Aug. 21, 1889, Brown and Ives Manufacturing Records, Mss. 9, Sub Group 10, Series D, Rhode Island Historical Society Manuscript Collections. For other examples, see vol. 6, July 31 and Dec. 26, 1883; vol. 12, July 25, 1889; vol. 13, loose sheet and May 5, 1890.

7. The banks were Atlantic National, Directors' and Stockholders' Minute Book, 1877–1912; Boylston National, Directors' and Stockholders' Minute Book, 1887–1909; Commercial National, Directors' and Stockholders' Minute Book, 1888–1900; Faneuil Hall National, Directors' and Stockholders' Minute Book, 1876–1902; Fourth National, Directors' and Stockholders' Minute Book, 1875–1900; and National City, Directors' and Stockholders' Minute Book, 1886–1903. The records of these banks are all in the Bank of Boston Archives. I traced the firms with unpaid debts through the Boston city directory in order to learn the names of all the local partners involved.

turned less frequently to their bank for funds. Thanks to the diaries of the Goddard Brothers Company, the firm that managed the Browns' various textile enterprises, the family's relationship with this bank can be followed in particularly close detail throughout the last quarter of the nineteenth century. William Goddard, a senior partner in the firm, was president of the Providence Bank during most of this period.[8]

As the diaries show, during the late nineteenth century Brown family enterprises continued to use the bank (now called Providence National) for a variety of purposes. The family's textile businesses kept funds on deposit there, and one of these firms, the Lonsdale Company, routinely had its payroll made up at the bank. The records also show that Goddard Brothers occasionally drew upon the bank for loans, sometimes of substantial size. For example, in November of 1879 the diaries record, "We discount at Prov. Nat^l Bank & Prov. Ins for Savings all Bills Receivable due Dec & Jan belonging to Lonsdale & Hope Co." A few years later, in November 1886, the notation appears: "Bk lends all its money to L Co & H Co @ 5%. Money still scarce about here."[9]

Goddard Brothers, however, was just as likely to be the bank's creditor as it was its debtor. In July of 1881 the firm lent the Providence National Bank $50,000 on call so that it could meet heavy drafts by the Providence Institution for Savings, which was also controlled by the Browns. A few days later the diaries noted, "The bank does little business as it owes $150000 to L Co & this is remittance day." In 1889 Goddard Brothers once again helped the bank meet heavy demands for funds by the savings institution.[10]

Indeed, the typical position of the Brown family's enterprises with respect to the money markets was that of creditor. For the better part of each year, revenue from sales poured into the Goddard Brothers' counting house, and the firm's main problem was to seek out suitable investment opportunities.[11] Only during the fall cotton-buying season did the family's enterprises have a substantial need for credit, and even then they were much less likely to borrow from the Providence National than they were from other institutions, especially those in Boston. According to notations in the diaries, Goddard Brothers negotiated loans totaling approximately $4,479,000 from banks and other kinds of financial intermedi-

8.   See also James B. Hedges, *The Browns of Providence Plantations: The Nineteenth Century* (Providence: Brown University Press, 1968), 255–6.

9.   Goddard Bros. Diaries, vol. 2, Nov. 17, 1879; vol. 9, Nov. 22, 1886.

10. Ibid., vol. 4, July 26 and Aug. 1, 1881; vol. 12, Oct. 23, 1889.

11. A large proportion of the diary entries are taken up with notations of purchases of commercial paper or money lent on call.

aries between 1878 and 1898. Of this amount only about $333,000 (7 percent) was lent by the Providence National Bank. Another $563,000 (13 percent) came from the Providence Institution for Savings, which the family also dominated, and $740,000 (17 percent) from the Rhode Island Hospital Trust Company, which the family had helped create but did not control. All the rest was borrowed from Boston institutions, which supplied the firm with approximately $2,793,000 in loans, or 63 percent of its total borrowing.[12]

As entries in the diaries indicate, Goddard Brothers turned to Boston banks for loans because interest rates in that city were generally lower than in Providence.[13] Family members, it seems, preferred borrowing out of town at good rates to using their leverage as insiders at the Providence National to obtain favorable terms for their own enterprises. Apparently they chose to protect their bank's earnings (and also the dividends on their extensive stockholdings) by lending out the bank's funds at the market rate of interest to creditworthy borrowers, even if that meant making money available to their business rivals. According to an entry for October 1896, "Our enemies have been borrowing heavily of Prov Bk In all they will have taken 50000 each or 200,000 on notes maturing this year at 6%." The diarist seemed pleased with the result, for he went on to note, "The City [of Providence] deposit is very convenient to us." For the Browns, by the late nineteenth century banking had become a business in its own right, an investment to be carefully managed and prized for its high, steady yields.[14]

The Providence National Bank may be an extreme example of the changes that were occurring in the banking sector, because the Brown family's ventures were so extraordinarily successful that they could command favorable credit terms in Boston as well as Providence. As the century progressed, however, an increasing number of banks found themselves for a variety of reasons with resources in excess of their directors' needs and at times even in excess of the needs of their communities. Some

12. Amounts for four loans (two from Providence National Bank, one from the Providence Institution for Savings, and one from an unnamed Boston institution) were not given. I estimated the missing amounts by calculating the average size of the loans from each source. Ibid., vols. 1–21.

13. See, for example, ibid., vol. 1, Dec. 23, 1878; vol. 21, Jan. 24, 1898.

14. Ibid., vol. 19, Oct. 9, 1896. The Providence National Bank paid dividends of 10% from 1870 to 1876, 7% from 1877 to 1879, and 8% from 1880 to 1900. By 1880 the Brown, Ives, and Goddard family group owned more than 60% of the bank's stock. Directors' and Stockholders' Minute Books, 1865–80, 1880–96, and 1896–1915, and Stock Ledger, 1857–85, Providence National Bank, Fleet National Bank Archives.

banks had surplus funds because their directors (like the Browns) were able to generate most of their own capital themselves or could turn to outside sources for funding. Other banks had surplus funds because the groups that controlled them were themselves no longer actively involved in business. In still other cases, as will be discussed below, the rise of deposit banking during the last third of the century enabled banks to attract lendable resources that far exceeded insiders' needs. Bankers nostalgically recalled the days when funds were scarce and applicants for loans anxiously "waited for the adjournment of the Board to learn if 'anything was done.'" To their dismay, "the proverb that 'the borrower is servant of the lender' [had] become reversed, and the lender now seeks the borrower."[15]

Whatever the reason, the appearance of these surplus funds had a snowballing effect that operated to reduce the incidence of insider lending throughout the economy. To the extent that banks had surplus funds to lend to outsiders, the funding opportunities for insiders at other banks increased. Moreover, to the extent that insiders turned to other institutions for loans, they freed up funds at their own banks for ventures in which they had no personal stake, which in turn freed up funds elsewhere, and so on.

II

As banks increased the proportion of funds they lent to outsiders, the problem of evaluating the creditworthiness of would-be borrowers took on increased urgency. When bankers lent their funds primarily to insiders, they were dealing with businessmen whose strengths and weaknesses were well known to them. But once they began to lend their funds to strangers, they needed to develop new ways of distinguishing worthy borrowers from the wider mass of applicants.

This problem became especially acute during the late nineteenth century as a result of two interrelated trends. The first was a shift in the kinds of commercial paper borrowers offered to banks. In response to the monetary disturbances of the Civil War era, manufacturers began to encourage customers to pay for goods in cash by offering them price discounts. Buyers reacted by changing the way they borrowed on the credit markets. Rather than paying for their purchases with an IOU that the seller then endorsed and discounted at a bank (making it two-name or "real" com-

15. Caleb H. Warner, *The National Bank of Commerce of Boston* (Cambridge, Mass., 1892 [privately printed]), 39–40; *Semi-Centennial of the National City Bank of Lynn* (Lynn, Mass., 1904 [privately printed]), 40–1.

mercial paper), buyers began to borrow from banks in advance of purchases in order to take advantage of the discounts. The result was a decline in the proportion of real bills on the market and a corresponding increase in what was called single-name paper. Backed only by the promise of the maker, single-name paper was effectively unsecured and was not linked directly to the completion of any particular commercial transaction. Whether it was a good investment or not depended on the borrower's financial soundness.[16]

This shift to a new kind of instrument coincided with the development of a national market for commercial paper, which compounded bankers' problems in evaluating the worth of these notes. During the early nineteenth century borrowers had typically restricted their dealings to one or two local banks, which in consequence had a clear sense of their customers' total obligations. Now, however, firms could issue their IOUs through note brokers, who would market them to banks and other financial intermediaries across the country. As a result, bankers lost their ability to assess a customer's total indebtedness. As an article in *Bankers' Magazine* reminded readers, by negotiating their loans through bill brokers, borrowers were "able to float much more paper in many cases than they could if they depended on one or two banks for funds. Herein is the risk of this new mode of lending money; a bank is utterly at sea concerning the ability of the borrower."[17]

The second trend that made the problem of evaluating borrowers' creditworthiness so critical was the declining profitability of banks during the last three decades of the nineteenth century. As a result of the passage of the National Banking Act during the Civil War, the economics of banking had changed in important ways. The Act required all nationally chartered banks to invest at least $30,000 or one-third of their capital (whichever was more) in U.S. government bonds, against which the banks would be permitted to issue currency up to 90 percent of the bonds' market value. It also required banks to maintain a reserve of 15 percent or more (depending on location) against their deposits. Not surprisingly, the region's state-chartered banks, which faced none of these requirements, proved reluctant to join the national system. The imposition in 1865 of a prohibitive tax on state banknotes radically altered their calculations, however, and most of the region's banks quickly applied for national charters.[18]

16. John A. James, *Money and Capital Markets in Postbellum America* (Princeton, N.J.: Princeton University Press, 1978), 55–9.
17. Vol. 48 (July 1893), 1–5.
18. Fritz Redlich, *The Molding of American Banking: Men and Ideas* (New York: Hafner, 1951), pt. II, 99–157; Phillip Cagan, "The First Fifty Years of

Despite their initial misgivings, their first years in the national banking system proved to be extremely profitable ones. During the late 1860s and early 1870s general economic conditions were extraordinarily favorable. In addition, bond prices were such that banks were able to earn a substantial premium by investing their capital in U.S. government securities, issuing currency on the basis of these securities, and then lending the currency out – rather than lending out their capital directly. As John James has pointed out, the premium was especially high for banks in the Northeast, where interest rates on loans were lower than in the rest of the country.[19]

The Panic of 1873 brought an abrupt end to this period of prosperity. During the ensuing depression the region's banks suffered severely and had to write off more than $3.7 million in losses in 1876, more than $5.4 million in 1877, and more than $5.6 million in 1878 (total loans and discounts in 1876 were $213.8 million).[20] Furthermore, although bank earnings rose again once the economy rebounded during the early 1880s, they never regained their previous levels. One reason was a decline in the profit that could be earned by issuing currency. The Treasury's policy of purchasing U.S. bonds to reduce the national debt pushed their prices skyward, and as a result during the period 1884 to 1891 the profit on note issues fell below the average rate of return on bank assets. Although currency issues became somewhat more profitable during the 1890s, depression-induced losses once again eroded banks' earnings.[21] Throughout this period, moreover, competition from new kinds of financial intermediaries increased. Particularly troublesome were the trust companies that state governments began chartering in greater numbers during the last two decades of the century. These institutions typically did not face

the National Banking System – An Historical Appraisal," in *Banking and Monetary Studies,* ed. Deane Carson (Homewood, Ill.: Irwin, 1963), 15–42; Ross M. Robertson, *The Comptroller and Bank Supervision: A Historical Appraisal* (Washington, D.C.: Office of the Comptroller of the Currency, 1968), 191–212; Andrew McFarland Davis, *The Origins of the National Banking System* (Washington, D.C.: Government Printing Office, 1910), 101–2.

19. Cagan, "The First Fifty Years of the National Banking System," 22–3; John A. James, "The Conundrum of the Low Issue of National Bank Notes," *Journal of Political Economy,* 84 (April 1976), 359–67. See also U.S., Comptroller of the Currency, *Annual Report* (1875), xvi–xviii.

20. U.S., Comptroller of the Currency, *Annual Report* (1876), lix, (1877), xxxiv, (1878), xlvii, (1900), 745–7.

21. Cagan, "The First Fifty Years of the National Banking System," 22–3; James, "The Conundrum of the Low Issue of National Bank Notes," 360.

the same regulatory restrictions as national banks but competed with them in every market save note issues.[22]

Whatever the cause, the profit rate of national banks in the region fell dramatically after the Panic of 1873 (see Table 4.1). Between 1871–5 and 1896–1900 the annual earnings rate of New England's national banks fell 48 percent (50 percent in Boston). Over the same period, the yield on a broad index of New England municipal bonds fell only 39 percent. By the end of the century, the earnings rate for national banks in Rhode Island was approximating the yield on municipal securities (a comparatively riskless asset), and Boston banks were performing only marginally better.[23]

One way banks responded to this decline in their earnings was by striving to increase deposits. As Table 4.2 shows, the ratio of deposits to capital rose sharply during the last thirty years of the century, so that by 1900 Boston banks were on average about ten times more leveraged than they had been during the 1850s. Most scholars have tended to view the growth of deposit banking as a demand-side phenomenon – that is, as a consequence of rising incomes (and an income elasticity for deposits that was greater than 1), a shift in preferences on the public's part to checks from cash for transaction purposes, and rising urbanization.[24] Some such demand-side changes were undoubtedly responsible for a significant share of the rise of bank deposits, but the growing eagerness of bankers to

22. Eugene Nelson White, "The Political Economy of Banking Regulation, 1864–1933," *Journal of Economic History*, 42 (March 1982), 33–40; James, *Money and Capital Markets in Postbellum America*, 39–40; George E. Barnett, *State Banks and Trust Companies Since the Passage of the National-Bank Act* (Washington, D.C.: Government Printing Office, 1911); Jon Moen and Ellis W. Tallman, "The Bank Panic of 1907: The Role of Trust Companies," *Journal of Economic History*, 52 (September 1992), 612–16.

23. National bank stock was a riskier investment than municipal bonds because in the event of default stockholders could recoup their investment only if the bank's remaining assets were sufficient to pay off its creditors in full. Moreover, if the funds raised by selling the bank's assets were inadequate to reimburse its creditors, under the national banking laws stockholders were liable for an assessment equal to 100% of the par value of their stock. The data on municipal bonds is from Sidney Homer and Richard Sylla, *A History of Interest Rates*, 3d ed. (New Brunswick, N.J.: Rutgers University Press, 1991), 286–8. For a similar analysis of bank earnings, see J. Van Fenstermaker, R. Phil Malone, and Stanley R. Stansell, "An Analysis of Commercial Bank Common Stock Returns: 1802–97," *Applied Economics*, 20 (1988), 813–41.

24. For a survey of this literature, see James, *Money and Capital Markets in Postbellum America*, 23–5.

Table 4.1. *Average annual earnings rates*
of national banks, 1871–1910

Period	Maine	Mass.[a]	Boston	N.H.	R.I.	New England[b]	U.S.A.
1871-5	11.3	10.3	9.0	9.5	9.8	9.8	10.2
1876-80	7.5	5.7	3.6	7.0	5.1	5.2	6.2
1881-5	6.9	6.4	5.1	6.8	6.1	6.1	8.2
1886-90	7.4	6.1	5.7	7.6	5.9	6.2	8.6
1891-5	6.0	5.0	4.6	5.4	4.8	5.1	6.6
1896-1900	6.6	5.3	4.5	6.2	3.8	5.1	6.6
1901-5	6.7	5.2	6.3	7.5	5.7	5.9	9.8
1906-10	6.9	7.3	8.7	9.1	7.9	7.7	9.7

Note: The average annual earnings rate is the ratio of net earnings to capital plus surplus.
[a]Includes Boston.
[b]Includes Connecticut and Vermont.
Source: U.S., Comptroller of the Currency, *Annual Report* (1871–1910).

solicit accounts, especially by offering to pay interest, was also a factor. Most individuals still did not maintain deposits in commercial banks during this period. Deposits came mainly from two sources: the cash reserves of business enterprises (monies that might otherwise have been invested in short-term interest-bearing assets) and the correspondent accounts of national and state banks in other localities. The latter were especially important to banks in the city of Boston, where by 1880 they amounted to a third of total deposits.[25]

Because attracting accounts from these sources depended on a willingness to offer competitive rates of interest, the rise of deposits was at least in part the result of a shift in bankers' attitudes toward this source of funds. In the first place, declining dividends made it more difficult for bankers to raise capital by selling stock, which, as we have seen, was the main source of lendable resources during the early part of the century. Indeed, the amount of money invested in bank stock increased only 1 percent over the entire period 1875–95.[26] Second, falling earnings also

25. U.S., Comptroller of the Currency, *Annual Report* (1880), clvi–clix. As mentioned above, the diaries of the Goddard Bros. Co. are filled with notations concerning possible investments for temporarily idle funds.
26. Ibid. (1900), 745–7.

Table 4.2. *Ratios of deposits to capital
for New England banks, 1870–1900*

Region	1870	1880	1890	1900
Maine	0.60	0.85	1.31	2.24
N.H.	0.52	0.77	1.49	2.70
Mass.[a]	0.93	1.54	2.22	3.95
Boston	1.19	2.10	2.77	5.50
R.I.	0.36	0.54	0.98	1.39

[a]Includes Boston.
Source: U.S., Comptroller of the Currency, *Annual Report* (1870), 554–7; (1880), clvi–clix; (1890), 250–3; (1900), vol. 1, 704–9, 730–1, 736–7.

raised the possibility that disappointed stockholders might attempt to encroach upon directors' managerial autonomy. Soliciting deposits thus became an increasingly attractive option, for it offered a solution to both these problems. As one writer put it, a higher ratio of deposits to capital permitted "larger dividends to the stockholders and also made the accumulation of a surplus an easier task."[27]

Whereas bankers had displayed little enthusiasm for soliciting deposits during the first half of the century, in the years that followed the Panic of 1873 their attitude completely reversed itself. As the directors of the Fourth National Bank of Boston reported to their stockholders in 1880, they "early saw the necessity of bringing to the bank as many good depositors as possible" and urged their shareholders "in future, [to] give us whatever influence it may be in their power to bestow, and bring to us all the business they can." Ten years later this same bank lent its cashier $1,000 for the purpose of purchasing enough stock to qualify for a directorship, "in consideration of the fact that this Bank can obtain the Boston account of the Nashua Trust Co provided the Cashier becomes a director."[28]

It is difficult to tell precisely when as a general policy banks began to pay interest on deposits. Bank examiners did not systematically collect such information until the 1890s, and minutes of directors' meetings contain little information on the subject. We do know, however, that in 1880 the directors of the Commercial Bank and the National Exchange

27. *Rhodes' Journal of Banking,* 15 (March 1888), 228.
28. Stockholders' meeting, Jan. 13, 1880, and Directors' meeting, Jan. 18, 1890, Directors' and Stockholders' Minute Book, 1875–1900, Fourth National Bank of Boston. See also the stockholders' meeting of Jan. 12, 1892.

Bank (both located in Providence) voted to pay 2½ percent interest on deposits of more than $500 and $100, respectively. The Massachusetts Bank, historically opposed to the payment of interest on deposits, appointed a committee in 1886 to consider reversing this practice (it did). Similarly, in 1892 the directors of the Merchants National Bank of Providence appointed a committee to consider "what, if anything, can be done to increase the business and profits of the Bank." Although the bank had paid interest on a few large deposits ('where the interests of the Bank will thereby be promoted') at least since 1871, the committee now recommended that the bank issue certificates of deposit for accounts worth as little as $500, payable on demand with interest rates from 2½ to 4 percent, depending on the length of time the deposit remained with the bank. Several months later the bank proceeded to advertise its new policy to the public, proclaiming at the same time that "liberal arrangements will be made for payment of interest on balances of Current accounts." In 1890 Commercial National in Boston also began to promote its deposit accounts by purchasing newspaper ads.[29]

According to bank examiners' reports, by the early 1890s Boston banks paid interest on 72 percent on average of their bankers' balances and 57 percent on average of their individual deposits. Providence banks also paid interest on the bulk of their accounts, including more than three quarters of their individual deposits. Country banks were somewhat less willing to offer interest to depositors, perhaps, as Richard Sylla has suggested, because they had more monopoly power, but in 1895 about two-thirds paid interest on at least some types of accounts.[30]

29. Directors' meeting, Nov. 29, 1880, Directors' and Stockholders' Minute Book, 1865–98, Commercial National Bank, Providence, R.I., Fleet National Bank Archives; directors' meeting, Dec. 6, 1880, Directors' and Stockholders' Minute Book, 1865–1905, National Exchange Bank, Providence, R.I., Fleet National Bank Archives; directors' meeting, Aug. 16, 1886, Directors' and Stockholders' Minute Book, 1883–1900, Massachusetts National Bank, Bank of Boston Archives; directors' meeting, Nov. 20, 1871, Directors' and Stockholders' Minute Book, 1865–91, and directors' meetings, Sept. 19, Oct. 31, and Dec. 5, 1892, Directors' and Stockholders' Minute Book, 1892–1909, Merchants National Bank, Providence, R.I., Fleet National Bank Archives; directors' meeting, Jan. 7, 1890, Directors' and Stockholders' Minute Book, 1888–1900, Commercial National Bank, Boston, Mass.

30. U.S., Comptroller of the Currency, Records of the Examination Division, Boston banks, 1892, and a sample of banks elsewhere, 1895; Richard Eugene Sylla, *The American Capital Market, 1846–1914: A Study of the Effects of Public Policy on Economic Development* (New York: Arno, 1975), 12, 92–3.

III

Increasing deposits, however, did not offset the downward trend in profits as much as bankers had expected. As Table 4.1 indicates, despite the sharp rise in the ratio of deposits to capital, earnings continued to drop. Moreover, as the following quantitative analysis of Boston institutions makes clear, banks that were most successful in attracting deposits did not always outperform their less leveraged competitors.

Data for this analysis came from several sources. The dependent variable (the profit rate for each Boston bank) was based on the annual reports of the U.S. Comptroller of the Currency, which included balance sheets for every national bank. Unfortunately, the Comptroller did not report earnings for these banks individually, so I had to construct estimates of their profits from the balance-sheet data along with information on annual dividends compiled by Joseph G. Martin for his history of the Boston stock market.[31] For purposes of this study, I have defined a bank's earnings in any given year as the amount of declared dividends plus the change in the amount credited to the bank's surplus and undistributed profits accounts.

This definition is not without its problems, however, because estimated earnings defined in this way are extremely sensitive to the manner in which each bank handled its delinquent debts. If a bank failed to charge off a bad loan at the time it was detected, its earnings for that year would be inflated, and of course the loss would not show up on the bank's balance sheets until it was written off.[32] Because year-to-year earnings were so prone to distortion by variations in the speed with which banks wrote off their losses, I have avoided all short-term analysis of banks' earnings in favor of treating their average performance over two longer periods of time: the decades 1876–85 and 1886–95.

Independent variables were derived from the annual reports of the Comptroller of the Currency, as well as from the manuscript returns of

31. Joseph G. Martin, *A Century of Finance: Martin's History of the Boston Stock and Money Markets* (Boston, 1898 [privately printed]), 100–11. The Comptroller collected information on earnings but reported only aggregate figures for reserve cities and states. A search at the National Archives, where the records of the Comptroller's office are, suggests that the figures for individual banks are no longer available.

32. For an excellent discussion of the problems of calculating banks' earnings, see Forrest Capie, "Structure and Performance in British Banking, 1870–1939," in *Money and Power: Essays in Honour of L. S. Pressnell*, ed. P. L. Cottrell and D. E. Moggridge (Basingstoke, Hants.: Macmillan, 1988), 80–9.

the national bank examiners for individual Boston banks.[33] These variables included such relevant balance-sheet magnitudes as the ratio of deposits to capital and bank size (measured by total assets). They also included a number of other measures that allowed me to control for managerial decisions that might affect profitability: the ratio of loans to total assets, the proportion of loans made on various types of personal and collateral security, and the average proportion of loans owed by directors.

The population included in this study consisted of each of the fifty-six national banks in Boston that were in operation during the entire twenty-year span. Excluded from consideration were all state banks and trust companies, one national bank that failed, two that voluntarily liquidated their affairs, one that left the city, and five that were founded after 1875.

Table 4.3 reports results for two regression equations estimated for each of the two time periods. In the first equation, the dependent variable is the banks' average profit rates; in the second, it is the variance in their profit rates over the ten-year period. These equations enabled me to compare the banks' track records according to two standards of performance: their ability to earn high average profits and their capacity to stabilize their returns from one year to the next.[34]

One of the most interesting aspects of the results in Table 4.3 is the poor performance of the size variable. There is a large body of literature that points to the existence of economies of scale in banking, but in neither the 1876–85 nor the 1886–95 period did large banks generally display higher earnings rates than smaller ones. Nor did they display a lower variance in profits, despite the greater opportunities for diversification that large size presumably entailed. Similarly, highly leveraged banks did not outperform their less highly leveraged rivals during the 1876–85 period: the deposit-to-capital ratio was not statistically significant in either of the equations. For the 1886–95 period, the ratio was significantly related to average profitability, but because the equation explained less than a quarter of the total variation in profitability, bankers could not have taken much comfort from the correlation.[35]

33. U.S., Comptroller of the Currency, *Annual Report* (1875–95), and Records of the Examination Division for the same period.

34. The variable for the variance in annual profit rates may be especially prone to error, however, because it is possible that bank managers timed their write-offs of bad loans with an eye to reducing the amount of variation in their annual profit figures.

35. The lack of statistically significant results was not a product of multi-collinearity. For the period 1876–85, the only high correlation among the independent variables involved SIZE and DIRECTORS' LOANS (the correlation

Table 4.3. *Determinants of profitability of national banks
in Boston, 1876–1895*

Independent variable	Dependent variable			
	1876-85		1886-95	
	AVEPROF	VARPROF	AVEPROF	VARPROF
CONSTANT	10.380***	-86.05	9.520***	7.002
	(3.60)	(-0.48)	(4.07)	(0.48)
SIZE	-0.030	-7.517	-0.032	-0.964
	(-0.23)	(-0.91)	(-0.32)	(-1.53)
DEPOSITS/CAPITAL	-0.243	9.415	0.393	1.895
	(-1.06)	(0.66)	(2.05)**	(1.58)
LOAN RATIO	-6.190*	111.463	-6.441**	6.468
	(-1.82)	(0.53)	(-2.39)	(0.38)
SINGLE-NAME	-12.076***	777.689***	0.872	5.956
	(-2.86)	(2.95)	(0.49)	(0.53)
COLLATERAL	-3.283	-99.871	5.033**	0.759
	(-0.91)	(-0.44)	(2.23)	(0.54)
DIRECTORS' LOANS	0.001	-0.022	-0.002	-0.011
	(0.21)	(-0.12)	(-1.39)	(-0.99)
Adjusted R^2	0.134	0.094	0.237	0.031
F-test probability	0.040	0.092	0.003	0.276

Notes: The T statistics are in parentheses. The definitions of the variables are as follows: AVEPROF, average annual profit rate for the period; VARPROF, variance in annual profit rates over the period; SIZE, total assets in millions of dollars at the beginning of the period; DEPOSITS/CAPITAL, ratio of all deposits (individual deposits and bankers' balances) to capital plus surplus at the beginning of the period; LOAN RATIO, ratio of loans to assets at the beginning of the period, where assets exclude required reserves and holdings of U.S. bonds; SINGLE-NAME, ratio of single-name paper to total loans at the beginning of the period; COLLATERAL, ratio of loans secured by collateral and payable on demand to total loans at the beginning of the period; DIRECTORS' LOANS for 1876–85, average ratio of directors' liabilities as payer to total loans over the period; for 1886–95, average ratio of directors' liabilities as both payer and endorser to total loans for the years 1891–95.
*Significant at the .10 level. **Significant at the .05 level. ***Significant at the .01 level.
Sources: See text.

The relatively poor showing of the size and leverage variables makes sense once one realizes that increasing the scale of a bank's operations by attracting additional deposits entailed special problems for bankers during the latter part of the century. In the first place, competition among banks for business pushed interest rates on deposits so high that bankers began to wonder whether increasing deposits was in fact remunerative at all. One writer went so far as to label the payment of interest on commercial deposits "the greatest menace in banking to-day."[36] Second, growing banks needed to find profitable outlets for their growing resources, and by the last few decades of the century this task had become increasingly arduous. The expansion of the banking system had so intensified the competition for good loans that it was more and more difficult to find investments that did not either earn low rates of return or reduce portfo-

---

was -0.54). Dropping the latter variable from the equations did not make the size variable statistically significant. For the 1886–95 period, SIZE had a negative correlation with DEPOSITS/CAPITAL (-0.52) and with DIRECTORS' LOANS (-0.44). Dropping both these variables from the equations still did not make size statistically significant.

On economies of scale in banking, see John A. James, "Cost Functions of Postbellum National Banks," *Explorations in Economic History,* 15 (April 1978), 184–95; Lyle E. Gramley, *Scale Economies in Banking* (Kansas City, Mo.: Federal Reserve Bank of Kansas City, 1962); George J. Benston, "Economies of Scale of Financial Institutions," *Journal of Money, Credit, and Banking,* 4 (May 1972), 312–41; Ernst Baltensperger, "Economies of Scale, Firm Size, and Concentration in Banking," *Journal of Money, Credit, and Banking,* 4 (August 1972), 467–88; George J. Benston, Gerald A. Hanweck, and David B. Humphrey, "Scale Economies in Banking: A Restructuring and Reassessment," *Journal of Money, Credit, and Banking,* 14 (November 1982), 435–56; James Kolari and Asghar Zardkoohi, *Bank Costs, Structure, and Performance* (Lexington, Mass.: Heath, 1987).

36. Frederick D. Kilburn, "Payment of Interest by Discount Banks upon Commercial Deposits," in *Practical Problems in Banking and Currency,* ed. Walter Henry Hull (New York: Macmillan, 1907), 78. The writer was a New York banker, but conditions in New England were similar. See, for example, Claudius B. Patten, *The Methods and Machinery of Practical Banking* (1891), 7th ed. (New York: Bradford Rhodes & Co., 1896), 339. James G. Cannon recognized "that banks cannot succeed without deposits," but he believed that "many institutions, in their mad rush for business, are putting forth every effort to augment their deposit lines, seemingly without considering whether the accounts secured are profitable." "Profit or Loss on Bank Accounts," *Proceedings of the Twentieth Annual Convention of the American Bankers' Association* (New York: American Bankers' Association, 1894), 42.

lio quality. Just how difficult it could be to keep a bank's funds fully invested can be seen from the diaries of the Goddard Brothers Company, the firm that managed the Brown family's textile enterprises and whose senior partner was also the president of the Providence National Bank. During periods of tight money, of course, it was not at all difficult for both the firm and the bank to find outlets for their resources. But during those periods when money was abundant, remunerative investments were hard to come by. The diaries are sprinkled with entries such as "Demand for money at bank much less. It is hard to find good paper"; "Bks heavily loaded with surplus funds"; "Bk finds no use for money"; and "Good paper scarce."[37] During such times not only were interest rates low, but it was difficult to find a sufficient number of qualified borrowers at any rate. In fact, bankers complained that it was precisely when their (interest-bearing) deposit accounts showed the greatest balances that the demand for loans was likely to be weakest: "When we cannot use the money profitably we are flooded with it, and when we can use it then it is largely withdrawn."[38]

As Table 4.3 indicates, the way in which bankers handled their growing portfolios was more likely to affect their profitability than were leverage ratios alone. Indeed, the variables that tended to perform best in the regressions were those that represented managers' investment decisions. Thus banks that lent out relatively more of their resources tended to be less profitable than those that invested a higher proportion of their funds in securities or other assets. Similarly, banks with high proportions of single-name paper generally earned lower profits and had a higher variance in returns during the 1876–85 period, whereas banks that lent a high proportion of their funds on demand on collateral security tended to do better during the period 1886–95.

None of these managerial strategies, however, could offer a real solution to the problem of declining profits. Although many national banks held stocks and bonds in their portfolios, legal restrictions on their ability to buy and sell securities limited their activity in these markets.[39] Moreover, legal restrictions also affected the availability of collateral loans. Because the National Banking Acts prohibited banks from lending on the security of real estate, collateral necessarily consisted for the most part of

37. Goddard Bros. Diaries, vol. 3, May 3, 1880; vol. 7, Jan. 28, 1884; vol. 8, June 22, 1885; vol. 14, Feb. 9, 1891.
38. E. H. Pullen, "Thirty-seven Years in a Bank," *Bankers' Magazine*, 57 (September 1898), 467–8. Pullen was vice-president of the National Bank of the Republic in New York City. See also Patten, *The Methods and Machinery of Practical Banking*, 406–7.
39. George M. Coffin, *Hand-Book for Bank Officers* (Washington, D.C.: McGill & Wallace, 1896), 53–4.

securities that commanded a ready market on the exchanges. As a result, this type of loan was most useful to businesses that issued marketable securities themselves, such as railroads (industrial securities were less frequently traded on the exchanges before the turn of the century), and to those engaged in the buying and selling of stocks and bonds. Collateral loans were of only limited use to most other borrowers, for the simple reason that businesses with surplus funds to invest in marketable securities were not likely to be those most in need of funds. Despite their obvious advantages for banks, then, collateral loans remained only a small part of their total portfolios. As late as 1890, 64 percent of the loans granted by Boston's national banks were still based entirely on personal security. Moreover, single-name paper accounted for an increasing proportion of these loans – 25 percent in 1890, as compared with 8 percent in 1875.[40]

IV

Declining profits in combination with the continued high proportion of personally secured loans (especially single-name paper) in banks' portfolios made it critical for bankers to find new ways of evaluating borrowers' creditworthiness and protecting themselves against default. One way they tried to do this was by requiring borrowers to maintain minimum deposits with them. Although this condition may initially have been a mechanism for enabling banks surreptitiously to earn interest in excess of the usury ceiling, falling interest rates had made the usury laws increasingly irrelevant by the last few decades of the century. The practice was nevertheless perpetuated because of the information it communicated about borrowers' creditworthiness and for the discipline it imposed on debtors' balance sheets. As one banker pointed out in *Rhodes' Journal of Banking:* "the *best* paper to accept is that offered by firms or individuals who are in the habit of carrying balances with their bank from whom the accommodation should be obtained. There appears to me *no* better means to determine the amount of risk a bank incurs than by regulating its loans according to the average balance carried." Another banker argued that the requirement to maintain compensating balances helped prevent losses by insuring that customers had a "cash reserve for emergencies."[41]

40. U.S., Comptroller of the Currency, *Annual Report* (1890), vol. 1, 141; Records of the Examination Division, Boston banks, 1875.
41. *Rhodes' Journal of Banking*, 20 (May 1893), 486–9; James B. Forgan, *A Good Note*, 1903 ed. (Chicago, 1920 [privately printed]), 17. Requiring deposits was also in theory a way to jack up earnings, but it is likely that any increases above market rates of interest were competed away.

Yet the protection offered by borrowers' deposits was limited at best. Although the relationship between the deposit and the loan amount varied widely from one institution to the next (so much so that writers found it impossible to generalize about the matter), the ratio was probably not an advantageous one from the banks' point of view, especially once the competition for deposits heated up during the latter part of the century. Critics repeatedly complained that banks tried to lure new depositors by promising them excessive lines of credit.[42]

In any event, such deposits were unable to stem the onslaught of heavy losses that banks experienced during the last few decades of the century, which for the average Boston bank increased 300 percent between 1876–85 and 1886–95.[43] Although much of the problem undoubtedly resulted from the troubled state of the economy, bankers were desperate to take whatever measures they could to improve their situation. By the 1890s they had become convinced that "by far the greater part of losses incurred by banks on commercial paper could have been avoided had their officers been possessed of sufficient information regarding the applicants at the time the loan was asked for."[44]

One thing seemed clear enough: bankers could no longer afford to base their credit decisions on a borrower's general reputation for wealth and probity. Even for country bankers, it was no longer sufficient to rely upon personal knowledge of customers' businesses, as one such banker learned when he decided to write down everything that he "positively knew, or could learn from unquestionable sources" about his borrowers. To his "astonishment," he discovered "how little I really knew." He concluded from this experiment that he and other bankers had been "granting credits on 'general reputation' unworthily."[45]

42. Albert R. Barrett, *Modern Banking Methods and Practical Bank Bookkeeping,* 5th ed. (New York: Bankers Publishing, 1907), 285; Forgan, *A Good Note,* 17. Bank records are usually silent regarding deposit arrangements. The one exception I have found is an agreement noted in the minutes of the Shawmut National Bank specifying that an out-of-town firm would be granted a $40,000 line of credit secured by collateral. In return it was expected that the firm would keep on deposit an amount equivalent to 20% of its debt. Directors' meeting, Sept. 27, 1875, Directors' and Stockholders' Minute Book, 1865–77, Shawmut National Bank, Shawmut Bank Archives.

43. U.S., Comptroller of the Currency, Records of the Examination Division, Boston banks, 1876–95.

44. *Rhodes' Journal of Banking,* 20 (June 1893), 585. See also *Bankers' Magazine,* 57 (September 1898), 384, 413–22.

45. *Bankers' Magazine,* 57 (August 1898), 286–7. See also *Rhodes' Journal of Banking,* 20 (February 1893), 137; (April 1893), 377.

For years bankers had supplemented their personal knowledge of borrowers' business dealings by subscribing to reports issued by the various commercial credit agencies such as R. G. Dun and Company. These reports were rarely based on financial statements filed by the firm in question. Usually they consisted of estimates of a firm's worth and of the character of its proprietors, based on the impressions of local lawyers and businessmen – precisely the kind of information that bankers were coming to regard as inadequate. Not surprisingly, then, by the 1890s trade publications were questioning the worth of such reports and arguing for more systematic methods of collecting information. Bankers, they insisted, would have to take charge of this function themselves by organizing credit departments within their own organizations and requiring financial statements from each of their customers. These more rigorous procedures would pay off because many applicants for loans were in fact unworthy of credit. In order to demonstrate "the value of a careful investigation of credits," one writer prevailed upon a New York bank with a credit department to prepare a summary of its investigation of 1,598 would-be borrowers. "Of these, 798, or practically 50 percent., were unsatisfactory and credit was refused." The obvious implication was that, without its credit investigation department, the bank would have been less able to discriminate among the various applicants for loans and would have faced heavy losses as a result.[46]

Banks were urged not only to require financial statements from their customers but to interpret these statements in a very specific way. A customer's resources should be divided into fixed assets, on the one hand, and quick or convertible assets, on the other. Only the latter were considered to be a proper foundation for loans. Loans, moreover, should not be granted if a borrower's liabilities exceeded 50 percent of his quick assets, a notion that gained currency as "the so-called 50 per cent. rule." Even on this basis, loans should be granted only for short periods of time – six months at most, and preferably less.[47]

46. *Bankers' Magazine*, 47 (January 1893), 535–6. See also Cannon, *An Ideal Bank*, 6–8. The increased importance of credit information placed new demands on bank officers, as William Goddard pointed out when he resigned the presidency of the Providence National Bank in 1905: "an obstinate lameness so tethers me to the spot in which I have spent my long life, that I feel disqualified from seeking elsewhere the information regarding the credit of borrowers, which I regard as of the highest importance to the successful management of a bank." Directors' meeting, Jan. 10, 1905, Directors' and Stockholders' Minute Book, 1896–1915, Providence National Bank.

47. James G. Cannon, "Bank Credits," in *Practical Problems in Banking and*

How this particular prescription emerged is a matter of some importance, because by definition it ruled out certain categories of loans to manufacturers. The emphasis on quick assets meant that much of the capital invested by manufacturers in their businesses, even if unencumbered, would not be considered a proper basis for making loans.[48] At the same time, the insistence on loans of short duration meant that manufacturers could not borrow from banks to finance improvements in plant and equipment that required a longer period of time to generate a return.

Many writers justified their emphasis on short-term commercial loans by emphasizing the greater need for liquidity necessitated by the growth of deposit banking. According to a pamphlet issued by the American Institute of Banking, "experience shows that a bank all of whose assets can be converted into cash within a few months without loss is altogether unlikely to be disturbed by lack of confidence, and should it be subjected to unfounded rumors no difficulty is experienced in securing the necessary funds from other banks."[49]

Yet the argument that short-term loans necessarily led to greater liquidity made little sense, as even the pamphlet's authors seemed to realize. Under crisis conditions, portfolios consisting entirely of short-term commercial loans could be as difficult to liquidate as those containing a significant proportion of long-term loans, because bankers typically had to renew their customers' notes in order to avoid alienating them or precipitating failures that would in turn render the loans themselves uncollectible.[50] Liquidity needs, bankers recognized, had to be met in other ways. Hence it was generally recommended that a bank invest 20 percent of its funds in high-grade bonds and securities, "such as are convertible at a moment's notice," and another 20 percent in commercial paper pur-

Currency, ed. Walter Henry Hull (New York: Macmillan, 1907), 47; Forgan, *A Good Note,* 8–10.

48. During the first two decades of the twentieth century a few writers did express doubts concerning the formula on precisely these grounds. See, for example, Albert N. Hogg, *The Sixth Sense* (Philadelphia: Corn Exchange Bank, 1915), 20; H. G. Moulton, "Commercial Banking and Capital Formation," *Journal of Political Economy,* 26 (May, June, July, November 1918), 484–508, 638–63, 705–31, 849–81; and even Cannon himself in "Bank Credits," 49–50.

49. *Loans and Investments* (New York: American Institute of Banking, 1916), 12.

50. Ibid., 14–15; Lloyd W. Mints, *A History of Banking Theory in Great Britain and the United States* (Chicago: University of Chicago Press, 1945), 216–19.

chased in the open market, which would be free of any pressure for renewal at maturity. With the liquidity of the institution thus safely assured, the bank could lend the remaining 60 percent of its funds locally for the benefit of its customers. But despite the recognition that these assets would generally be unavailable in times of emergency, most writers still insisted that "the conclusion should not be drawn . . . that the loans made to such regular customers need not possess the quality of liquidness." Loans to regular customers should also be granted for brief periods only and should be based solely on the firms' short-term assets.[51]

Careful study of the pamphlets promoting such advice suggests that at the heart of the matter was concern about information and monitoring problems, not liquidity per se. Short-term loans based on quick assets were desirable because they helped discipline the borrower. Bankers expected "that borrowers will use the proceeds of loans which they are to repay in a few months more wisely than might be the case if the payment were indefinitely deferred." Moreover, because the information contained in a borrower's financial statement reflected current conditions, which were liable to "change radically for the worse" with the passage of time, such a statement was clearly "a basis of short time credit only."[52]

V

By the last decade of the century, then, declining profit rates, in conjunction with the increasing amount of single-name paper on the market, had prompted banks to develop new methods of evaluating their customers' creditworthiness, particularly by soliciting financial statements from all their borrowers and by forming credit departments capable of processing the requested information. At the same time, it was necessary for bank managers to devise some way of monitoring borrowers with whom they had no personal connections. To this end, financial writers urged bankers to restrict themselves to short-term loans and to interpret customers' financial statements according to the "50 per cent. rule": that is, loans should be granted on the basis of quick assets only, and total indebtedness should be limited to half the value of those assets. This policy made it more difficult, however, for banks to satisfy the credit needs of manufacturing ventures. To the extent, then, that it was implemented, its effect

51. E. T. Coman, "Requisites of a Good Loan," in *Practical Problems in Banking and Currency*, ed. Walter Henry Hull (New York: Macmillan, 1907), 66–77; *Loans and Investments*, 14–15.

52. *Loans and Investments*, 14–15.

would be to encourage banks to specialize increasingly narrowly in the business of commercial lending. As the next chapter will show, this tendency to specialize was reinforced by another information problem that banks faced during the latter part of the century – the problem of communicating their own soundness to investors and especially to depositors, on whom they were becoming more and more dependent for funds.

5

Professionalization and specialization

One of the most fundamental principles of good banking is that the bank should not furnish the capital for its customers to do business upon. The customer should possess his own capital, and require assistance from the bank only at certain seasons and for specific purposes.

David R. Forgan[1]

I

At the same time as the decline in insider lending made it more difficult for banks to assess the creditworthiness of their borrowers, it also made it harder for depositors and investors to evaluate the soundness of a particular bank. Because only a small proportion of loans now typically went to insiders, the identity of a bank's directors conveyed little information to the public about the contents of the institution's loan portfolio. Worse, the identity of the directors also conveyed little information about the quality of the bank's management team, for directors tended to lose interest in overseeing a bank once their need for its funds diminished. Indeed, by the last third of the nineteenth century, many directors had begun to neglect their formal responsibilities, failing to attend regular board meetings and delegating more authority to their executive officers. Attendance reached an all-time low at the weekly meetings held to scrutinize recent discounts. Only two of the seven directors of the Boylston National Bank of Boston, for example, were present for at least 70 percent of the board's meetings in 1880. Only three of the Massachusetts National Bank's nine directors had an equivalent attendance record, and only one of the nine directors of the People's National Bank of Roxbury. This pattern was repeated at many other institutions.[2]

1. "Banking as a Profession," *Bankers' Magazine*, 57 (September 1898), 384. Forgan was president of the Union National Bank of Chicago.
2. Directors' and Stockholders' Minute Book, 1864–87, Boylston National Bank of Boston, Bank of Boston Archives; Directors' and Stockholders' Minute Book, 1865–83, Massachusetts National Bank of Boston, Bank of Boston

The growing indifference of directors to their responsibilities was a serious problem, because it opened the door to opportunistic behavior on the part of the bank's active managers (the president and/or cashier and the few participating directors). In a small number of cases these men were able to use their positions of authority to lend themselves considerable sums of money without the rest of the board's consent and also, of course, without the knowledge of the general public. Whether these loans were more likely to generate losses than the insider loans so common among early-nineteenth-century banks is difficult to say. But because credit was now abundant, the motivation for such behavior may well have been to secure loans for ventures that would not otherwise have met banking standards, or to obtain larger lines of credit than bankers were normally willing to grant. In any event, contemporaries increasingly regarded such behavior as dangerous, and by the last few years of the century it had become a commonplace that large loans to opportunistic managers were the major cause of bank failures. In the words of Comptroller of the Currency William Barret Ridgely, "The practically universal rule is that all failures are due to excess loans to one interest or group of interests, generally owned or controlled by the officers of the bank itself."[3]

But how were investors and depositors to know which banks were engaged in such dangerous practices? And how were banks that eschewed such practices to communicate this fact to the public at large? At stake here was more than just banks' ability to raise funds. Unless people were able to distinguish among the various banks, the failure of any one of

Archives; Directors' and Stockholders' Minute Book, 1864–83, People's National Bank of Roxbury, Mass., Bank of Boston Archives. For additional examples, see Directors' and Stockholders' Minute Book, 1873–88, Manufacturers National Bank of Boston, Bank of Boston Archives; Directors' and Stockholders' Minute Book, 1875–1900, Fourth National Bank of Boston, Bank of Boston Archives; Directors' and Stockholders' Minute Book, 1864–89, First National Bank of Warren, R.I., Fleet National Bank Archives; Directors' Minute Book, 1885–1900, Phenix National Bank, Phenix, R.I., Fleet National Bank Archives. Attendance remained high at some banks. For examples, see Directors' Minute Book, 1874–95, First National Bank of Boston, Bank of Boston Archives; Directors' and Stockholders' Minute Book, 1865–80, Providence National Bank, Providence, R.I., Fleet National Bank Archives.

3. Quoted in Edward Preston Moxey, "Bank Defalcations – Their Causes and Cures," *Annals of the American Academy of Political and Social Science*, 25 (1905), 33.

them threatened to undermine confidence in the banking system as a whole and with it the public's willingness to leave funds on deposit.

The root of the problem was depositors' lack of information about individual banks. As one writer complained in 1888, it was "much more difficult to secure trustworthy information in regard to the standing of a bank than it [was] in regard to the standing of a commercial firm."[4] Although each national bank published a financial statement several times yearly, these documents contained no information at all concerning the contents of the bank's loan portfolio. Moreover, the balance sheets of many banks looked roughly similar. In 1885, for example, the average ratio of capital plus surplus to total liabilities for Boston banks was about 35 percent, with nearly half the banks falling within the range of 30 to 40 percent. Five of the nine banks with ratios below 25 percent were among the most successful in the city in attracting accounts, a record that suggests that depositors did not regard such information as particularly useful.[5]

As Charles W. Calomiris and Gary Gorton have pointed out, whenever lack of information makes it difficult for depositors to monitor the performance of individual banks, the likelihood of panics increases. Whenever depositors believe that some banks are in danger of failing but are unable to identify the particular institutions at risk, they may react by withdrawing their savings indiscriminately, precipitating a systemwide crisis.[6] Contemporary bankers understood this danger all too well. As one writer in *Bankers' Magazine* explained, "We are in a most important sense directly responsible for each other, and cannot avoid being disturbed by the ignorance, selfishness or immoral conduct of our most remote members." Or, as another writer succinctly put it, "Every bank that fails through mismanagement weakens the surrounding ones." The danger was dramatically illustrated in early 1884 when several failures, "all attributable to the madness of speculation by bank officers," caused depositors to panic. In Vermont the failure of the First National Bank of St. Albans (allegedly

4. *Rhodes' Journal of Banking*, 15 (March 1888), 232.
5. U.S., Comptroller of the Currency, *Annual Report* (1885), 62–83. Banks were difficult to distinguish in other ways as well. Most had been founded before the Civil War and had long records of success. Most, moreover, still occupied modest quarters. In Boston, for example, the second stories of buildings along State and adjacent streets still housed the vast majority of the city's banks.
6. "The Origins of Banking Panics: Models, Facts, and Bank Regulation," in *Financial Markets and Financial Crises,* ed. R. Glenn Hubbard (Chicago: University of Chicago Press, 1991), 109–73.

caused by an "unfortunate speculation in stocks by its president and cashier") led to a run on the National Union Bank of Swanton, even though the solvency of the latter institution was regarded by informed opinion as beyond question. ("To meet only $52,000 due depositors, it held $117,000 of good, short time paper.") That same year the *Bankers' Magazine* despaired that "many business men are suspicious of other banks, and, by withdrawing their deposits, are doing their utmost to bring on the very condition of things they deplore."[7]

Even the most prestigious banks were vulnerable to runs, as William Goddard learned during the late 1870s when a savings-bank panic spread to the rock-solid Providence Institution for Savings, operated in conjunction with his own Providence National Bank. Over the course of the run the savings bank lost nearly $500,000 in deposits. On the worst day of the panic about $195,000 was withdrawn. That night the Providence National Bank had to stay open until ten-thirty in order to honor checks drawn on it by the savings institution. Cash ran low, and Goddard had to arrange for $425,000 to be shipped in express from New York.[8]

Some idea of the extent to which bankers like Goddard worried about depositors' confidence can be gauged from their willingness to bail out banks that failed as a result of excessive loans to insiders. When the manufacturing empire of Rhode Island's Sprague family ran into financial trouble after the Panic of 1873, for example, the family's obligations at the three Providence banks where it held sway amounted to three-quarters of a million dollars apiece. As a result of the failure, the First National Bank of Providence was forced to write down its capital by more than 80 percent, Second National by 40 percent, and Globe National by

7. Vol. 38 (May and June 1884), 886, 901–2; 39 (July 1884), 45; 42 (August 1887), 83.

8. See Goddard Bros. Diaries, vol. 1, April 8, 12, 26, 27, 29, and 30 and May 1 and 2, 1878, Brown and Ives Manufacturing Records, Mss. 9, Sub Group 10, Series D, Rhode Island Historical Society Manuscript Collections; directors' meeting, April 27, 1878, Directors' and Stockholders' Minute Book, 1865–80, Providence National Bank; *Providence Journal*, April 29, 1878, p. 2. Although national bank failures in New England were actually fairly rare (between 1880 and 1900 there were only six in Massachusetts, two in New Hampshire, and none at all in either Maine or Rhode Island), the general financial crises that periodically racked the economy kept bankers on edge. During the last two decades of the century alone there were serious monetary disturbances in 1884, 1890, and 1893. U.S., Comptroller of the Currency, *Annual Report* (1900), 502–11; O. M. W. Sprague, *History of Crises Under the National Banking System* (Washington, D.C.: Government Printing Office, 1910).

50 percent. These banks were saved from failure by the combined efforts of other Providence banks (including Goddard's Providence National), which agreed to contribute as much as 3 percent of their capital to guarantee the deposits of the endangered banks.[9]

In order to prevent such incidents from recurring, bankers joined forces to organize clearinghouses. Just as their predecessors in the early nineteenth century had developed the Suffolk system to guard against monetary excesses by country banks, so bankers now responded by organizing a new mechanism to regulate the behavior of their colleagues. The Boston Clearing House, the region's first such institution, was dominated by the families that controlled two of the city's most important banks, Merchants National and Second National. Franklin Haven, president of the former institution, served as president of the clearinghouse from its inception in 1856 until 1859. His son, who succeeded him to the presidency of the Merchants National Bank, also served as president of the clearinghouse from 1902 until 1907. James H. Beal, president of Second National, headed the clearinghouse from 1871 until 1887, and two other members of the Beal family followed in his footsteps during the next century.[10]

Both families were known for their conservative views. Haven senior was one of the first men in Boston to rise through the ranks of bank employees, starting out as a teller in the Globe Bank and then moving to the Merchants as cashier when that bank was founded. Made president at the time of Panic of 1837, he instituted a policy of discounting only real commercial paper, that is, paper that was self-liquidating and not subject to renewal at maturity. In his own words, his goal was to "exert an influence, limited perhaps, but salutary, against a disposition to over-bank or over-trade in this community."[11] James H. Beal had been elected

9. Howard Kemble Stokes, *Chartered Banking in Rhode Island, 1791–1900* (Providence: Preston & Rounds, 1902), 56–7; directors' meeting, Oct. 29, 1873, Directors' and Stockholders' Minute Book, 1865–1905, National Exchange Bank, Providence; directors' meeting, Oct. 29, 1873, Directors' and Stockholders' Minute Book, 1865–91, Merchants National Bank, Providence; directors' meeting, Nov. 3, 1873, Directors' and Stockholders' Minute Book, 1865–80, Providence National Bank. These records are all in the Fleet National Bank Archives.

10. *100th Anniversary: The Boston Clearing House Association, 1856–1956* (Boston, 1956 [privately printed]). According to the *Manual* put out by the Maverick National Bank (Boston: Wright & Potter, 1887), seven other New England cities had clearinghouses by the late 1880s (p. 93).

11. Richard P. Chapman, *One Hundred Twenty-five Years on State Street! "Merchants National of Boston" (1831–1956)* (New York: Newcomen Society, 1956). The quotation is taken from pp. 12–13.

president of the Granite Bank (later Second National) during the Panic of 1857, when that institution's fortunes were at a low ebb. He promptly severed all his other business ties, devoting himself exclusively to the bank, and pioneered in the systematic collection of credit information. Beal and his son Thomas P., the bank's next president, were so cautious about their investments that they insisted on leasing offices rather than constructing a bank building. As they stated their position, "Capital tied up in bricks and mortar was of little use as a protection to depositors or for the purpose of extending credit to customers in times of stress."[12]

As Franklin Haven and the other founders originally envisioned it, the primary purpose of the Boston clearinghouse was to facilitate the settling of accounts among the city's numerous banks. But its potential usefulness as an instrument of regulation soon became apparent. In addition to clearing checks, the organization was also valuable as a means of instilling public confidence. By serving as a lender of last resort for temporarily insolvent banks, it was well positioned to safeguard the public's deposits and thereby prevent runs on its membership.[13] Because this service was available only to members, moreover, admission to the clearinghouse became a prize that could be granted as a reward for sound management practices or denied as a punishment for financial transgressions. The Pacific National Bank of Boston, for example, was excluded from the clearinghouse because the city's leading bankers disapproved of its management and "decidedly and successfully opposed its admission."[14]

Unlike the Suffolk system, however, the clearinghouse had only limited effectiveness as a regulatory tool. In the first place, banks like Pacific National typically arranged to clear their checks through an allied member institution, a practice that potentially jeopardized the latter's sound-

12. Alexander S. Wheeler, *The History of the Second National Bank of Boston from 1860 to 1896* (Boston, 1932 [privately printed]); Thomas P. Beal, *The Second National Bank of Boston* (Boston, 1958 [privately printed]), 8–9, 11–12.

13. Gary Gorton, "Clearinghouses and the Origin of Central Banking in the United States," *Journal of Economic History*, 45 (June 1985), 277–83; Gorton and Donald J. Mullineaux, "The Joint Production of Confidence: Endogenous Regulation and Nineteenth Century Commercial-Bank Clearinghouses," *Journal of Money, Credit, and Banking*, 19 (November 1987), 457–68.

14. Claudius B. Patten, *The Methods and Machinery of Practical Banking* (1891), 7th ed. (New York: Bradford Rhodes & Co., 1896), 357. Patten was cashier at Boston's State National Bank, a member of the clearinghouse. On the admission policies of clearinghouses, see also Edward Carroll, Jr., *Principles and Practice of Finance: A Practical Guide for Bankers, Merchants, and Lawyers* (New York: Putnam, 1895), 132–3.

ness. When the Pacific National Bank failed in 1881, for example, its correspondent, Central National, faced heavy losses and had to be rescued by the associated banks.[15] Second, the organization could not afford to be overly selective, because denying membership to a significant number of institutions would have undermined its effectiveness both in clearing checks and maintaining public confidence in the banking system.[16] Third, such balance-sheet information as the clearinghouses routinely collected did not provide any data about loan portfolios. Although clearinghouse officials had the authority to conduct full-scale investigations of member banks' affairs, such powers were usually reserved for emergencies.

Even when information concerning unsound practices materialized, moreover, clearinghouse officials were not always willing to act. Fearful of precipitating a crisis, they sometimes chose to overlook the transgressions of their membership. The Maverick National Bank is a case in point. One of Boston's largest banks, it collapsed as a result of large loans made to shore up the speculative investments of its president, Asa P. Potter, and several of its directors. After Potter's partner, Irving A. Evans, went bankrupt and committed suicide a month before the Maverick's collapse, there were rumors that the bank was also in trouble. The clearinghouse, however, took no action at all until the Winthrop Bank, of which Evans's brother was president, refused to honor one of the Maverick's certified checks. (Potter later claimed that the brother blamed him for the suicide and used this means to exact revenge.) Other clearinghouse members were appalled by the Winthrop's action, but as the cat was now out of the bag, the association had no choice but to initiate an investigation, which culminated in the pronouncement that the Maverick National Bank was indeed insolvent.[17]

Not only were the association's monitoring efforts of limited effectiveness, but by the end of the century the clearinghouse was backing away from its role as a lender of last resort. In 1899, for example, it refused to bail out the failed Broadway National Bank and ceased its rescue operations at Globe National once the unsound practices of that bank's management became known.[18] Apparently bankers had begun to worry that the clearinghouse would end up sheltering poorly managed institutions at

---

15. Patten, *The Methods and Machinery of Practical Banking*, 357.
16. A. S. Bolles, "The Functions of Clearing Houses – The New York Clearing House Controversy," *Proceedings of the Convention of the American Bankers' Association* (New York: William B. Greene, 1890), 127–31.
17. *Boston Evening Transcript*, Nov. 2, 1891, pp. 1–2; Nov. 3, 1891, p. 8.
18. Ibid., Dec. 16, 1899, p. 9; Dec. 18, 1899, p. 1; *Boston News Bureau*, Dec. 16, 1899, p. 1; Dec. 18, 1899, p. 1; Dec. 22, 1899, p. 2.

great cost to the rest of the membership, and they decided to be more selective about offering their backing. Ironically, however, this new refusal automatically to come to the aid of clearinghouse members would exert, as I shall argue below, a more powerful disciplinary influence over the banking sector than the association's original attempt to monitor members' behavior.

Government oversight of banks was also weak during this period. Agents of the U.S. Comptroller of the Currency regularly examined the books of all nationally chartered banks, but the Comptroller could do little about violations of sound practice, or even of law, as long as the banks involved were fundamentally solvent. For example, although the National Banking Acts prohibited loans to any one individual, firm, or corporation in excess of 10 percent of capital, this provision was relatively easy to evade and difficult to enforce. All the Comptroller could really do was make violations known to the offending banks' boards of directors. The only other sanction he had at his disposal was to institute proceedings to revoke the banks' charters, a remedy far too drastic to be invoked with any frequency. The statutory limit notwithstanding, therefore, over 40 percent of the national banks reporting to the Comptroller in 1900 had at least one loan on their books exceeding 10 percent of their capital.[19]

II

During the last three decades of the nineteenth century, movements developed in many sectors of American society to systematize and rationalize human activity – to put it on a firm scientific basis. The new "professionals" who promoted this cause appeared in fields as disparate as railroad management, medicine, and history.[20] They had their counterparts in

19. *Bankers' Magazine*, 37 (December 1882), 445; Albert R. Barrett, *Modern Banking Methods and Practical Bank Bookkeeping*, 5th ed. (New York: Bankers Publishing Co., 1907), 289.

The regulatory authority of the Comptroller, moreover, appears to have declined during this period. Competition between state and federal governments for the business of chartering banks led, on the one hand, to a general erosion of standards and, on the other, to an increase in the number of institutions not subject to federal regulation. Eugene Nelson White, "The Political Economy of Banking Regulation, 1864–1933," *Journal of Economic History*, 42 (March 1982), 33–40; John A. James, *Money and Capital Markets in Postbellum America* (Princeton, N.J.: Princeton University Press, 1978), 36–40.

20. See Robert H. Wiebe, *The Search for Order, 1877–1920* (New York: Hill &

banking, too, as a group of self-conscious professionals emerged from the ranks of career bank managers, trade-journal publicists, and government regulators. Claudius B. Patten, for example, made his way up through the clerical ranks at Boston's Suffolk and State banks, ultimately becoming cashier of the latter institution. Subsequently he wrote a long series of articles for *Rhodes' Journal of Banking* with the aim of promoting the sound banking practices that were exemplified by his own career, as well as providing other aspiring employees with the benefit of his knowledge and experience. His publisher, Bradford Rhodes, would later eulogize him as the very model of the new professional: "He loved his profession and sought continually to formulate better and safer methods in the transaction of the banking business. . . . Selfishness had no place in his nature, and he was opposed to taking out a patent on a new idea and putting it under lock and key in his own bank."[21]

Rhodes himself had originally come to New York to work as a reporter. After a stint with the business department of the *Daily Commercial Bulletin,* he established his own bankers' trade journal, which proved highly successful and provided him with an influential forum from which to pronounce upon monetary and banking issues. By 1899 Rhodes had acquired the competing *Bankers' Magazine,* assumed the presidency of the Mamaroneck Bank and the Union Savings Bank (both in Westchester County), served several years in the New York legislature (where he chaired the Committee on Banks), and played a leading role in a variety of bankers' groups, heading the local section of the New York State Bankers' Association and sitting on the executive council of the national organization.[22]

Another spokesman for professional standards in banking was John Jay Knox, who was appointed Comptroller of the Currency during the Grant administration. Like Patten and Rhodes, Knox began his career in private

Wang, 1967); Alfred D. Chandler, Jr., *The Visible Hand: The Managerial Revolution in American Business* (Cambridge: Harvard University Press, 1977); Olivier Zunz, *Making America Corporate, 1870–1920* (Chicago: University of Chicago Press, 1990); John Higham, *History: Professional Scholarship in America* (New York: Harper & Row, 1973).

21. Bradford Rhodes, Introduction, in Patten, *The Methods and Machinery of Practical Banking,* iii. See also *Rhodes' Journal of Banking,* 13 (May 1886), 417–18.

22. *National Cyclopedia of American Biography,* vol. 10, 416. I have included some examples from outside New England because for all practical purposes these professionals constituted a national movement. They traveled to promote their views, and their publications were read throughout the country. Because New York was the nation's financial center, many of them operated out of that city.

employment. After working for a succession of upstate New York banks, where he rose from teller to cashier, he journeyed westward with his brother in the late 1850s to set up a private banking firm. In 1862 he published an article in *Hunt's Merchants' Magazine* proposing the formation of a system of national banks. The article caught the attention of Secretary of the Treasury Salmon P. Chase, thus inaugurating a career in government that culminated in Knox's appointment in 1872 to a twelve-year term as the nation's chief bank regulator. Knox used the platform provided by his office to travel around the country promoting sound banking practices.[23]

Conservative bankers like the Havens and the Beals found the new professionals to be valuable allies in their drive to assert some control over competitors' lending practices. Both groups indeed had much to gain from a shift in the way banks conducted their business, and both were particularly eager to forestall opportunistic behavior by bank managers. As we have already seen, conservatives worried that opportunism in one bank could threaten the stability of the entire financial system. The professionals, on the other hand, believed that such behavior ran counter to the values of objectivity and impartiality upon which their movement was founded. They also recognized that as long as businessmen could secure capital for their ventures by involving themselves in the management of a bank, so long would the professionalization of the banking system be stymied.

With the formation of this alliance, then, insider lending took on the proportions of an evil to be destroyed.[24] In books on banking practice, trade-journal publications, newspaper articles, and addresses to profes-

---

23. *Dictionary of American Biography*, vol. 10, 477.
24. This position was not completely new. A few conservatives, such as Nathan Appleton, A. B. Johnson, and even Franklin Haven, Sr., had voiced similar opinions before the Civil War (see esp. Johnson, *A Treatise on Banking: The Duties of a Banker, and His Personal Requisites Therefor* [Utica, N.Y.: R. Northway & Co., 1850]), but it was not until the last quarter of the century that their ideas acquired widespread appeal.

   By this time, however, preoccupation with the issue was largely internal to the banking system. There was no general hue and cry against insider lending. Instead public attention focused largely on the question of the money stock (whether the government should issue greenbacks, whether silver should be monetized) and also on the level of interest rates that banks charged for loans, particularly in the western parts of the country. For a discussion of these concerns, see Irwin Unger, *The Greenback Era: A Social and Political History of American Finance, 1865–1879* (Princeton, N.J.: Princeton University Press, 1964). See also such works on populism as

sional societies, both conservatives and professionals directed a steady stream of criticism at bank officers and directors who enriched themselves at their institutions' expense – at officials "who appreciate[d] the utility of a bank – to them":

> They direct emphatically and direct in such a way as always to serve first their own interest. Their idea of a bank is that it is an institution existing mainly for their own benefit, and they do not hesitate to use it in the promotion of their own interests, however much others may suffer by their conduct.[25]

The most obvious solution to the problem of opportunistic behavior, proponents of professional banking agreed, was to prohibit bank officers from having "any special interest in parties or concerns that borrow money from their institutions." Bank presidents in particular should be "engaged in no outside interest of considerable importance."[26] Whereas presidents had previously been chosen for their prominence in the world of business, reformers now proposed that they be selected for their expertise in banking. The likeliest pool of candidates consisted of men who had worked their way up through the ranks of bank officers. These men were well versed in all facets of bank management. More important, because they had made banking their career, they, and not businessmen, would be more likely to put the interests of their institutions above personal considerations and apply strict and objective standards in evaluating applications for credit.[27]

The professionalization of bank officers could be only a partial solution

Lawrence Goodwin, *The Populist Moment: A Short History of the Agrarian Revolt in America* (New York: Oxford University Press, 1978).

25. The quotation is from *Bankers' Magazine*, 36 (April 1882), 733–5. See also 37 (March 1883), 656; 38 (June 1884), 963; 42 (January 1888), 511; James G. Cannon, *An Ideal Bank* (New York, 1891 [privately printed]), 10; Patten, *The Methods and Machinery of Practical Banking*, 266; B. B. Comegys, "How a Banker Should Treat His Dealers and the Public; or, What Matter of Man Should a Banker Be," *Proceedings of the Twentieth Annual Convention of the American Bankers' Association* (New York: American Bankers' Association, 1894), 39. See also the fundamental principles of banking as articulated by Hugh McCulloch, first Comptroller of the Currency, quoted in Barrett, *Modern Banking Methods,* 305.

26. *Bankers' Magazine*, 38 (June 1884), 908; 39 (July 1884), 8, 35. See also 39 (October 1884 and January 1885), 243, 483–7.

27. On this point, see esp. Patten, *The Methods and Machinery of Practical Banking,* 272–3. See also Barrett, *Modern Banking Methods,* 25; Comegys, "How a Banker Should Treat His Dealers," 37–8; *Bankers' Magazine*, 38 (June 1884), 963.

to this problem, however, because ultimate authority over a bank's lending practices rested not with its president but with the board of directors,
at whose pleasure the president and all other officers served. It was unre-
alistic to expect a businessman to forsake his outside interests to assume a
position on the board, because under such circumstances no one would
willingly take upon himself a job that involved, as one writer put it, "a
deal of gratuitous work, unwelcome and wearing responsibility, and very
little of what business men deem compensation."[28] It was in fact precisely
because of his outside interests – and his consequent ability to attract
business to the bank – that a director's services were valued in the first
place. Moreover, because the promise of accommodation and access to
credit in periods of monetary stringency undoubtedly helped make this
unremunerative job attractive to otherwise busy men, most reformers
were unwilling to support an absolute ban on loans to these officials.
What they did insist upon was that the loans remain within legal limits.
As James G. Cannon, vice-president of the Fourth National Bank of New
York and a leader of the bankers' reform movement, argued, "If a director
will give proper security, and keep within the limits prescribed by the
National Bank Act, and will ask no more than his account entitles him to
receive, there is no reason why he should not be accommodated as a
borrower of the bank in which he is a director."[29]

Yet because excessive loans to directors were widely believed to be the
major cause of bank failures, some means had to be found of restraining
the behavior of those who would abuse their positions. Because staff
members had no authority over directors, reformers could not confine
their attention to the issue of professionalization but had to focus as well
on the lending decision itself. They had to develop a set of "fundamental
principles" to govern the granting of loans, principles that could be applied easily by both stockholders and directors to monitor the behavior of
the less scrupulous members of the board.[30] Most fundamental of all was
the idea that banks, to the greatest extent possible, should restrict their
business to the discount of "real" commercial paper, that is, to the discount of notes issued in the course of actual commercial transactions.

28. Patten, *The Methods and Machinery of Practical Banking*, 271.
29. Cannon, *An Ideal Bank*, 18. See also E. T. Coman, "The Requisites of a
     Good Loan," in *Practical Problems in Banking and Currency*, ed. Walter
     Henry Hull (New York: Macmillan, 1907), 73–5. For a contrary view, see
     Boston Evening Transcript, March 27, 1900, p. 1.
30. The phrase is Hugh McCulloch's. See Barrett, *Modern Banking Methods*,
     305–6.

III

This preference for "real bills," though frequently expressed in New England during the first two-thirds of the century, had not previously been of much influence in shaping either banking policy or practice. Now, however, the increased interdependence of the banking system and the need to monitor the actions of bank directors enhanced the doctrine's appeal.[31] In the first place, loans on commercial paper were considered desirable because (it was thought) they were self-liquidating: once a wholesaler had disposed of goods he had bought from a manufacturer, for example, he could redeem the IOU he had issued to cover his initial purchase. Second (and more to the point), such loans were thought to make the lending process more objective: because a manufacturer had to scrutinize a wholesaler's standing before risking his credit by endorsing the latter's note, bankers were relieved of the need to conduct further credit investigations. As the conservative Chicago banker James B. Forgan counseled an audience of Providence bank employees, "The strength of the promise is not in this case of prime importance, and need not therefore be as closely considered."[32]

Some commentators even went farther and argued that because commercial paper bore a one-to-one correspondence to the actual wealth-generating activities of the economy, it was for all practical purposes as good as gold. As one writer explained: "Commodities are, after all, the only things that are really wealth. . . . It is only by convertibility into food, fuel, clothing, and shelter that anything becomes of value. Gold is wealth because of its convertibility; and in the same way, credit is wealth."[33]

If credit based on real bills was tantamount to wealth, then it mattered little to whom a bank granted its discounts. As long as all the notes in its portfolio were bona fide commercial paper, the bank was safe, and greedy directors could do it no real damage. This belief in fact was incorporated

31. On the real-bills doctrine, see Lloyd W. Mints, *A History of Banking Theory in Great Britain and the United States* (Chicago: University of Chicago Press, 1945), 206–10; Richard Sylla, "American Banking and Growth in the Nineteenth Century: A Partial View of the Terrain," *Explorations in Economic History,* 9 (Winter 1971–2), 197–227. See also Robert Craig West, *Banking Reform and the Federal Reserve, 1863–1923* (Ithaca, N.Y.: Cornell University Press, 1977), 136–62.

32. *A Good Note,* 1903 ed. (Chicago, 1920 [privately printed]), 8.

33. Thomas F. Woodlock, "Banking Conditions in Wall Street," in *Practical Problems in Banking and Currency,* ed. Walter Henry Hull (New York: Macmillan, 1907), 24.

into the National Banking Acts: Section 5200 of the federal code prohibited banks from lending in excess of 10 percent of their capital to any one person or company. There were two exceptions to this provision, however. The first exempted "the discount of bills of exchange drawn in good faith against actually existing values" – in other words, real commercial paper. The obvious presumption here was that, because such loans were based on tangible commodities, no bank would be endangered by discounting large amounts for a single firm.[34]

The second exception, "the discount of commercial or business paper actually owned by the person negotiating the same," is similarly instructive. The provision applied mainly to professional brokers, whose growing presence in the money markets offered reform-minded bankers another means of guarding against the dangers of opportunism. Not only were brokers responsible for evaluating the creditworthiness of the notes they offered for sale, but by interposing themselves between banks and would-be borrowers they made the lending process more impersonal and thus more objective. For this reason, as one eminent banker explained, "buying paper through brokers is not without its advantages."

> Paper can be so bought with cool deliberation and free from the personal influence which the needy customer studies how best to exercise. . . . The human susceptibility of the banker to be influenced by relationship, friendship, good-fellowship, neighborliness, return for favors received, sympathy for the distressed, flattery, personal interest and other extraneous considerations is eliminated. It counts for a great deal in arriving at a decision to be relieved of these influences.[35]

If bankers would grant credit only on the basis of real bills, thought reformers, the stability of the banking system would be assured. But the reformers also recognized the unlikelihood of achieving such a goal, given the decline in the volume of real bills relative to other kinds of business paper during this period. The prospective supply simply was not sufficient to absorb the banking system's foreseeable demand for lendable funds.[36] Should banks move away from real commercial paper, however, opportunities for favoritism threatened to widen. In calculating the amount of collateral required for a loan, for example, bankers were prone to overvalue the assets of enterprises with which they were involved, as a rash of

34. See George M. Coffin, *Hand-Book for Bank Officers* (Washington, D.C.: McGill & Wallace, 1896), 64.
35. Forgan, *A Good Note*, 21–2. See also Comegys, "How a Banker Should Treat His Dealers," 40–1.
36. On this point, see West, *Banking Reform and the Federal Reserve*, 157–62. See also James, *Money and Capital Markets in Postbellum America*, 55–9.

bank failures during the early 1880s dramatically illustrated. According to trade-journal analysts, the cause of these failures was loans "on very poor security" made by bank officers who had "a pecuniary interest in the enterprises that received the money." As one writer reflected, the officers in question "well knew in most of these cases, probably, that the securities were of a hazardous nature. And they never would have accepted such securities, except for their own interest in these outside undertakings."[37]

In order to guard against such willful misjudgment, conservative bankers began (without abandoning the real-bills doctrine) to promulgate new and objective standards for other types of loans. In the case of collateral loans, objective criteria were relatively easy to come by, for the market provided an evaluative mechanism. By implication, then, the securities of closely held corporations had to be avoided at all costs. Because such instruments were not traded on the exchanges, their worth was difficult to establish, and this uncertainty made it possible for bank officers to overvalue the assets of enterprises with which they were associated.

Willful misjudgment was more difficult to guard against in the case of unsecured loans, but the faith of these reformers in the objective worth of real commercial paper helped them devise another set of lending criteria that they thought would obviate the problem. Although they recognized that real commercial paper was increasingly scarce, they believed that banks could create an equally effective substitute by restricting their business to short-term loans based entirely on quick assets. We have already seen how this type of loan was embraced as a solution to the problem of evaluating the creditworthiness of outside borrowers. That it might also represent a solution to the objectivity problem is suggested by an article entitled "Requisites of a Good Loan," written by a bank cashier named E. T. Coman. Like most other writers on the subject at the time, Coman recommended that banks invest 20 percent of their funds in high-grade bonds and securities, and another 20 percent in commercial paper purchased in the open market. Such investments, in the amounts prescribed, would virtually guarantee a ratio of liquid assets sufficient to meet all but the most critical exigencies, yet Coman nonetheless insisted that all remaining loans be based solely on borrowers' "current business," by which he meant advances on "the market value of commodities in the process of conversion into money." If not specified for sixty or ninety days, such loans "should mature upon the definite happening of an event which is of reasonable certainty of occurrence . . . , the maturity of a crop, the completion of a contract." Loans of indeterminate length were a

37. *Bankers' Magazine*, 38 (June 1884), 908.

recipe for disaster. Especially to be avoided were "loans which have the character of a permanent investment in the business of the borrower."[38]

It is clear from this pamphlet that the author, who goes on to fret about the problem of insider lending, made these recommendations not primarily for the purpose of insuring liquidity but because he believed they were the best means of guaranteeing that loans would be granted according to objective criteria, such that a banker would exercise "no arbitrary discretion when he extends or refuses accommodation to the borrower."[39] By adopting a standard for loans resembling as closely as possible the ideal of real commercial paper, banks could avoid those entanglements between borrower and lender that distorted the latter's judgment and potentially jeopardized the security of the banking system.

As Coman's pamphlet suggests, long-term loans were considered prima facie evidence of just such potentially ruinous entanglements between borrowers and lenders. Hence, as conservative bankers and professionals redefined the parameters of the banking business during the latter years of the century, they proscribed this sort of lending entirely. As David R. Forgan emphasized in 1898, "One of the most fundamental principles of good banking is that the bank should not furnish the capital for its customers to do business upon." This notion was expressed even more forcefully by Hugh McCulloch, the former Comptroller of the Currency, in a statement that was widely quoted in the practical banking literature: "Banks are not loan offices. It is no part of their business to furnish their customers with capital."[40]

IV

As a result, then, of their determination to curb opportunistic behavior by bank managers, the allied conservatives and professionals articulated a vision of sound lending policy that sharply narrowed the scope of banking operations to short-term loans based on commercial paper or easily convertible assets. This change in policy was extremely important because, to the extent that it came to be embodied in actual practice, it made it more difficult for firms in the industrial sectors of the economy to obtain bank financing for their ventures. If short-term assets were considered the only proper basis for loans, the credit-evaluation process was clearly biased against manufacturing enterprises with proportionally

38. Coman, "Requisites of a Good Loan," 69–71.
39. Ibid., 66.
40. Forgan, "Banking as a Profession," 384; Barrett, *Modern Banking Methods*, 305. See also *Bankers' Magazine*, 57 (August 1898), 284–6.

large investments in fixed capital. Borrowers unable to meet the specified ratio of convertible assets to liabilities might be granted credit on the basis of good collateral, but this kind of loan was inevitably restricted to firms that issued marketable securities (mainly railroads in the late nineteenth century) or were engaged in the buying and selling of stocks and bonds. As we have seen, collateral loans were of only limited use to most other borrowers, because businesses with surplus funds to invest in marketable securities were not likely to require credit. What manufacturers really needed were loans secured by equity in their firms, but this sort of lending was specifically frowned upon, owing to the judgment problems it entailed.

Unfortunately, there is no way to test directly the effectiveness of the reformers' campaign, but changing management practices suggest that it did have a genuine effect, at least in the region's larger cities. By 1895 two-thirds of a sample of more than thirty Boston banks had presidents who were either no longer actively engaged in business or had worked their way up through the hierarchy of bank employees.[41] Indeed, whenever a bank's president now died or retired, there was a growing tendency to select his successor from the ranks of banking professionals rather than of prominent businessmen, as had been common earlier in the century. The directors of the People's Bank of Roxbury, for example, elected their cashier president in 1886 and subsequently amended the bank's bylaws to increase his managerial authority. Charles R. Lawrence, the cashier of Boston's Bunker Hill National Bank of Charlestown, was promoted to its presidency in 1889. He was succeeded in 1906 by Fred K. Brown, who had replaced him as cashier. At Boston's Atlantic Bank, after President T. Quincy Browne resigned in 1898 (because a personal business failure had forced him to assign all his assets, including his stock in the bank), the directors selected the bank's cashier to head the institution. And the team of financiers that rescued the Massachusetts Bank at the turn of the century chose as its president Daniel G. Wing, a product of the banking hierarchy in his home state of Nebraska who had served as a national bank examiner and as receiver for two failed Boston banks.[42]

41. This information was abstracted from the reports of the national bank examiners to the U.S. Comptroller of the Currency for Boston banks in 1895. The records of the Examination Division are stored at the National Archives in Washington, D.C., Record Group 101. The banks in the sample were not chosen at random, but were picked in order to match up with other records or fill gaps in coverage.

42. Directors' meeting, Aug. 3, 1886, Directors' and Stockholders' Minute Book, 1884–98, People's National Bank, Roxbury, Mass.; *A Century of Banking in Historic Charlestown* (Boston, 1925 [privately printed]), 25–6;

The professionalization of bank presidents is also apparent in their salaries. During the early nineteenth century presidents were offered at most token payments, and many received no remuneration at all. By mid century, salaries for bank presidents had become the general rule, but typically presidents earned only a fraction of the amount paid to cashiers, who were the real day-to-day managers. During the last three decades of the century, however, presidents' responsibilities and salaries generally increased relative to those of cashiers, surpassing them when it became common for cashiers to be promoted to the presidency.[43]

At the same time as bank presidents were becoming more professional, new associations of bank clerks were being organized in cities like Providence and Boston. While the ostensible purpose of these organizations was to furnish old-age and disability benefits for their membership, they also provided a forum through which upwardly mobile bank clerks could be indoctrinated with the values of their profession. Reformers were often the featured speakers at association meetings, and their writings were touted as recommended reading for aspiring clerks.[44] That bank officers might absorb values that put them at odds with their own directors can be seen from the case of the Maverick National Bank. Several years before the bank's failure, its cashier, John Eddy, had quietly resigned. As he later told reporters, "I could not hold the position of Cashier of the Maverick Bank and sanction as I was obliged to all that I was expected to."[45]

There is also some evidence that bank directors were once again becoming more conscientious about their duties. During the 1870s and

directors' meetings, Dec. 31, 1898, and Jan. 5, 1899, Directors' and Stockholders' Minute Book, 1877–1912, Atlantic National Bank of Boston, Bank of Boston Archives; N. S. B. Gras, *The Massachusetts First National Bank of Boston, 1784–1934* (Cambridge: Harvard University Press, 1937), 152–4, 159.

43. See for example, the records of the Atlantic, City, Faneuil Hall, First, Fourth, Manufacturers, Massachusetts, and Shoe and Leather National banks of Boston, all in the Bank of Boston Archives.

44. *Rhodes' Journal of Banking*, 12 (February 1885), 131; 12 (March 1885), 207; 13 (May 1886), 347–52. In addition, the American Bankers' Association devoted an increasing proportion of its program to practical banking matters. There was also a movement to form local Bankers' Institutes, "voluntary association[s] of gentlemen engaged in banking, or otherwise interested in banking affairs, who organize for the purpose of advancing the interests as well of their profession generally as of the individual members of it." The quotation above is from *Rhodes' Journal of Banking*, 12 (1885), 184–5.

45. *Boston Evening Transcript*, Nov. 3, 1891, p. 8.

early 1880s attendance at directors' meetings had reached an all-time low. By 1895, however, this situation had begun to reverse itself. All six directors of the Boylston National Bank were present for 80 percent or more of the meetings in 1895, and four were present for at least 90 percent of them. Attendance was still low at the Massachusetts National Bank, but at People's four of the directors attended at least 70 percent of the time.[46] To encourage this trend, many banks began to pay their directors a nominal fee, usually two dollars (sometimes more) for each meeting attended. Although these payments were largely symbolic, they reflected the power that the reformers' vision had begun to exert over the entire banking community.[47]

Doubtless there are explanations besides the reform campaign for each of these changes in management practice. But the point to emphasize here is not so much the cause of these changes as their collective effect. As bank officers became more professional, they were more likely to follow the recommendations of the reformers in their day-to-day operations. Similarly, as directors began to take their oversight responsibilities more seriously, they were more likely to apply professional standards in evaluating the performance of their banks' executive staffs. Here is where the Comptroller of the Currency could play an important role – by reviewing the reports of the national bank examiners and notifying the directors of any breaches of law or sound banking practice. Although the Comptroller did not have any real power to enforce his views so long as a bank remained solvent, he could (and did) warn directors that they were personally liable for any losses resulting from violations of law. That such warnings could have an educational effect can be seen from the experience of the Phenix National Bank, a country bank in southern Rhode Island. The bank's records contain copies of letters from the Comptroller criticizing its management for excessive loans to one particular manufacturing concern. Subsequent letters in 1898 and 1899 indicate that the bank had brought these loans into compliance with the statute (though

46. Directors' and Stockholders' Minute Book, 1887–1909, Boylston National Bank, Boston; Directors' and Stockholders' Minute Book, 1883–1900, Massachusetts National Bank, Boston; Directors' and Stockholders' Minute Book, 1884–98, People's National Bank, Roxbury, Mass.

47. See, for examples, directors' meeting, Nov. 6, 1882, Directors' and Stockholders' Minute Book, 1873–88, Manufacturers National Bank, Boston; directors' meeting, Feb. 5, 1885, Directors' Minute Book, 1874–95, First National Bank of Boston; directors' meeting, Jan. 18, 1886, Directors' and Stockholders' Minute Book, 1883–1900, Massachusetts National Bank, Boston; stockholders' meeting, Jan. 10, 1888, Directors' and Stockholders' Minute Book, 1886–1903, National City Bank, Boston.

the Comptroller still found other practices to complain about). Interestingly, when the bank was rechartered in 1900 as a trust company under Rhode Island law, it copied verbatim Section 5200 of the national code (the provision limiting loans to any one individual or firm to 10 percent of capital) directly into its new bylaws.[48]

Again, when the Comptroller discovered in September of 1899 that the president of the Globe National Bank of Boston had surreptitiously used overdrafts to make illegally large loans to several manufacturing concerns, the bank's directors hastily came to their senses. Although they had not paid much attention to bank matters previously, they now forced the president to make good on his loans and resign his position. Their actions, however, came too late to save the bank from collapse. The failure of one of its major borrowers, in conjunction with a sharp decline in the price of certain securities with which the bank's managers were prominently identified, precipitated a run on the bank that even a substantial loan from the clearinghouse was unable to staunch.[49]

Clearinghouses too created incentives for banks to adhere to the professionals' prescriptions. By the end of the century it had become apparent that these associations would extend emergency credit only on the security of loans backed by readily marketable stocks and bonds or good commercial paper. When the Broadway National Bank of Boston failed in 1899, for example, the clearinghouse refused to come to its rescue on the ground that the bank held $600,000 of paper from the failed John P. Squire and Company meatpacking firm, only a third of which was adequately secured. (The Squire family had a controlling interest in the bank.) The clearinghouse's loans to the Globe National Bank were backed by readily marketable stocks, but when it was learned that this bank too was compromised by its extensive involvement with Squire and other manufacturers, the association abandoned its support. For other Boston banks the lesson was unmistakable. The clearinghouse would not come to a bank's assistance unless its loan portfolio conformed to the professionals' conception of sound practice. The association would concentrate its efforts instead on protecting from the resulting financial tur-

48. The letters are loose in Directors' Minute Book, 1885–1900, Phenix National Bank, Phenix, R.I. See also the 1900 bylaws in Directors' and Stockholders' Minute Book, 1900–37, Phenix Trust Company. Both record books are in the Fleet National Bank Archives.

49. *Boston Evening Transcript*, Nov. 7, 1899, p. 9; Dec. 14, 1899, pp. 1, 3; Dec. 22, 1899, pp. 1, 4; Dec. 23, 1899, pp. 1, 7; Dec. 26, 1899, p. 1; *Boston News Bureau*, Nov. 8, 1899, p. 1; Dec. 16, 1899, p. 1; Dec. 21, 1899, p. 1; Dec. 22, 1899, p. 2; Jan. 6, 1900, pp. 1, 4; Jan. 10, 1900, p. 1.

bulence banks that met the new standards. In the words of a clearing-house official, "Any bank in Boston that can show a proper condition will get all the assistance it needs."[50]

V

It remains to assess the extent to which these new principles affected everyday banking practice, that is, the extent to which the injunction to make only short-term loans based on readily convertible assets actually inhibited banks in supporting manufacturing ventures. Writing during the second decade of the twentieth century, the economist H. G. Moulton argued that, notwithstanding the prescriptions of the practical banking literature, "the distinction between commercial and investment operations is ignored in practice." Moulton firmly believed that banks should play an active role in supporting manufacturing investment, and in order to demonstrate that such lending would in no way undermine the safety of the banking system, he undertook to prove that a considerable portion of existing loans already financed fixed investment. Moulton conceded that banks decided whether or not to make unsecured loans by calculating the ratio of a firm's debt obligations to its quick assets. He also admitted that such loans were rarely granted for periods in excess of six months. But he argued that many short-term loans were regularly renewed and that once a loan had been granted, banks had no control at all over the uses to which the funds were put. As a practical matter, the proceeds of a loan could as easily be used to pay for investments in plant and equipment as to finance goods in the stream of production. Based on his own (undescribed) "investigations extending over a period of several

50. The quotation is from *Boston News Bureau*, Dec. 18, 1899, p. 1. See also Dec. 16, 1899, p. 1; Dec. 22, 1899, p. 2; *Boston Evening Transcript,* Dec. 14, 1899, pp. 1, 3; Dec. 16, 1899, pp. 1, 9; Dec. 18, 1899, p. 1; Dec. 22, 1899, p. 4; Feb. 1, 1900, p. 5. According to the financial press, which was highly critical of the clearinghouse's decisions, the Broadway was actually in better shape than it appeared to be and would have weathered the Squire failure. Without the backing of the clearinghouse, however, the Comptroller would not allow the institution to reopen. The clearinghouse defended its action by asserting that "one concern owed the [Broadway National] bank three times the amount of its capital," that "the management that asked for clearing house support was the one responsible for this condition of affairs," and that "1500 out of 2000 shares were owned by a failed concern, which made improbable the collection of assessment." *Boston Evening Transcript,* Feb. 2, 1900, p. 5.

years," Moulton claimed that as much as 20 percent of the banking sector's unsecured commercial loans were in actuality used for investment purposes.[51]

Moulton's assertions are difficult to verify, because the banking records that remain from this period rarely contain data on lending practices. There is, however, a brief run of complete loan records for the Suffolk National Bank in Boston, one of the city's leading conservative banks.[52] Analysis of these records shows that 46 percent of the bank's portfolio consisted of collateral loans, 84 percent of which were granted to brokers and other intermediaries who dealt in the securities markets.[53] The other 54 percent of the portfolio consisted of short-term loans based on personal security, and it is unlikely that many of these loans could have supported investments in plant and equipment. Fully two-thirds (by value) were notes purchased on the commercial-paper market, that is, bought from firms or individuals who served neither as principals nor endorsers for the notes. Although many of the signatories on these loans were manufacturers, they were not themselves customers of the bank and hence could not expect their notes to be renewed at maturity. In fact, only 19 percent of the bank's loan portfolio consisted of notes backed by personal security that were discounted for the benefit of customers who were signatories, and only 41 percent of this amount involved manufacturing enterprises. Most of the bank's customers (accounting for 75 percent of its personal loans and 88 percent of its collateral loans) were brokers or distributors. In other words, the bulk of this prominent bank's business was commercial lending pure and simple.

It is possible, of course, that the Suffolk Bank was unusually specialized in the commercial lending business and that the loan portfolios of other institutions would have looked quite different. Unfortunately, most other bank records contain only scattered information on loans, with no infor-

51. "Commercial Banking and Capital Formation," *Journal of Political Economy*, 26 (June 1918), 638–63.
52. Vol. 75, Discount Register, 1899–1902; vol. 101, Discounted Notes Balance, 1900–2; vol. 102, Discount Ledger, 1901–2, Suffolk National Bank, Boston, Mass., Mss. 781, Baker Library, Harvard Graduate School of Business Administration. I analyzed all loans granted in the months of January, April, July, and October 1901.
53. Moulton also argued that collateral loans to brokers and other intermediaries who dealt in the securities markets indirectly underwrote the investment activities of the firms that had issued the securities in the first place. This argument has some validity, but he unrealistically assumed that the amount of investment activity thus generated was fully equal to the value of these loans.

mation at all about their terms or the kinds of security that backed them. Fragmentary records, for example, are available for a handful of Rhode Island banks (National Bank of Rhode Island in Newport for 1888, First National Bank of Warren for 1886, National Hope Bank of Warren for 1889, National Warren Bank of Warren for 1888 and 1898, National Niantic Bank of Westerly for 1893, and the First National Bank of Bristol for 1898). But in none of these records is it possible to distinguish loans to regular customers from short-term commercial paper bought in the open market. A proxy for this distinction can be devised, however, by assuming that all loans to local firms (that is, loans whose principals or endorsers were listed in the local city directories) were loans to customers and that all other loans consisted of purchased commercial paper. Such a calculation reveals that loans to local customers who were manufacturers ranged from a low of none to a high of 20 percent of the total, with most banks clustering at between 14 and 20 percent. There is no reason to assume, moreover, that every loan in this category supported investments in fixed capital. A large proportion undoubtedly financed bills receivable.[54]

The small number of loans to local manufacturers in many of these banks' portfolios may, however, have been a function of a lack of demand.

54. Directors' Minute Book, 1862–1902, National Bank of Rhode Island, Newport; Directors' and Stockholders' Minute Book, 1864–89, First National Bank of Warren, Warren; Directors' and Stockholders' Minute Book, 1873–92, National Hope Bank, Warren; Directors' and Stockholders' Minute Book, 1887–99, National Warren Bank, Warren; Directors' and Stockholders' Minute Book, 1865–1905, National Niantic Bank, Westerly; and Directors' and Stockholders' Minute Book, 1865–1901, First National Bank of Bristol. These records are all in the Fleet National Bank Archives.

A couple of other examples: In 1887 the Shoe and Leather Bank lent a considerable proportion of its funds – as one would expect – to various wholesale dealers in the shoe and leather business. Most of its other borrowers were merchants and brokers. Only around 5% of its portfolio consisted of loans to local manufacturers. At a second bank (the Monument National) a list of loans outstanding on the eve of its 1905 merger with the Bunker Hill National Bank shows 26% granted to local manufacturers, but this figure is probably an overestimate. The loan totals were less than $200,000, at least one-third below normal, and it is likely that many of the bank's commercial loans had been retired in anticipation of liquidation. The only way for two national banks to merge during this period was for one bank to liquidate the other. Directors' and Stockholders' Minute Book, 1885–93, Shoe and Leather National Bank, Bank of Boston Archives; loose sheets in Directors' Minute Book, 1892–1905, Monument National Bank, Mss. 781, Baker Library, Harvard Graduate School of Business Administration.

Reports of national bank examiners to the Comptroller of the Currency indicate that country banks in communities such as Warren, Rhode Island, could not find sufficient local outlets for their funds and had to buy much of their paper in neighboring cities. The same reports show that banks in industrial towns such as Lewiston, Maine, Fall River, Massachusetts, Pawtucket, Rhode Island, and Concord, New Hampshire, had significant dealings with local manufacturers.[55] This last group of reports also contains frequent hints of insider lending. For example, the First National Bank of Pawtucket's generous loans to the Blair Camera Company were endorsed by a director who was "largely interested" in the firm. Similarly, the Pacific National Bank of the same city lent large sums to the Narragansett Machine Company, the Excelsior Webb and Tape Company, and the Hope Webbing Company, all firms with which its directors were affiliated. As one bank examiner wrote in 1895 concerning the First National Bank of Fall River, Massachusetts: "The business of this bank is in connection with the mill corporations of Fall River, and is quite prosperous. The directors and officers are largely interested in this class of property and familiar with the various lines of paper they carry."[56]

Banks in industrial towns like Fall River, in other words, were still functioning in a manner reminiscent of the first half of the century. Although insider lending had declined from the extraordinary levels that prevailed earlier, the officers and directors of these banks still for the most part consisted of prominent businessmen from the community, and the professionalization movement had not really affected them yet. In contrast to the case of Boston, the vast majority of the presidents (about 80 percent) were actively involved in business ventures, mainly as merchants and manufacturers, and they operated their institutions with the needs of their own and other local enterprises in mind.[57] As long as their loans

55. Compare, for example, U.S., Comptroller of the Currency, Records of the Examination Division, report on the National Hope Bank, Nov. 18, 1885, and report on the National Warren Bank, Nov. 19, 1885, with report on the First National Bank of Lewiston, Me., Feb. 19, 1880, report on the First National Bank of Fall River, Mass., May 16, 1890, report on the Pacific National Bank of Pawtucket, R.I, June 3, 1885, and report on the Mechanicks National Bank of Concord, N.H., July 17, 1890.

56. Report on the First National Bank of Pawtucket, R.I., for Feb. 5, 1895, report on the Pacific National Bank of Pawtucket for Dec. 3, 1895, and report on the First National Bank of Fall River, Mass., for July 29, 1895.

57. This estimate is based on a sample of national examiners' reports for about 40 banks in New England, not including the cities of Boston and Providence, in 1895.

were properly documented and remained within legal bounds, the Comptroller posed no objections to them. Moreover, because the soundness of these banks was not so crucial to the health of the financial system as a whole, the national examiners' reports were relatively cursory and did not serve unambiguously as instruments to spread professional values.

The situation in Boston, a reserve city under the National Banking Acts, was quite different, however. There the examiners' reports were extraordinarily thorough, often running to ten pages or more of attachments in closely written script. In 1890, for example, the examiner provided the Comptroller with richly detailed descriptions of each bank's portfolio of collateral loans, including item-by-item discussions of loans whose security he regarded as doubtful. These descriptions serve as indicators both of the extent to which the professionals' values dominated current banking practice and of the pressures applied to individual banks to conform to the new standards. Not surprisingly, banks whose officers were actively involved with the clearinghouse had portfolios of collateral loans that adhered closely to the reformers' prescriptions. At the Merchants National bank, for example, 95 percent of the loans were backed by "various kinds of stocks and bonds which are of a readily salable character." The bulk of the remainder was secured by other kinds of acceptable collateral, mainly promissory notes and commercial paper. Similarly, 79 percent of the collateral loans of the Second National Bank were secured by readily salable stocks and bonds. Another 10 percent were backed by western securities which, though not quoted on the exchanges, found an active market among dealers. Most of the rest were backed by promissory notes.[58]

For the city as a whole, the average proportion of collateral loans backed by marketable securities was about 70 percent, with virtually every bank above the 50 percent mark.[59] Most of the remaining loans were also judged by the examiner to be backed by acceptable collateral, but there were occasional exceptions that elicited his lengthy critical comments. The examiner was especially hard on loans that appeared to be supplying capital for manufacturing ventures. For example, he criticized the People's Bank of Roxbury for loans of $5,000 to the Hallet and Davis Piano Company and $10,000 to an officer of the Whittier Machine Company, each on the security of its respective company's stock. As the examiner himself put it, "the policy of carrying for a long time a loan for a

---

58. Report on the Merchants National Bank of Boston, May 13, 1890; report on the Second National Bank of Boston, March 21, 1890.

59. This statement is based on a sample of national examiners' reports for 24 banks in Boston in 1890.

company on the security of its own shares seems questionable even though the stock is a dividend paying stock."[60]

At the end of the century, therefore, professionalization was still confined mainly to the region's largest cities, but there it was beginning to have a significant effect. Slowly but surely it was changing the way banks defined their business, fostering among them an increasingly narrow specialization in the business of granting short-term commercial and brokers' loans and thus encouraging them to abandon the direct role in economic development that they had played earlier in their history.

60. Report on the People's National Bank of Roxbury, Boston, June 5, 1890.

6

The merger movement in banking

The most striking characteristic of American banking at the present moment is the universal tendency to smaller profits. Not only is money getting cheaper, but competition is so keen that the temptation to gain business by doing it for nothing is proving too strong for many bankers. This tendency will help to hasten the day of the trained professional banker in preference to the amateur who spent the best part of his life at something else.

David R. Forgan[1]

I

Despite all the efforts bankers made during the last three decades of the nineteenth century to improve their collection of credit information and promote sound lending practices, earnings in the banking sector continued to fall. After a brief recovery during the late 1880s, the profit rate for national banks in New England resumed its downward trend, with the result that earnings for the period 1896–1900 were nearly 50 percent below their level for 1871–75 (see Table 4.1). Many people felt there were simply too many banks in the region and "that too many of them have too much capital and too large expense accounts for the amount of business they do."[2] But despite dwindling returns, there were no significant efforts to restructure the banking sector before the late 1890s. Indeed, as Table 6.1 indicates, the number of banks in the region continued to grow, from 505 in 1860 to 724 in 1895 (including both national and state institutions). In Boston, the region's financial center (where one might expect the process of restructuring to have gone farthest), the number of banks actually increased by more than 80 percent over the course

---

1. "Banking as a Profession," *Bankers' Magazine*, 57 (September 1898), 386. Forgan was president of the Union National Bank of Chicago.
2. *Boston Evening Transcript*, Jan. 2, 1897, p. 6. See also *Bankers' Magazine*, 39 (July 1884), 40; A. S. Wheeler, *Banking in Boston: A Paper Read Before the Bank Presidents' Association* (Boston: Cotton & Gould, 1890), 7; *Providence Journal*, June 10, 1899, p. 4.

Table 6.1. *Number and capital of banks in the region, 1860 and 1895*

Region	1860		1895			
			National banks		State banks[a]	
	No.	Capital in $000	No.	Capital in $000	No.	Capital in $000
Maine	69	7,533	82	11,121	17	1,461
Mass.[b]	178	66,482	268	97,142	31	10,375
Boston	40	37,732	60	53,750	13	7,450
N.H.	51	4,941	50	5,880	0	0
R.I.	90	21,152	58	19,537	14	3,733
New England[c]	505	123,560	644	213,831	80	18,944

[a]Includes trust companies.
[b]Includes Boston.
[c]Includes Connecticut and Vermont.
Sources: Maine, Bank Commissioners, *Annual Report* (1860), 75–6; Massachusetts, Secretary of the Commonwealth, *Abstracts of the Returns from the Banks* (1860), 78–9; Massachusetts, Board of Commissioners of Savings Banks, *Annual Report* (1896), 672–703; New Hampshire, Bank Commissioners, *Reports* (1860), 92–3; Rhode Island, State Auditor, *Annual Statement Exhibiting the Condition of the Banks* (1860), 35; Richard Eugene Sylla, *The American Capital Market, 1846–1914: A Study of the Effects of Public Policy on Economic Development* (New York: Arno, 1975), 251–2; U.S., Comptroller of the Currency, *Annual Report* (1896), vol. 1, 696–701, 771; (1900), 745–7.

of the period. Only in Rhode Island did the banking sector contract significantly – from 90 banks in 1860 to 72 in 1895 – but even there the end result was still one bank for every 5,400 residents (see Table 6.2). Moreover, although the amount of capital invested in banking per Rhode Islander fell by 50 percent between 1860 and 1895, the increase in leverage ratios over the same period more than compensated for the drop, so that bank assets per person actually increased from $179 in 1860 to $216 in 1895.

One reason there was so little restructuring was that the interests of bank officers and stockholders diverged. Stockholders, of course, were primarily interested in profits from their investments. If the return on a bank's assets was unremunerative but the bank was otherwise in good financial shape, they stood to benefit from closing the institution, selling off its assets, dividing the proceeds among themselves, and then investing in more profitable enterprises. Bank directors were also concerned about

Table 6.2. *Density of banks and bank capital in 1860 and 1895*

Region	1860		1895	
	Persons per bank	Capital per person ($)	Persons per bank	Capital per person ($)
Maine	9,100	12	6,800	19
Mass.*a*	6,900	54	8,700	41
Boston	4,500	212	6,800	123
N.H.	6,400	15	7,900	15
R.I.	1,900	121	5,400	60
New England*b*	6,600	37	7,200	45
U.S.A.	19,900	13	17,900	11

*a*Includes Boston.
*b*Includes Connecticut and Vermont.
Sources: See Table 6.1. Also U.S., Comptroller of the Currency, *Annual Report* (1896), vol. 1, 718; U.S., Department of Commerce, *Historical Statistics of the United States: Colonial Times to 1970* (Washington, D.C.: Government Printing Office, 1975); Massachusetts, Bureau of Statistics of Labor, *Census of the Commonwealth of Massachusetts, 1895* (Boston: Wright & Potter, 1896), vol. 1, 11.

the rate of return on their institution's stock; they were, after all, shareholders themselves. In 1895, for example, directors of Boston banks owned an average of seventy-five shares in their own institutions.[3] But unless profits were low enough to threaten the integrity of the bank, they were generally loath to support liquidation proposals, for they stood to lose both position and prestige. The president, who was the only salaried member of the board, faced the loss of a substantial income. The other directors were only minimally compensated for their services, but they too had much to lose, namely, the status associated with board membership and their privileged access to loans. Many directors presided over banks that had been associated with their families for decades, and their standing in the community derived in part from their ability to control access to credit. Closing the bank threatened to erode their base of influence and hence was to be avoided at all costs.

Although bank directors typically held only a minority interest in their institutions' stock (in Boston, the average stake of the banks' boards of

3. U.S., Comptroller of the Currency, Records of the Examination Division, Boston, 1895. These are manuscript records stored at the National Archives, Record Group 101.

directors was only 10 percent of capital in 1895),[4] the remaining stock
was so widely dispersed that directors' decisions were almost never ques-
tioned. Stockholders' meetings were typically very poorly attended, and
because directors were rarely willing to vote themselves out of office, the
only way to dislodge them was for contenders to buy up a controlling
number of shares. Successful challenges of this type did, however, arise in
both Boston and Providence during the last few years of the century,
evidence that conflict was indeed brewing between the banks' directors
and the stockholders they were supposed to represent.

The Boston challenge resulted from a peculiar set of circumstances.
Savings institutions were restricted by law to a few categories of investments. One type of security they were permitted to buy was bank stock,
and when earnings were high during the early 1870s, they made heavy
purchases at premium prices with the expectation that the trend in profits
would continue. In 1865, for example, savings institutions in Massachusetts held $10.4 million worth of bank stock (evaluated at par). Over
the next ten years they increased their holdings to $24.8 million (also
evaluated at par), but the actual growth in their investment was much
higher, because stock prices rose during those years. When bank earnings
commenced their long downward slide in the late 1870s, these institutions were caught with large investments which were paying a declining
rate of return but which they could not unload without disrupting the
market and causing even more serious losses. Because these stock holdings, substantial though they were, were typically only a small part of the
institutions' total portfolios, and because there was always the hope that
bank profits would revive in the future, most continued to hold onto their
stock. As late as 1898, Massachusetts savings institutions collectively
owned as much as 40 percent of the banking capital in Boston.[5]

By the mid 1890s, however, the hope of better earnings had receded as
dividends shrank to their lowest levels ever. Evaluated at 1870 prices, 44
percent of the institutions' investments in bank stock yielded them less
than 4 percent per year over the period 1886–95, and another 31 percent
yielded less than 5 percent per year.[6] When the economic recovery of the

4. Ibid. This figure includes only stock owned by the directors themselves and
   does not include any additional shares that may have been owned by members of their families.
5. Massachusetts, Commissioner of Savings Banks, *Annual Report* (1867–96).
   See also *Boston News Bureau,* Oct. 4, 1898, p. 1.
6. This calculation assumes that savings institutions bought all their stock at the
   lowest price recorded for the year 1870 by Joseph G. Martin in *A Century of
   Finance: Martin's History of the Boston Stock and Money Markets* (Boston,
   1898 [privately printed]), 102. Stock purchased earlier would most likely

late 1890s again failed to produce any improvement in bank earnings, the officers of these institutions finally determined to do something to resolve the situation. Recognizing their common plight, they formed a committee in 1896 with the goal of reducing the number and capital of banks in Boston. After a year or so of negotiations, the committee secured the liquidation of the National City Bank (which had by then stopped paying dividends entirely) and a reduction in the capital stock of the Freeman's, Tremont, Revere, and Suffolk National banks.[7] The managers of most of the other banks resisted the committee's appeal, however. Finally, in the fall of 1898, the frustrated representatives turned for assistance to the private banking house of Kidder, Peabody and Company. Eager for a large national bank to help finance its flourishing underwriting business, Kidder, Peabody agreed to head a syndicate that would merge several of the city's banks into a larger institution. By purchasing the savings institutions' most concentrated stock holdings, the syndicate promptly secured control of nine national banks (Market, Boston, Columbian, Hamilton, Howard, North, Eagle, Revere, and the National Bank of North America). It then forcibly liquidated all of them and consolidated their business with that of the Shawmut Bank, which already had a long-standing relationship with Kidder, Peabody and other private banking houses in the city. As Shawmut's new president the syndicate chose James P. Stearns, vice-president of the old Shawmut National Bank, whose son was a member of the Kidder, Peabody firm.[8]

Without the effective control that the savings institutions' concentrated stock holdings permitted, it is unlikely that the syndicate could have carried off a merger of such scope, because most of the banks' officers and directors were vehemently opposed to the idea. News of the scheme hit

have been cheaper, but the large quantities procured over the next five years would have cost considerably more. Quoted prices for bank stock fell only slightly between 1875 and 1895, probably because there were relatively few sales. Had the savings banks and other large institutional investors begun to dump their stock, values would have plummeted.

7. *Boston News Bureau*, Dec. 17, 1897, p. 1; Jan. 3, 1898, p. 1; Jan. 11, 1898, p. 1; Sept. 29, 1898, p. 1; directors' meetings, Dec. 14 and 24, 1897, and Feb. 15, 1898, and "Minute," 345, Directors' and Stockholders' Minute Book, 1886–1903, National City Bank, Boston, Bank of Boston Archives.

8. These events can be followed on an almost daily basis in the pages of the *Boston News Bureau* and the *Boston Evening Transcript* from Sept. 29, 1898, through mid January 1899. See also Asa S. Knowles, *Shawmut: 150 Years of Banking* (Boston: Houghton Mifflin, 1986), 75–83; U.S., Comptroller of the Currency, Records of the Examination Division, report on the Shawmut Bank, Oct. 14, 1890.

the affected directors like a bombshell. The response of W. S. Draper, cashier of the National Bank of North America, was typical:

> The plan is an imposition and in every way unjust. I do not know why our bank was included in the list. We are on a good financial standing and although, with all the banks, have been seeing some hard times, there is no reason why in a short time we cannot be paying six percent on investments as we used to. I am sure we have no sympathy for the plan.[9]

Most of the nine targeted institutions made a concerted effort to block the deal. The officers of at least five of them sent out circulars defending their own performance and urging shareholders not to sell their stock. They claimed "that the price offered by the liquidation for the shares is a very low one" and that the syndicate would earn a handsome profit from commissions at the stockholders' expense.[10] As a counterproposal, they offered to take it upon themselves to liquidate the banks without charge, "if it be the wish of their stockholders," although one director who supported the syndicate's plan reminded readers of the *Boston Evening Transcript* that in the past the banks' managers had steadfastly ignored such requests: "The fact is that, in spite of assertions to the contrary, the management of most of the banks in question would refuse to liquidate if they were asked, and would not liquidate unless they were compelled to do so." Indeed, earlier that same year at the annual meeting of the Continental National Bank, a prominent shareholder had moved that directors call a special meeting of the stockholders to consider the question of liquidation. The president ruled the motion out of order and refused to put the matter to a vote.[11]

In a broader attempt to rally support, the managers of the nine banks also sought to arouse the opposition of the general business community to the deal, arguing that the consolidated institution would not be so responsive to the needs of local borrowers as the individual banks it would replace. As one bank officer told a reporter for the *Boston Evening Transcript:* "We know our customers well and are used to carrying them along under varying circumstances, but the new bank may not have the same feeling toward them. . . . I do not see how there can fail to be some disaster to individual business men if the deal goes through."[12] Finally,

9. *Boston Evening Transcript,* Sept. 30, 1898, p. 1. See also Oct. 1, 1898, p. 1, and *Boston News Bureau,* Sept. 30, 1898, p. 1.
10. *Boston Evening Transcript,* Sept. 30, 1898, p. 1; Oct. 1, 1898, pp. 1, 4; Oct. 4, 1898, p. 1; Oct. 6, 1898, p. 3; Oct. 15, 1898, p. 9.
11. Ibid., Oct. 6, 1898, p. 3; *Boston News Bureau,* Jan. 12, 1898, p. 4; Jan. 14, 1898, p. 1.
12. *Boston Evening Transcript,* Oct. 3, 1898, p. 8.

bank managers threatened to sabotage the syndicate's plan by paying out surplus funds and liquidating assets in advance of the mergers, and only the syndicate's obvious ability to control a majority of the banks' stock (which carried with it the power to force the rebels out of office) prevented them from making good on their threats. The bankers also vowed to – and in some instances likely did – encourage customers to take their business elsewhere; one bank's officers went so far as to organize a competing institution under its original name and locate it directly across the street from its predecessor.[13]

The importance of the managers' interest in shaping the outcome of these mergers can also be seen by contrasting the Shawmut case with the nearly contemporaneous wave of mergers negotiated by the Industrial Trust Company in Rhode Island. Under the aggressive leadership of Samuel P. Colt, Industrial set out in 1899 on an ambitious plan of acquisition, taking over one bank after another in Providence and elsewhere in the state. Although the managers of some Rhode Island banks rejected Industrial's overtures (sometimes successfully), most of the takeovers occurred with the cooperation of the banks' officers and directors. The directors of the First National Bank of Pawtucket, for example, wrote stockholders that they considered "this offer of the Industrial Trust Company a very satisfactory one, and its acceptance to be of much greater advantage to the stockholders than the continuance of the operation of the bank." Similarly, the directors of the First National Bank of Bristol agreed that "it is for the interest of the stockholders of the bank that the bank should liquidate" and so voted.[14]

13. Ibid., Oct. 3, 1898, p. 8; Oct. 4, 1898, p. 1; Oct. 5, 1898, p. 3; Oct. 6, 1898, p. 3; Oct. 24, 1898, p. 8; Dec. 27, 1898, p. 10. The syndicate reduced the level of opposition somewhat by placing four of the banks' presidents on the new Shawmut board. See Knowles, *Shawmut*, 82.

14. Letter from the directors to the stockholders, Jan. 31, 1900, Directors' and Stockholders' Minute Book, 1879–1900, First National Bank of Pawtucket; directors' meeting, Oct. 17, 1900, Directors' and Stockholders' Minute Book, 1865–1901, First National Bank of Bristol (both in Fleet National Bank Archives). For additional examples, see the minutes of the following directors' meetings: Feb. 2, 1900, Directors' and Stockholders' Minute Book, 1898–1900, Pacific National Bank, Pawtucket; March 29, 1900, Directors' Minute Book, 1862–1902, National Bank of Rhode Island, Newport; July 13, 1904, Directors' and Stockholders' Minute Book, 1899–1904, National Warren Bank, Warren; and April 29, 1901, Directors' and Stockholders' Minute Book, 1851–1901, Pascoag National Bank, Pascoag (all in Fleet National Bank Archives). See also *Bristol Phoenix*, Oct. 16, 1900, p. 2; Nov. 13, 1900, p. 3; *Newport Daily News*, March 31, 1900, p.

This difference in attitude was a direct consequence of a clause in Industrial's charter that permitted branch banking. When the Industrial Trust Company acquired a bank it rarely closed it down – unlike Shawmut – but continued operating it as a branch. The existing board of directors was transformed into a board of managers and the staff left largely intact. When two or three banks were combined into a single branch, some staff members might lose their positions, but the board of managers was usually enlarged to include important directors from each of the constituent units, and as much of the staff was retained as possible.[15] At least in the early years, moreover, these boards of managers possessed a great deal of autonomy. Branches were forbidden to make investment decisions or hold investment securities but seem to have been given complete freedom in the area of loans. The minutes of the trust company's board of directors and executive committee for the years 1900 to 1905 reveal only one instance where the officers of the central bank even discussed a loan made by a branch. There is also only one instance in which they recommended that a branch make a loan to a particular party.[16] Despite the mergers, the officers of Industrial's constituent banks were able to retain a great deal of their former authority.

Although eventually they agreed to merge with Industrial without protest, Rhode Island's small country bankers had originally opposed granting the trust company permission to operate branches. Colt, however, occupied a strategic position in the hierarchy of the state's dominant

5; July 29, 1905, p. 9; Sept. 8, 1905, p. 5; *Warren Gazette,* July 15, 1904, p. 4; *Wickford Standard,* Jan. 17, 1902, p. 2; *Woonsocket Evening Call,* June 16, 1900, p. 3; Dec. 28, 1901, pp. 1, 4.

    In a couple of instances there was resistance to the Industrial Trust Company's plans. Managers of the Slater National Bank in Pawtucket, for example, obtained a new trust-company charter from the state in order to avoid a merger. See directors' meeting, Feb. 1, 1900, and stockholders' meeting, Nov. 8, 1900, Directors' and Stockholders' Minute Book, 1865–1900, Slater National Bank, Pawtucket, Fleet National Bank Archives; *Providence Journal,* Feb. 3, 1900, p. 1; *Pawtucket Evening Times,* Feb. 2, 1900, p. 6; Feb. 3, 1900, p. 7.

15. For examples that illustrate the continuities in local management, see *Bristol Phoenix,* Nov. 13, 1900, p. 3; *Newport Daily News,* March 31, 1900, p. 5; *Pawtucket Evening Times,* Feb. 3, 1900, p. 7; *Warren Gazette,* July 15, 1904, p. 4; *Westerly Daily Sun,* Dec. 2, 1904, p. 5; *Woonsocket Evening Call,* June 15, 1900, p. 5; Feb. 7, 1902, p. 3.

16. See the Minute Books of the Board of Directors and the Executive Committee of the Industrial Trust Company, Providence, Fleet National Bank Archives.

Republican party, and his influence eventually won out in the legislature.[17] In Massachusetts, on the other hand, small bankers succeeded in
fighting off all attempts to introduce branch banking, and they were
similarly successful at the national level. Indeed, under the national banking laws two banks were permitted to merge only if the acquiring institution completely liquidated its partner's assets. Not until 1918 was the law
changed to permit national banks to establish branches – and even then
branching was allowed only in states that had legalized such operations
for their own institutions.[18]

In the absence of branching, the only way the interests of both stockholders and directors could be satisfied was to negotiate a series of smaller mergers that combined the operations of two or at most three preexisting banks. Not only did such consolidations reduce the number and
capital of banks in the area, thus improving the earnings potential of
those that remained in operation, but they also allowed a significant
portion of the acquired banks' directors to obtain positions on the new
(expanded) boards. The formation of the Shawmut and the Industrial
Trust combinations triggered a number of these smaller mergers in both
Boston and Providence. At least a dozen were organized in Boston alone
between 1898 and 1904. When Central National took over and liquidated the Lincoln National Bank in late 1898, for instance, several of
Lincoln's directors joined Central's board, and Benjamin R. Perkins, Lincoln's cashier, was made a vice-president. Similarly, the directors of the
Continental National Bank fended off the liquidation proposal of one
prominent shareholder by negotiating a merger with the Manufacturers
National Bank.[19]

The net result of this series of mergers was a dramatic decline in the
number of banks. By 1910 the number of national banks in Boston had
dropped to 23, little more than a third of the 60 banks operating in that
city in 1895 (the number of trust companies simultaneously increased by

17. One reason Colt succeeded was that the legislature had previously granted
the right to operate branches to another trust company, which, however,
had not yet exercised the privilege. See Andrew J. F. Morris, "Restless
Ambition: Samuel Pomeroy Colt and Turn-of-the-Century Rhode Island,"
unpub. honors thesis, Brown University, 1991, 102–6.
18. Eugene Nelson White, "The Merger Movement in Banking, 1919–1933,"
Journal of Economic History, 45 (June 1985), 285–91.
19. *Boston News Bureau*, Oct. 29, 1898, p. 1; Nov. 9, 1898, p. 1; Nov. 14,
1898, p. 1; Edwin A. Stone, *A Second Chapter in Boston Banking* (Boston:
Berkeley Press, 1906), 5. In only one case that I have found – that of the
Massachusetts National Bank – did directors fend off a threat by buying up
the stock themselves. See *Boston News Bureau*, Dec. 22, 1899, p. 4.

only 10, from 13 to 23). Over the same period, the number of national banks in Providence fell from 25 to 9; the number of trust companies held steady at 4. But though the number of banks declined, the average size of the remaining institutions increased dramatically. In Boston the average assets of banks and trust companies rose from $4.3 million in 1895 to $11.7 million in 1910. In Providence the average size of a bank or trust company rose to $11.1 million.[20]

This change in the structure of the banking system had a dramatic effect on earnings. As Table 4.1 indicated, the ratio of net earnings to capital plus surplus among Boston's national banks (including the Shawmut) increased 63 percent between 1891–1900 and 1901–10, and the earnings rate for national banks in Rhode Island (excluding the Industrial Trust Company, which did not have a national charter) increased 58 percent. Even more striking, banks in these two localities improved their performance relative to other banks in the region (where there were no significant mergers) as well as to the nation as a whole. The ratio of the earnings rate of Boston banks to those in both New England and the United States increased from 88 percent and 68 percent, respectively, in 1896–1900, to 113 percent and 90 percent in 1906–10. Over the same period, the ratio of the earnings of Rhode Island banks to those in the region increased from 75 to 103 percent, and to those in the nation from 58 to 81 percent. This increase in relative profitability suggests that the improvement was not exclusively a consequence of the economy's return to prosperity but derived from the reorganization of the banking system in these two areas.

II

Against this general backdrop of profitability, both the National Shawmut Bank and the Industrial Trust Company proved to be extraordinarily successful enterprises. In the first decade of the twentieth century, for example, Shawmut earned a rate of return of 9.3 percent, compared with the 5.7 percent earned by the old Shawmut Bank for the decade 1886–95, and the 2.9 to 5.2 percent recorded by the nine banks it had liquidated. Industrial Trust had an even more impressive record, earning an average rate of return of 14.5 percent over the decade 1901 to 1910.[21]

20. U.S., Comptroller of the Currency, *Annual Report* (1895), vol. 2, 403–22; (1910), 550, 662; Massachusetts, Bank Commissioner, *Annual Report* (1910), pt. 1, xliv–xlv; Rhode Island, Bank Commissioner, *Annual Report* (1910), 126–204.

21. Profit rates were calculated from information in U.S., Comptroller of the

One possible explanation for the mergers' enhanced profitability was that the disappearance of so many previously competing banks increased their market power. Some such phenomenon may indeed have accounted for the particular profitability of the Industrial Trust Company, which acquired many or, in some cases, all of the banks in a number of Rhode Island communities. In 1895, for example, there were six banks in Woonsocket, but by 1910 only three remained to compete with Industrial's local branch. The situation was much the same in Pawtucket, which had three national banks in 1895. Fifteen years later only one was left, now reorganized as a trust company, the other two having been absorbed by Industrial. By 1910 the company faced no competition at all in Bristol, Warren, and a couple of smaller communities where it had acquired all preexisting banks.[22]

Monopoly power alone, however, cannot account for the success of the Shawmut Bank, which in 1910 still faced competition from twenty-two national banks and twenty-three trust companies in Boston proper, not to mention banks headquartered outside the city. For that matter, even Industrial Trust faced outside competitors, as well as the immediate rivalry of the eleven independent banks and trust companies located in Providence itself. In addition, it faced the specter of potential competition in the countryside, where there was nothing to prevent another trust company from setting up additional branches. This threat of renewed competition undoubtedly had a restraining effect on the rates of interest that both Shawmut and Industrial charged for loans. Nonetheless, it seems likely that both institutions benefited from the sharp reduction in the number of competitors, as did the remaining banks in these areas.

Another possible explanation for the mergers' success was that the size of the new institutions helped them reduce unit costs and capture economies of scale. Clearly the National Shawmut Bank benefited from such savings. As early as 1900 its business volume was already 83 percent of the 1895 total for all ten banks involved in the original merger, yet it paid the salaries of only one set of officers and maintained only one banking facility to service its customers. Economies in expense were also available to the Industrial Trust Company, though to a somewhat lesser extent. The trust company's Providence office absorbed only two national banks in

Currency, Annual Report (1885–95) and (1900–10); Knowles, *Shawmut*, 88, 115; Rhode Island, State Auditor, *Annual Statement Exhibiting the Condition of the Banks* (1900–7); Rhode Island, Bank Commissioner, *Annual Report* (1908–10); Martin, *A Century of Finance*, 104–5.

22. Rhode Island, Bank Commissioner, *Annual Report* (1910), 258–63, 266–7; U.S., Comptroller of the Currency, *Annual Report* (1910), 662–3.

1899, and only one more after that. Although Industrial arranged for the liquidation of four additional Providence banks in 1901, it merged them into a separate entity called the United National Bank, in which it retained a controlling interest.[23] Outside Providence the trust company turned most of its acquisitions into branches, though in the event that it obtained more than one bank in a given area, it typically combined their operations to reduce expenses. In Bristol, for example, it merged two national banks and two savings institutions into a single facility. In several localities, however, it acquired only one bank.

One might have expected that large banks operating during the last quarter of the nineteenth century would also have benefited from economies in expense. As the quantitative evidence presented in Chapter 4 suggested, however, even had such economies existed, they were not sufficiently important to influence profitability. The problem was that banks that expanded by increasing deposits faced the difficult task of finding outlets for their funds that did not either earn low rates of return or reduce portfolio quality. Mergers, on the other hand – whether large or small – offered a way out of this bind. By liquidating their competitors and taking over the cream of their business, banks were able to increase both their size and degree of leverage (and thus reduce unit expenses) without having to choose between lower earnings and higher risk. Strictly in terms of size, the reorganized National Shawmut Bank was less than the sum of its parts, but it was able to earn higher profits than the banks it absorbed simply by being selective about the kinds of business it assumed from them.

Finally, because they were so large, the Shawmut and Industrial Trust combinations could enter lucrative sectors of the credit market that had effectively been closed to their smaller predecessors. Both these institutions made use of their connections with private banking houses to participate in a number of new underwriting ventures. Kidder, Peabody and Company placed three of its representatives on Shawmut's board, and the bank subsequently helped the firm finance securities issues for railroad, gas, electric, telephone, and mining companies, as well as for foreign

23. According to a memoir written by one of the company's employees, the scheme was a concession to "the nationwide protest against the absorption of so many small banks." It may also have reflected a desire to maintain United's national charter and thus its ability to issue currency, which it would have lost had it been acquired by the trust company. See "Some Recollections of 50 Years with the Industrial" in folder labeled "Industrial: Charter: History: Laws," Industrial Trust Company, Providence. The author of the memoir is unknown.

governments.[24] In 1902 the Industrial Trust Company increased its capital by $300,000 to enable several large New York financial interests, including the Mutual Life Insurance Company, Morton Trust, James Stillman of National City Bank, George F. Baker of First National Bank of New York, and Jacob H. Schiff of Kuhn, Loeb and Company, to buy blocks of its stock. The resulting alliance gave the trust company entree to major underwriting syndicates and other investment opportunities in New York. In fact, beginning around 1904, a committee of the company's New York directors assumed responsibility for authorizing all its investments.[25]

III

Despite its beneficial effect on the profitability of the banking sector, the merger wave did nothing to reverse the late-nineteenth-century trend toward specialization in short-term commercial loans. Indeed, at the same time as the largest of these combines were moving into the underwriting business, they were coming under increasing pressure to adhere to the professionals' precepts in their everyday lending activities. Although it is beyond the scope of this study to trace the policies of these institutions into the twentieth century, it is clear that the merger movement in some ways heightened the tendency toward professionalization and specialization that was already under way. In the first place, the giant banks that resulted from the mergers were too large to be managed by businessmen whose primary interests lay elsewhere. Hence James P. Stearns, Shawmut's president, was a banker by profession. Although he had entered the business through family connections (he had married the daughter of William Bramhall, one of Shawmut's previous presidents), he made banking his career and worked his way up through the ranks, attaining the position of vice-president several years prior to the merger.[26] Unlike Stearns, Industrial's president, Samuel P. Colt, was deeply involved in other ventures, including the presidency of the U.S. Rubber Company. His busy schedule, however, forced him to delegate much of the respon-

24. Knowles, *Shawmut*, 84–6. Two other private banking houses also had representatives on Shawmut's board.
25. *Providence Journal*, Aug. 2, 1902, p. 3; "Reminiscences of W. E. Smith," 6–7, in folder marked "Industrial: Charter: History: Laws," Industrial Trust Company, Providence. On the financial activities of large trust companies, see also Larry Neal, "Trust Companies and Financial Innovation, 1897–1914," *Business History Review*, 45 (Spring 1971), 35–51.
26. Knowles, *Shawmut*, 75, 77.

sibility for the bank's day-to-day operations to the professional members of its staff. As one of his employees, Ward E. Smith, later recalled, "Col. Colt was not at the bank so very much." Even when he was living in Rhode Island (which was not always the case), his "custom was to leave at 2 o'clock Tuesdays to attend the Rubber Company meeting and other business in New York, returning to Providence at 2 P.M. Saturday afternoon."[27]

Changes in the size and composition of the banks' boards of directors also reinforced the tendency toward professionalization. Seats were added to accommodate the financiers who bankrolled the mergers and also to cement alliances with important private banking houses. Shawmut's board, for instance, was increased from ten to seventeen at the time of the merger, and the bank's Articles of Association were amended in 1908 to permit as many as thirty directors. In 1909 they were amended once more to allow thirty-two, and in 1912 the limit was raised to forty. Industrial's board grew in size from eighteen in 1898 to thirty-two just seven years later. In 1905 stockholders amended the company's bylaws to permit up to forty directors.[28]

As the boards increased in size, their membership grew more diverse. Shawmut's postmerger board included five directors from the old Shawmut National Bank, four from liquidated institutions, three from Kidder, Peabody, and two from other private banks involved in the syndicate.[29] As previously mentioned, Industrial's board was broadened in the early twentieth century to include such prominent New York financiers as Elbridge T. Gerry and Jacob H. Schiff.

As a result of these changes in size and membership, boards of directors became less clubby than they had been in the premerger environment, which in turn decreased the likelihood that members would wink at opportunistic behavior by one of their number. More important, the presence of representatives of private banking houses on these boards meant that some members now had the expertise to make sure that managers conformed to professional banking standards. The change was immediately apparent in the case of Shawmut. Its lending business was

27. "Reminiscences of W. E. Smith," 2, 8. For a description of Colt's many other activities, see Morris, "Restless Ambition."

28. Directors' Minute Book, 1877–98, Shawmut National Bank, Boston, and Organization Certificate and Amendments to Articles of Association, Directors' Minute Book, 1898–1903, National Shawmut Bank, Shawmut Bank Archives; stockholders' meetings, Jan. 18, 1898, Jan. 20, 1903, and Jan. 17, 1905, Stockholders' Minute Book, 1896–1917, Industrial Trust Company, Providence.

29. Knowles, *Shawmut,* 82.

normally handled on a day-to-day basis by an executive committee, whose decisions the board of directors convened weekly to ratify. Each year the board appointed its own agents to scrutinize the state of the bank's loan and investment portfolios, and in the reports of these examining committees there is clear evidence that managers were being held to the standards of professional bankers. In 1903, for example, the examiners chastised the bank's managers for accepting as collateral certain securities that were not traded actively on the market: "We disapprove in loaning on the stock of a Corporation where we are loaning direct to the Corporation, especially to Officers, except on listed and active and saleable stocks." The examiners also devoted a significant portion of their report to criticizing "the large and apparently permanent Loans to Corporations and Individuals which appear like furnishing a steady Capital for business enterprises." To reduce the number of such loans, the examiners recommended "converting a certain class of Time Loans that usually have to be renewed at the option of the borrower, and a part of what we call Steady Demand Loans, into Loans that when they come due cannot possibly have any claims on the Bank." To this end they advised the executive committee to make purchases "in the open market of Commercial paper and Collateral Loans."[30]

In the case of the Industrial Trust Company, one finds similar evidence that monitoring was going on. Even before the expansion of the late 1890s, for instance, the New York firm of Morton, Bliss and Company held a large block of the institution's stock and consequently was allotted representation on the board. When George T. Bliss objected to Colt's policy of lending money to himself, Colt promptly responded "that my entire indebtedness to the Industrial Trust Co. is liquidated. . . . I beg to add that I am in full accord with the principle you have stated, that an officer, and especially the President of a Trust Co., should in no way be indebted personally to the Company." Colt promised he would never again borrow money from the institution and further reassured Bliss that "we now have a standing vote that no loan shall be made upon any kind of security to exceed $100,000, without the authority of the full Board of Directors."[31]

Colt was not so easily controlled, however. The Industrial Trust Company was in many ways a very different kind of institution from the

30. Report of the Committee to Examine the Loans and Securities of the Bank, April 23, 1903, Directors' Minute Book, 1898–1903, National Shawmut Bank, Boston.
31. Directors' meeting, Nov. 27, 1894, Directors' Minute Book, 1887–95, Industrial Trust Company, Providence.

National Shawmut Bank. Because it was chartered by the state of Rhode Island, it did not come under the jurisdiction of the Comptroller of the Currency but was subject only to the more perfunctory oversight of the state. As a trust company, moreover, Industrial combined savings-bank functions with commercial banking activities, and as a result was permitted to make long-term loans to businesses on the security of real estate. Although the directors at first limited the quantity of such loans to the amount on deposit in the company's "participation" (savings) accounts, they quickly repealed the restriction. Under Colt's administration, moreover, Industrial's standards were laxer than those recommended by conservative bankers, even with respect to the strictly commercial end of its business. Rather than follow the 50 percent rule, for example, the executive committee adopted a more lenient formula: "that it shall not be the policy of this Company to loan to Corporations whose quick assets do not exceed their liabilities." Firms that did not meet this criterion could still obtain loans on the security of "a satisfactory endorser or endorsers." In addition, the minutes of the company's executive committee record large loans to businesses with which Colt was personally associated. For example, Industrial made extensive call loans to the National India Rubber Company in Bristol, Rhode Island, which Colt controlled before it was acquired by U.S. Rubber. These loans sometimes exceeded the self-imposed ceiling of $100,000 to any single borrower. The trust company also allowed U.S. Rubber to overdraw its account by more than $55,000 and advanced the corporation at least $100,000 as a first installment to help it purchase a majority interest in the Joseph Banigan Rubber Company, one of the combine's most important competitors. Subsequently the company advanced U.S. Rubber $500,000 on the security of its stock in the Banigan subsidiary.[32]

These policies, coupled with Industrial's aggressive campaign of acquisitions and its vigorous competition for deposits, affronted the conservatives who managed Providence's most elite financial institutions, such as the Providence National Bank and the Rhode Island Hospital Trust Company.[33] There was not much they could do about the situation, however,

32. Directors' meetings, Sept. 6 and Oct. 4, 1887, Directors' Minute Book, 1887–95; directors' meeting, March 28, 1899, Directors' Minute Book, 1895–1903; executive committee meetings, July 14 and Sept. 1, 1896, Minutes of the Executive Committee, 1895–7; executive committee meetings, April 19, 1898, and Feb. 28, 1899, Minutes of the Executive Committee, 1897–9, Industrial Trust Company, Providence.

33. The Rhode Island Hospital Trust Co. was chartered in 1869 by a group of the city's leading financiers in order to create (according to one of those involved) "a financial institution of high credit and powerful resources and,

until the Panic of 1907 finally provided them with an opportunity. The episode was triggered by a run on the Union Trust Company, another institution in the conservatives' disfavor. As the run rapidly spread to Industrial, officers of Hospital Trust made a public gesture of entering their competitor to conduct an inspection. They emerged to proclaim Industrial in sound financial health, a demonstration of support that apparently succeeded in staunching the outflow of funds. But their support, ratified later that same day by a broad committee of the city's leading bankers, did not come cheap. In tandem with Industrial Trust's New York investors, who also disliked Colt's management practices, the conservatives forced Colt to resign the presidency, allegedly on account of his deteriorating health. Colt was in fact ill at the time, but when he nonetheless balked at resigning, his lawyer sent him a blunt message through his brother: "I am satisfied from the talks that I have had with several of the New York interests and the Providence people, that it will be a question of his doing this, or their resigning from the Board and their official positions."[34] Colt was given the largely honorific title of chairman of the board of directors, and Cyrus P. Brown was elected president in his stead. To a much greater extent than Colt, Brown fit the mold of the professional banker, having worked his way up through the ranks at the trust company, where he had started out in 1887 as a lowly clerk. At the same time as Colt was deposed, monitoring was improved by adding the bank's auditor to the board of directors and giving him the title of vice-president.[35]

When Colt returned from his illness to assume his duties as chairman of the board, he found the new president studiously disregarding his opinions. As he later complained, "Not only was my advice not asked by the President on any subject, but any suggestion from me was absolutely ignored." He also learned that Brown "had antagonized men outside of the Industrial Board simply because they were friendly with [me] or were

at the same time, prove a pecuniary help to Rhode Island Hospital, a benevolent institution in its infancy" that had recently been founded by many of the same men. The company was required by its charter to pay one-third of its profits in excess of 6% to the hospital. In 1880 the charter was amended, and in lieu of future payments the trust company gave the hospital a large block of stock. Florence Parker Simister, *The First Hundred Years* (Providence: Rhode Island Hospital Trust Co., 1967), 10–15, 30.

34. Letter from John J. Watson, Jr., to LeBaron B. Colt, Jan. 13, 1908, quoted in Morris, "Restless Ambition," 188.
35. Morris, "Restless Ambition," 185–8. At the same time the conservatives orchestrated the reorganization of the Union Trust Company and put it under the management of one of their own.

in some way associated with the Rubber Company."[36] Worse still, he discovered that the bank's management had disposed surreptitiously of two thousand of his own shares of Industrial Trust stock and that some of this stock had been purchased by Brown himself.[37]

Colt was down but not out. He still owned a large block of Industrial Trust stock, and a few years later he used it as a base from which to launch a proxy fight to regain control of the company from the professionals. Like his banking practices, Colt's campaign was waged largely on the nineteenth-century terrain of personal contacts. He and his allies called in all personal debts, and the tactic produced immediate and tangible results. As one grateful stockholder responded, "Of course, I will sign a proxy in Colonel Colt's favor for the Industrial meeting. I bought my stock through him and am willing to do anything he wishes me to do in respect to it."[38] The Colt forces were especially strong in Bristol, Colt's hometown. They were correspondingly weakest in Newport, the base of political opposition to Colt's abortive 1906 run for the U.S. Senate. Wherever direct personal contacts were lacking, however, the Colt group made alliances with prominent businessmen who could exert influence over local stockholders. Colt's nephew, for instance, enlisted the help of an intermediary to contact a man named Miller in Pawtucket who was "exactly the man to do most energetic work. He knows everybody, is very close with the Goff family, with whom he does a large amount of business, is popular and influential among the investors in Pawtucket." The intermediary apparently did his job well, for Miller "agreed to do all in his power to help the situation." Similarly, Colt's brother noted that a member of the Rodman clan had secured proxies from all the stockholders in southern Rhode Island's Pawtuxet valley, "except Pendleton in Westerly, who is expected to sign today."[39]

Industrial Trust's embattled managers responded by conducting a

36. *Providence Journal,* Dec. 24, 1911, p. 1; letter from Charles A. Emerson to Samuel P. Colt, Nov. 20, 1911, Colt Family Papers, Group 78, Series XV, Box 90, Folder 69, University Library Special Collections, University of Rhode Island.

37. During his illness Colt apparently had been asked to sign a transfer for the shares on the ground that the stock was needed as collateral for a loan. The bank then sold the stock without his knowledge or approval. Morris, "Restless Ambition," 189–90.

38. Quoted in a letter from John D. Carberry to Samuel P. Colt, Nov. 13, 1911, Colt Family Papers, Group 78, Series XV, Box 90, Folder 68.

39. Letters from LeBaron C. Colt to Samuel P. Colt, Nov. 3 and 22, 1911, ibid., Folders 68 and 70; letter from Lebaron B. Colt to Samuel P. Colt, Nov. 22, 1911, Folder 70; Morris, "Restless Ambition," 192–4, 196–7.

proxy campaign of their own – only theirs was fought on the terrain of professional standards by raising fears that Colt's entrepreneurial style of banking would undermine the soundness of the institution. They publicly accused Colt of attempting to seize personal control of the company, and warned stockholders that Colt was demanding changes in Industrial's bylaws that "would give him sole control of every commercial activity in which the bank might be concerned, would permit him to assume entire supervision of every act of the President, the Treasurer and the trust officers, and would make the office of chairman of the board, which Col. Colt now holds, the one dominating factor in the entire situation."[40] Brown and his allies canvassed stockholders through a team of prominent businessmen who hinted darkly "that there was a great deal more to this contest that would yet come out, that it would even go back of 1907, bringing out things . . . that would make Colonel Colt sit up and take notice."[41] One conservative banker went so far as to write U.S. Senator Nelson Aldrich, a long-time Colt patron, seeking his help in beating back the challenge: "Some of us bank men are really anxious as to the fate of the [Industrial Trust Company] if Colt once more assumes control. As to his speculative tendencies and selfish purposes in its management I need tell you nothing."[42]

Both sides amassed considerable support, but the final outcome depended on the disposition of large blocks of stock controlled by New York financial interests. Gerry threw his support to Brown and even refused Colt an audience, pleading a severe attack of the gout. Schiff also declined to grant Colt a proxy: "If it be the intention to turn out or change the present management, which appears to be conservative and doing well for the interests of the stockholders, I think I would prefer not to take sides against it."[43] George F. Baker, who controlled the dispensation of 1,590 shares belonging to himself, his brother, and the Mutual Life Insurance Company, also refused Colt's request. Instead of siding with Brown or maintaining a position of strict neutrality, however, Baker decided to put his stock up for sale. In this way he both avoided the consequences of the proxy fight and made a killing on the shares. Colt secured this entire block by offering the astronomical sum of $300 per

40. *Providence Journal*, Dec. 20, 1911, p. 1.
41. Letter from Waldo M. Place to Samuel P. Colt, Dec. 21, 1911, Colt Family Papers, Group 78, Series XV, Box 90, Folder 75.
42. Letter from Robert Gammell to Nelson W. Aldrich, Dec. 27, 1911, quoted in Morris, "Restless Ambition," 205.
43. Letters from Elbridge T. Gerry to Samuel P. Colt, Nov. 20 and 24, 1911, Colt Family Papers, Group 78, Series XV, Box 90, Folders 69 and 71; letter from Jacob H. Schiff to Samuel P. Colt, Nov. 13, 1911, Folder 68.

share ("We were 'held up,'" as Colt's agent, John D. Carberry, later put it).[44] However outrageous the price, the purchase gave Colt effective control of the trust company and turned the tide of proxy votes in his favor. Even Schiff ultimately conceded his proxy, though Gerry never retracted his support for Brown.[45]

When the stockholders finally convened at Industrial Trust headquarters on January 16, 1912, the Colt forces won an easy victory. With a margin of more than four thousand shares, they deposed Brown as president, substituting one of their own, H. Martin Brown, a director who had remained loyal to Colt. At the same time, they purged Colt's enemies from the board and elected their own slate of directors, composed entirely of Rhode Islanders. In part this choice was a response to charges that Colt would move control of the bank to New York (where he often resided), but it was also a symbolic declaration of independence from the constraints imposed on his operations by the New York financiers.[46]

The case of Industrial Trust shows that a determined entrepreneur like Colt could staunch the tide of professionalization, at least for a time. But it also shows how difficult this was to accomplish. Regular commercial bankers resented the competition for resources that such free-wheeling institutions represented, and they continually sought to rein them in — force them to conform to their own conceptions of sound banking. Finan-

44. Letters from John D. Carberry to Samuel P. Colt, Nov. 27 and 28, 1911, ibid., Folder 72. Other stock was sold (or offered) during the proxy fight for between $22 and $32 less per share. See letters from John D. Carberry to Samuel P. Colt, Nov. 18, 1911, Folder 69, and Waldo M. Place to Colt, Dec. 28, 1911, Folder 72.

45. Letter from Samuel P. Colt to Henry A. C. Taylor, Jan. 12, 1912, ibid., Box 91, Folder 78.

46. Colt explained this change to a disgruntled former New York director by claiming that he had made the decision just one day prior to the meeting: because "the other side made such a handle of my wishing to take control of the Industrial Trust Company over to New York, . . . we decided it best to have no one on the new Board but residents of Rhode Island." But a list of prospective directors (the list is undated, but its contents indicate that it was drawn up earlier in the month) makes it clear that Colt had planned to exclude the New Yorkers from the board if at all possible. Colt was unsure of his strength, however, and begged George F. Baker to allow his name to be submitted temporarily as a director if "it seems desirable." Baker agreed, but the move did not prove necessary, "finding we were as strong." Letters from Samuel P. Colt to George F. Baker, Jan. 13 and 17, 1912; Colt to Charles H. Allen, Jan. 17 and 30, 1912, Folder 78; list of present and prospective board members, undated, Folder 79.

cial crises provided the leverage they needed to impose their will. Thus runs on the Union and Industrial Trust companies during the Panic of 1907 put these institutions at the mercy of conservatives. For both, the price of rescue was the same: the ousting of the old management and the substitution of a new team acceptable to local bankers. In the case of Industrial Trust, Colt was able to win back his authority, but only after a bitter and exorbitantly expensive proxy battle. Few entrepreneurs had the resources to wage such a costly struggle for control.

IV

According to Joseph A. Schumpeter, entrepreneurs and bankers should play fundamentally different economic roles. As Schumpeter saw it, entrepreneurs were extraordinarily talented individuals whose fertile minds devised new products and production processes and whose innovations were responsible for increasing the economy's productive capabilities. The function of bankers, on the other hand, was to create the purchasing power that entrepreneurs needed to put their ideas into effect. The bankers' role in the growth process, though vital, was thus essentially passive, because the funds they amassed were useless until entrepreneurs borrowed them and invested them in productive assets.[47]

Schumpeter recognized that the fundamentally different roles of entrepreneurs and bankers might sometimes be combined in one and the same person, but he suggested that the increasing specialization that accompanied economic development would tend to split these functions off from one another. This differentiation of function, moreover, he believed would improve the operation of the economy. Banks, Schumpeter argued, must "be independent of the entrepreneurs whose plans they are to sanction or to refuse. This means, practically speaking, that banks and their officers must not have any stake in the gains of enterprises beyond what is implied by the loan contract." Bankers who were independent were better able to discriminate among potential borrowers and hence better able to channel their funds to legitimate innovations.[48]

This study of banking in nineteenth-century New England has shown

47. Joseph A. Schumpeter, *The Theory of Economic Development: An Inquiry into Profits, Capital, Credit, Interest, and the Business Cycle* (Cambridge: Harvard University Press, 1934), esp. chap. 2.
48. Ibid., 76–7. The quotation is from *Business Cycles: A Theoretical, Historical, and Statistical Analysis of the Capitalist Process* (New York: McGraw-Hill, 1939), vol. 1, 118.

that the process of specialization that Schumpeter described did in fact occur. During the early part of the century most banks were controlled directly by entrepreneurs, who funneled the institutions' resources into their own enterprises. Indeed, starting a bank was an important way of obtaining financing for entrepreneurial ventures. By the end of the century, however, banks were no longer simply the financial adjuncts of their directors' enterprises. They had become businesses in their own right. Staffed by professionals, they earned profits by collecting local savings and lending the proceeds to creditworthy borrowers in the form of short-term commercial loans.

Contrary to Schumpeter, however, this study suggests that the differentiation of function that occurred in New England in the latter decades of the nineteenth century was not necessarily a good thing, because it removed bankers from the business of financing economic development and may actually have made it more difficult for entrepreneurs to gain access to funds. Although bankers' increasing specialization in short-term commercial lending occurred at a time when other sources of capital (for example, the securities markets) were expanding, there is reason to believe that it nonetheless had a detrimental effect on economic development in the region. Why this was so can be seen by exploring banks' role in the financial life cycle of firms.

In theory, as firms grow and mature their sources of funding should change. This is because as firms become better established, more information is available about them, and as a result they can take advantage of cheaper techniques for tapping outside pools of savings. When firms are first getting a start in business (stage one), they have to rely on internal sources of funding – the wealth of their founders' families and whatever earnings they are able to plow back into the enterprise. When firms are well established and have track records that can easily be evaluated by outsiders (stage three), they can go to the equity markets for capital. In between the first and third stages firms often need assistance from banks to raise funds in order to expand. Because collecting information about firms in this stage is too costly for investors to take on individually, this function must be performed by intermediaries, such as banks, whose responsibility it is to serve as "delegated monitors" – that is, to collect information about and monitor closely the institutions to which they grant credit. Under the oversight of banks, then, firms grow and mature until they are able to tap the capital markets on their own. Banks, moreover, can help this transition to independence along by underwriting a firm's stock issues and purchasing for themselves a share in the enterprise. Their willingness to invest their own funds in the firm signals to other investors that the stock is of high quality. German banks performed this function particularly well during the late nineteenth and the early twentieth century.[49]

New England banks, on the other hand, did not. Even after the merger wave in banking, when large institutions like the National Shawmut Bank and Industrial Trust began to participate in underwriting syndicates, there was little connection between the banks' regular lending business and their activities in the equity markets.[50] Private investment bankers in New York and Boston put the underwriting syndicates together, and banks merely contributed their funds. In their regular lending business, moreover, banks shunned any kind of direct involvement in their borrowers' businesses. (Industrial Trust's support of International Rubber was a partial exception, but this connection resulted from Colt's position as president of both institutions and was severely frowned upon by the conservative bankers who tried to displace him.) Not surprisingly, only the nation's largest firms gained access to the securities markets during this period. Indeed, the only industrials traded on the national exchange in the early twentieth century were giant consolidations formed with the assistance of major private bankers like Morgan. Even on the regional exchanges, access was limited to firms with long track records in the area.[51]

It is beyond the scope of this study to examine the experiences of individual firms in the credit markets, but a recent study by Charles W. Calomiris provides some sense of the costs that conservative banking practices imposed on the manufacturing sector. Comparing the United States and Germany, Calomiris found that the capital–output ratio, the share of equipment in the capital stock, and the rate of growth of labor productivity were all higher in the latter nation than in the former – evidence that is consistent with the idea that Germany's more aggressive banking system lowered the cost of finance for firms. He also presented evidence that equity finance was significantly more expensive and access

49. This discussion draws on Charles W. Calomiris, "The Costs of Rejecting Universal Banking: American Finance in the German Mirror, 1870–1914," in *Coordination and Information: Historical Perspectives on the Organization of Enterprise*, ed. Naomi R. Lamoreaux and Daniel M. G. Raff (Chicago: University of Chicago Press, forthcoming).

50. This was also the case in the 1920s, when banks began to organize affiliates to market securities.

51. Thomas R. Navin and Marian V. Sears, "The Rise of a Market for Industrial Securities, 1887–1902," *Business History Review*, 29 (June 1955), 105–38; Martin, *A Century of Finance*, 126–44. Martin added only about a dozen new manufacturing firms to his list of stock quotations over the entire period 1865–97.

to equity markets more restricted in the United States than in Germany, a pattern that he argued was a direct result of German banks' greater willingness to take an equity position in the firms to which they lent money and in that manner ease the transition from bank to equity finance.[52]

There is also reason to believe that banks in New England were not doing a good job of easing firms through the transition from stage one to stage two of the financial life cycle. Although in theory the function of banks is to solve information problems, in practice the uncertainties that the region's bankers faced when they began to lend most of their funds through arm's-length relationships encouraged them to adopt a conservative posture and lend only to the tried and true. The most extreme manifestation of this conservatism was the injunction (evident in the loan portfolio of the Suffolk National Bank and in the report of Shawmut's committee of stockholders) to channel more and more lending through the commercial-paper market, where information problems were less serious. Although the commercial-paper market was somewhat more accessible than the securities markets, it was a viable source of credit only for firms with established reputations or wealthy and important backers. As a result, up and coming firms, particularly in new industries, could find it difficult to gain access to funds.

One cannot help wondering whether bankers' increasing conservativism during the late nineteenth century accounts for one of the most prominent (and ultimately most damaging) characteristics of the New England economy – its persistent specialization in a few leading industries, such as textiles and shoes. Whatever localization economies caused these industries to cluster initially in New England, over time one might have expected the region's economy to become more diverse. New England had a large force of both skilled and unskilled workers that entrepreneurs could readily turn to other tasks. It also boasted a vibrant machine-tool and machine-building sector. More important, New England was a center of invention for all kinds of manufacturing industries (not just textiles and shoes) and consistently exhibited the highest per capita patenting rates in the nation.[53] Might not the region's history have been different if banks had been willing to nurse innovative industries along?

52. Calomiris, "The Costs of Rejecting Universal Banking."
53. Naomi R. Lamoreaux and Kenneth L. Sokoloff, "The Location of Invention and Technical Change in Late-Nineteenth- and Early-Twentieth-Century America: A Research Project and Preliminary Report," unpub. paper, 1993.

Conclusion

On January 2, 1991, Rhode Islanders awoke to the somber news that Governor Bruce Sundlun had declared a bank holiday and closed all of the state's privately insured banks and credit unions. Each of the affected institutions was a member of the Rhode Island Share and Indemnity Corporation, or RISDIC, as it was commonly known. RISDIC, it turned out, was insolvent – bankrupted by the failure of one of the largest banks it insured, and because state law forbade banks and credit unions to operate without insurance, RISDIC's member institutions were forced to shut their doors. Over the next few days, the news only worsened. When the closed institutions applied for federal insurance to enable them to reopen, it quickly became apparent that only some of them would qualify. Federal regulators rejected applications from the rest on the grounds that their portfolios contained too high a proportion of real-estate loans, especially commercial ones, and that their default rates were unusually high. As news reports revealed, at the root of both problems were excessive loans to developers who were closely connected with the institutions' managers.[1]

To most Rhode Islanders, the insider lending uncovered by the RISDIC collapse had no redeeming social value. It was corruption pure and simple – comparable to the bribes and kickbacks that repeatedly surfaced in investigations of Rhode Island's state and local government. Most Americans, moreover, viewed the situation in a similar light, as the contem-

---

1. These events can be followed on the front pages of the *Providence Journal* for the first few weeks of January 1991. See also Vartan Gregorian, *"Carved in Sand": A Report on the Collapse of the Rhode Island Share and Deposit Indemnity Corporation* (Providence: Brown University, 1991) and *Supplement and Supplemental Appendix* (Providence: Brown University, 1991). Gregorian's supplemental report reprinted an earlier document authored by special assistant attorney general Robert S. Stitt, which detailed "unduly concentrated loans to officers, directors and 'other insiders'" at RISDIC-insured institutions. See also the special *Providence Journal* series on the Central Credit Union in North Providence, published June 23–28, 1991.

poraneous savings-and-loan debacle suggested. Popular explanations blamed rapacious businessmen for looting formerly healthy savings banks, leaving taxpayers with empty shells and billions of dollars in depositors' claims to pay off. According to one popular account, "Swindlers, mobsters, politicians, greedy S&L executives, and con men capitalized on regulatory weaknesses created by deregulation and thoroughly fleeced the thrift industry."[2]

How different these attitudes toward insider lending were from those of early-nineteenth-century New Englanders. Not that our ancestors were insensitive to problems of corruption and conflict of interest. Indeed, politics during the Jacksonian era was rife with such concerns. But early New Englanders perceived insider lending as corrupt only to the extent that they regarded banks as public institutions. Although the privileges that banks received by virtue of their special legislative charters gave them a quasi-public status, once the number of banks began to increase dramatically in the decades following the War of 1812, it became ever more difficult to conceive of them as anything other than private enterprises whose lending decisions were nobody's business but their own.

Jacksonian New Englanders still lived in a world where kinship and other personal connections retained their primacy – where it was considered normal and proper to satisfy the claims of relatives and friends before those of more distant acquaintances, and certainly those of complete strangers. Businessmen as a matter of course channeled favors toward close associates, and bankers were not expected to behave any differently. Many banks in fact were founded by kinsmen who intended to use the institutions to raise capital for their private ventures. Nor was there anything underhanded or deceptive about the aims of these founders. It was well known that many banks were formed for such purposes, and investors could assume that when they bought stock in a bank they were actually investing in the enterprises of its directors.

In the context of the early-nineteenth-century New England economy, moreover, insider lending seems to have had few negative consequences. Individual banks discriminated against outsiders when they made their lending decisions, but the rapid expansion of the financial system kept the consequences of these distortions to a minimum by enabling numerous kinship groups to found their own banks. Some banks failed as a result of

---

2. Stephen Pizzo, Mary Fricker, and Paul Muolo, *Inside Job: The Looting of America's Savings and Loans* (New York: McGraw-Hill, 1989), 453. Many scholars have blamed government policy and trends in interest rates for the thrifts' problems, but the popular literature has focused on the behavior of bank insiders.

excessive loans to their own officers and directors, but the low levels of leverage characteristic of early-nineteenth-century banking kept such failures to a minimum and isolated other institutions from their consequences. Stockholders, it is true, bore the brunt of any losses from bad debts, but the risks they faced were minimized by an incentive structure that helped to keep loans to insiders within reasonable bounds. Because a bank failure would deprive directors of their main vehicle of capital accumulation and at the same time seriously damage their business reputations, members of the board monitored each other's lending behavior to prevent excessive borrowing. Obviously this system was imperfect, but it worked well enough so that stockholders generally showed little interest in curbing insider lending and, where the law required it, even voted to raise the amount that directors could borrow. Banks' earnings were generally high and steady, and money flowed into the market for bank stock at a pace that, in the 1850s at least, exceeded the rate of growth of investment in manufacturing. Bank funds in turn were plowed back into economic development by means of the directors' diversified investments in manufacturing, transportation, commerce, and real estate.

Circumstances ultimately transformed this insider-oriented banking system into a more professional and impersonal one, but the change occurred much later and in a very different fashion than most scholars have traditionally assumed. According to modernization theorists, the appearance of banks and other corporations sounded the death knell of kinship-based forms of business enterprise by freeing entrepreneurs from the need to depend upon their relatives for capital. Although this proposition makes some theoretical sense, in practice banks as well as other types of corporations could be – and were – used by kinship groups to expand the amount of capital they could raise for their ventures and to give their enterprises a permanent institutional base. Indeed, the multiplication of these institutions during the first half of the nineteenth century actually operated to provide more and more kinship groups with the opportunity to expand their businesses and thereby challenge the hegemony of groups that earlier had used their own resources to achieve positions of economic dominance.

Rather than the corporate device per se, it was economic development that set in motion the series of changes that ultimately brought an end to this personal style of banking. As additional banks and other financial institutions were chartered, New England was gradually transformed from a capital-scarce region into one rich in capital. And as credit became easier to obtain, entrepreneurs found it less necessary to exercise control over a bank in order to secure loans. Although insider lending did not completely disappear – at some institutions insiders still absorbed significant amounts of lendable resources as late as the 1890s – the practice became relatively less common by the last quarter of the nineteenth century.

Other changes that occurred at about the same time made such insider lending as persisted seem more dangerous than ever before. As banks lent increasing amounts of resources to outsiders, they found it necessary to develop systematic credit-evaluation procedures. Once they had done so, loans to insiders that were not subjected to equivalent scrutiny came to seem increasingly problematic. At the same time, once bank directors no longer needed their banks to provide them with credit, they tended to withdraw from active management and delegate more and more authority to a few active members and salaried employees. They even stopped attending the regular board meetings at which managers' lending decisions were routinely reviewed. This decline in attentiveness meant that many members of the board were no longer in a position to monitor the activities of their colleagues, and as a result it was now much easier for unscrupulous officers and directors to behave opportunistically – to loan too much money to themselves and their favorites.

One effect of these changes was that the identity of a bank's directors no longer conveyed much information to the public about the contents of a bank's portfolio or even about the quality of its management. This loss of information had especially serious consequences during the post–Civil War period as a result of the growth of deposit banking. Once deposits became a significant proportion of total liabilities, bankers had to worry about runs, and that made insider lending seem still more dangerous. The collapse of a bank as a result of opportunistic behavior by insiders might trigger runs on other institutions as well, because the public had no way of knowing whether they were similarly imperiled.

Conservative bankers responded to these new threats, and particularly to the dangers that opportunism now posed for them all, by trying to reform business practices throughout the industry. By promoting new lending standards that could be monitored easily by a few conscientious directors and stockholders, they sought to reduce the likelihood that bank managers would engage in irresponsible lending behavior. In this endeavor they were aided by members of an increasingly numerous group of banking professionals intent on enhancing their own position within the field – bank employees determined to expand opportunities for themselves in the upper echelons of management, trade-journal publicists seeking to enlarge their influence and readership, and government regulators eager to expand their authority over the industry. The values promoted by these rising professionals ran counter to the ethic of private collaboration that had provided justification for insider lending in the earlier part of the century. Moreover, members of these groups had much to gain from changing the way in which banks conducted their affairs. As long as businessmen could secure capital for their enterprises by involving themselves in the management of a bank, so long would the professionalization of the banking system be thwarted.

In their drive to devise objective and easily monitored lending criteria, conservative bankers and their professional allies drew inspiration from a set of principles known as the real-bills doctrine. Long an important (though largely dormant) element of banking theory, this doctrine held that banks should restrict their business to the discount of "real" commercial paper, that is, to notes issued in the course of actual commercial transactions. Loans on real commercial paper were considered desirable because they were thought to be self-liquidating. Moreover, because they bore a one-to-one correspondence to the actual wealth-generating activities of the economy, they were regarded as tantamount to wealth.

During the last several decades of the century, however, changes in the way firms conducted their transactions made real commercial paper increasingly scarce. Professionals nonetheless believed that banks could create an equally effective substitute by restricting their business to short-term loans based solely on borrowers' quick assets. This type of loan had a number of advantages. In the first place, it minimized information problems by keeping borrowers on a short leash and forcing them to reapply for loans every six months or so. Second, because it was based on quick (or readily convertible) assets, this type of loan resembled the self-liquidating, wealth-based character of real commercial paper. Hence it provided banks with an objective standard that could be used to insure that managers exercised no arbitrary discretion in their lending decisions.

This new standard was applied with increasing frequency during the last two decades of the century as bank management became more professional. The change was most pronounced in cities like Boston and Providence, where bank presidents were now chosen mainly from the ranks of bank employees rather than from among prominent businessmen, as had been common earlier. Presidents promoted from within were less likely to have outside business interests that might influence their lending decisions. Moreover, thanks to the numerous professional organizations that had sprung up to improve the training and status of bank employees, they were more likely to have internalized the conservatives' ideas of sound banking practice. The new standards received another important boost (at least in urban areas) as a result of the merger wave at the turn of the century. The giant banks that resulted had close ties with leading private bankers in cities like New York and Boston. These men had both the knowledge and the authority to monitor the activities of the banks' managers, and they took care to insure that the professionals' prescriptions were being observed.

As the new ideas about sound lending practice spread through the region's financial centers, banks in these cities came to play a much narrower role in economic life. Rather than emulate the policies of their forebears by generously granting accommodation credit, they adopted the contrary policy of restricting their business to short-term commercial loans. Such specialization undoubtedly helped bankers reduce their vulnerability to failure, but the solution also had important consequences for other sectors of the economy, for the new lending rules made it more difficult for entrepreneurs to obtain bank loans, especially for investment in new manufacturing industries. Entrepreneurs in new industries were unlikely to possess the marketable securities needed to guarantee collateral loans. At the same time, the requirement that loans on personal security be backed by unencumbered quick assets worth twice the value of the debt made it difficult for them to secure credit to improve or enlarge their plants. Although the equity markets were expanding during this period, only large, well-established firms had access to them. Small firms needed banks' credit and support to make the transition to equity finance, but this was a role that late-nineteenth-century institutions were unwilling to play. Paradoxically, then, the ultimate consequence of New England's transformation into a capital-abundant economy was to make it more difficult for innovative manufacturers to gain access to funds. At the root of this paradox lay the information problems created by the substitution of arm's-length for insider lending.

It is important to understand that the decision to specialize in short-term commercial lending was not imposed on bankers by the government. The regulatory system was extremely weak during this period, and this weakness was part of the problem. Indeed, the rules that regulators most successfully enforced – for example, the prohibition against branching by national banks – were themselves indicators of the strength of bankers vis-à-vis the government. In other respects, regulatory oversight was minimal. In the case of lending behavior, for example, government officials could do little more than counsel bank managers to obey the law.[3]

---

3. John A. James has argued that even the legal prohibition against loans on real estate was frequently violated by national banks. See *Money and Capital Markets in Postbellum America* (Princeton, N.J.: Princeton University Press, 1978), 29, 46.

Although conservative bankers found regulators, like other professionals, to be useful allies in their struggle to induce colleagues to follow sound lending practices, the principles they preached grew out of their own concerns. The reform movement was in essence an attempt to alleviate the consequences of interdependence in a system where there was no central control. The growing importance of deposits had made all bankers vulnerable to each other's transgressions, yet the anarchic structure of the industry and the large number of individual institutions – even after the turn-of-the-century merger movement – made it difficult to prevent dangerous abuses.[4]

Ironically, it would be a strengthened federal government during the 1930s that ultimately alleviated the conditions that had fostered banks' specialization in short-term commercial banking. The creation of the Federal Deposit Insurance Corporation in 1933 (followed by other federal and state deposit-insurance programs over the next several decades) dramatically reduced the interdependence of the banking system by protecting banks against runs triggered by the unsound policies of one of their number. As a result, pressures to conform to a single pattern of lending behavior abated, and bankers began gradually to lengthen the terms of their loans and to experiment with a variety of new lending instruments capable of supporting investment in manufacturing. By the

4. New left historians have made similar arguments, attributing government regulation itself to bankers' desire to assert control over their industry. See Gabriel Kolko, *The Triumph of Conservatism: A Reinterpretation of American History, 1900–1916* (New York: Free Press, 1963), chap. 6; James Livingston, *Origins of the Federal Reserve System: Money, Class, and Corporate Capitalism, 1890–1913* (Ithaca, N.Y.: Cornell University Press, 1986).

German banks, whose lending policies evolved very differently from those in the U.S., never faced similar problems of vulnerability. During the 1870s (before deposits were an important source of lendable funds) large banks in Berlin began to absorb smaller banks in the provinces and to create *Interessengemeinschaften*, or groups of mutual interest, by (among other means) exchanging shares of stock with provincial institutions. These communities of interest extended the control of the Berlin banks into the countryside, limiting the provincial banks' independence of action and effectively stabilizing the entire banking system. See Holger L. Engberg, *Mixed Banking and Economic Growth in Germany, 1850–1931* (New York: Arno, 1981), 43–83, 199; P. Barrett Whale, *Joint Stock Banking in Germany: A Study of the German Creditbanks Before and After the War* (London: Macmillan, 1930), 26–35; J. Riesser, *The German Great Banks and Their Concentration in Connection with the Economic Development of Germany* (Washington, D.C.: Government Printing Office, 1911), 156–65.

end of the New Deal, theorists had even begun to mount a significant challenge to the real-bills doctrine.[5]

Bankers' renewed ability to support economic development did not mean, however, that they could also return to the insider lending of the early nineteenth century. Under the new regime, that practice proved more dangerous than ever before, because deposit insurance further weakened the incentive structure needed to hold loans to insiders within reasonable bounds. As Rhode Island's RISDIC scandals and the national savings-and-loan failures would dramatically illustrate, bankers operating in an insured environment feel little inclination to restrain their levels of risk and cannot be trusted to keep their own borrowing within sustainable limits. Nor can depositors be given responsibility for monitoring banks' soundness. Because the provision of insurance encourages them to regard their money's safety as independent of the quality of a bank's portfolio, they look only at the rate of return in deciding where to place their funds. Thus bankers seeking additional resources for their own ventures have only to offer slightly higher yields in order to attract deposits. In a banking system characterized by deposit insurance, then, the only way to keep risk levels under control is strict government regulation. Insiders cannot be trusted to monitor themselves.

To use Marxian, or Hegelian, terminology, the post-1930s deposit-insurance regime might be regarded as a synthesis that combined the support for economic development characteristic of early-nineteenth-century banks with the more impersonal value system that had evolved by the latter part of the century. It was a synthesis that permitted banks to lend funds in arm's-length relations and still provide long-term credit to manufacturing ventures. It thereby rescued them from the straightjacket they had voluntarily donned at the end of the nineteenth century and enabled them once again to play a more active role in economic life. Undoubtedly this synthesis has imposed costs on the economy in the form, alternately, of regulatory rigidity and lax regulatory oversight, but the new regime has to be understood as the product of a path-dependent process – the outcome of our particular historical experience with financial institutions and our evolving system of values.

Other societies, of course, have had very different histories and operate in accordance with different value systems. In many other parts of the world, for example, favoritism toward kinsmen and other close associates is still an accepted part of daily life. It is important, therefore, that we not react moralistically when confronted with the insider lending that often

5. See, for example, Lloyd Mints, *A History of Banking Theory in Great Britain and the United States* (Chicago: University of Chicago Press, 1945).

characterizes financial institutions in such societies. The lesson of our own history is that under certain circumstances a banking system based on insider lending can function very well. Rather than attempt to impose our own modern values and institutions on others, therefore, our efforts at assistance might better be directed toward helping these societies arrange incentives in a way that puts insider lending to productive use.

Index